SATISFACTION

Women, Sex, and the Quest for Intimacy

Anita H. Clayton, M.D.,
with Robin Cantor-Cooke

Ballantine Books　New York

ISBN 978-1-4000-6452-6

Printed in the United States of America on acid-free paper

www.ballantinebooks.com

2 4 6 8 9 7 5 3 1

First Edition

Book design by Fearn Cutler de Vicq

Just a Few Words Before I Get Going

This is a book about women, and why we are the way we are about sex. It is a little bit about the way women's brains work and a lot about the way women think, both of which have an enormous effect on the way we become aroused, feel desire, and abandon ourselves to passionate lovemaking—or not. With women, it can go either way: just because a woman feels stirrings of arousal doesn't mean she's going to hop a streetcar named desire and rush headlong into a cathartic bout of ecstasy. She might, but she might also feel her arousal fizzle unless all the stars in constellation Eros are aligned just so. It's different with men: when a guy becomes aroused, he gets an erection, and when he gets an erection, he wants to have sex, end of story. But a woman can fall into her husband's arms and be tingling under his touch when suddenly she remembers there's a wad of wet laundry that's been solidifying in the washer for two days, and she'll be out of that bed so fast, the poor man won't know what hit him (a clammy camisole, most likely).

I became interested in studying sexuality in the late 1980s, when I was a psychiatrist in the Navy and a significant number of my (mostly male) patients reported problems with delayed ejaculation. These men happened to be taking a widely prescribed antidepressant and complained at a much greater rate than was reported in the package insert. I thought it would be useful to find out how many people taking antidepressants—men and women alike—were experiencing sexual dysfunction and set about developing a patient questionnaire that would yield some reliable data. Fifteen years and reams of research later, we had our questionnaire, administered it to 6,300 people, and published a study examining the prevalence of sexual dysfunction with all antidepressants available since 1988.[1] The results were enlightening and also tossed an unanticipated wedge into my résumé, not to mention my family room, when one of its findings found its way into the 20th Anniversary Edition of Trivial Pursuit: "What percent of men taking antidepressants experienced sexual dysfunction in Dr. Anita Clayton's 2001 study (17, 37, or 57%)?"* I suppose it's fair to say that you never know where you may come across my patients.

The patients you will come across in this book are based on real people I have treated in my practice; most are composites of several persons whose symptoms would be recognizable were they presented on their own. Because this book talks frankly about sex, I have assiduously disguised even seemingly innocuous details: if a woman has two children, these pages may bless her with three or with one; if her lover is a stonemason, he may be thus transformed into a carpenter; an African-American woman who teaches college chemistry may manifest as a patent attorney of unspecified ethnicity. Which leads me to the question of why there is no racial diversity in these pages, and the answer is that I have chosen not to identify patients according to race. I have two reasons for this: one, because doing so might make them recognizable within their communities; and two, because race is simply not a factor in the cases included here. In those instances where a patient's ethnicity or nationality was a factor in her situation, I included the information, likewise altered. For instance, the last chapter features a woman born in Colombia, whereas the patient on whom she is based was born in a Central American country. My goal is to present these women as fully as possible without divulging facts that may reveal their identities, or those of their family members.

You may also find yourself wondering why a particular story is located in one chapter while it might have applied just as well to another, and yes, you're right: themes in many of these stories overlap. Peg's story, which appears in the chapter about shame, might also have fit into the previous chapter, about repressed resentment. The intertwined nature of women's sexuality seldom allows for tidy boundaries between causes and effects,

---

*37 percent (you get a piece of pie!).

symptoms and diagnoses, and it is this complexity that makes us so interesting to love and live with, and to study and write about.

Finally, I offer these profiles not as tales of psychiatric triumph over sexual adversity but rather as stories of real women whose sexual circumstances may in some ways mirror your own and whose hard-won insights may cast light on your own quest for erotic satisfaction. There are, after all, patients whose outcomes are not as successful as we would have liked them to be, and some of their stories are included here. Moreover, in no way do I mean to suggest that insights leap, articulate and fully formed, into my patients' consciousness in a rapturous moment of mind-blowing revelation—far from it. Sometimes I work with a patient for months and interpret something over and over again before she sees it. I might repeat the same explanation week after week, like a mantra of her melancholy: "There's that abandonment theme again; here you are once more, getting angry because someone rejected you." And she might say, "No—that's not what happened at all!" And I'll be pretty convinced that it is, but no matter. If she isn't ready to see it, we might as well be looking at one of those black-and-white graphics where one person sees two nose-to-nose profiles and another sees a Grecian urn: it's right there in front of you, but you just can't see it. You stare at it and squint at it and then suddenly, *zing!*—there it is, two profiles, as clear as could be. You cannot imagine how you managed to miss it, but it was utterly invisible to you until the moment it became the most obvious thing in the world. The odd thing is, once you see the profiles, you have a hard time seeing the urn again; it's as if the urn never existed. All that has changed, of course, is the way you are perceiving the image, which is how psychiatry works as well. What changes is the patient's perception of the problem and acknowledgment of his or her complicity in it. Once that happens, everything else changes, too.

That is my hope for this book: that it will offer you a different way of perceiving both yourself and the part you have played and continue to play in creating your sexual self. Once that happens, everything—and everyone—can change.

Contents

SATISFACTION

CHAPTER 1

Am I Normal?

Why are so many women dissatisfied with their sex lives?
With the possible exception of Paris Hilton (and the mademoiselle who once had the room next to mine at the Hilton Paris), women are not enjoying sex as much as they would like to, or even as much as they used to. I know this because of what I hear from patients in therapy, volunteers in medical studies, friends in restaurants, and well-dressed women in business class who learn I'm a psychiatrist and, if the flight is long enough, share a lot more with me than an armrest. Something has gone out of their intimate lives, they say. They're not interested in sex anymore, or they are interested but can't get aroused, or they can get aroused but have neither the desire nor the energy to follow through. Their relationships are suffering, and they want to know what's wrong with them.

It's not just the people I happen to encounter who feel this way; millions of women across the country—as well as across ethnic, cultural, and economic lines—want to enjoy sex more. If you have frank conversations with your female friends, this probably isn't news. But it was big news indeed back in 1992, when social scientists conducted a study of adult sexual behavior and found that 43 percent of American women were unhappy with their sex lives[1]—which doesn't sound that bad unless you believe, as I do, that the other 57 percent were lying.

If you wish I had quoted a more recent study, I don't blame you; I also wish we had newer numbers to look at. That we don't have fresher research reveals a void in the literature of female sexuality: coy conversations with girlfriends aside, we just don't know that much about it.

Moreover, what we do know isn't necessarily the gleanings of rigorous research. For example, several years ago, the television show *Primetime Live* aired a segment on sexuality based on the results of a telephone poll it had conducted the previous summer. The interviewers were all women (people are allegedly more willing to disclose intimate details to female voices than to male ones) who rang up 1,500 randomly selected Americans—undoubtedly in the middle of dinner—to ask them about their sex lives. And while a few juicy morsels did emerge—three out of four men said they always had an orgasm during sex, while only three out of ten women said they did; and a strapping 57 percent of women and men said they'd had sex either outdoors or in a public place—an informal survey of this kind hardly qualifies as a scientific study.[2] To make things even murkier, when sex researchers do learn something new, it's often reported in a way designed less to illuminate the issue than to sell the one on the newsstand. A *Newsweek* cover story in June 2003 proclaimed, "Sexless Marriage on the Rise: 15 to 20 Percent of Couples Have Sex No More Than 10 Times a Year." Uh-oh—you could almost hear a gasp sweep the heartland: *Is that me? I know we're having sex less often than we used to, but it's not that bad . . . or is it? Is my marriage* sexless? Well, wait a minute—what does *sexless* mean? To me, it doesn't mean ten times or eight times or one time. It means zero times—no sexual contact, no physical intimacy, nothing. But this headline says that having sex every five weeks or so is the same as having no sex at all. It implies that making love infrequently is the same as never doing it—the implication being that either way, you're screwed.

The message resonates throughout the land: everyone is getting more and hotter sex than you are, especially if you're a woman. You have to have a certain kind of look (drop-dead gorgeous), a particular kind of body (microscopic rear, bountiful breasts), and unassailable self-confidence to qualify as sexually viable. It's different for guys; they can be awkward, goofy, grungy, or all three and still end up in bed with the star by the end of the show. But if humanness makes men more appealing, it does the opposite for us. For a woman to be sexy, she's got to be more than human—sleeker, surer, supremely in control. You've seen these creations in the movies and on television: supple, gleaming, straight-talking gals who render guys mute with withering glances and keen-edged dialogue. These women are hip, glib, and quick; they are exquisitely in touch with their feelings and never lack words to express them. They may be inner-city detectives or winsome wives and mothers, but no matter: whether they're packing lunches or .38s, they are firm and unflappable, with nerves, buns, and coiffures of steel. They know what they want, especially in bed, and neither stammer nor apologize when telling their husbands, boyfriends, and lovers what feels good, what doesn't, and what drives them to ecstasy. Like the lusty protagonists of HBO's classic *Sex and the City,* these women know good sex, and they know how to get it.

But these women aren't real; when it comes to sex, no one is as self-aware and sure of herself as these figments of a screenwriter's imagination. Real women, such as the ones I see in my practice, are fascinating flesh-and-blood contradictions: perceptive and unaware, intelligent and ill informed, partnered yet lonely. This one has a husband and three young children, that one is barely out of childhood herself, another has a married lover eighteen years her senior. They have little in common, yet they are alike: they are all women, and they all wish the sex were better.

The thing is, many of them don't know the sex *could* be better. They figure that lusty, chandelier-swinging lovemaking isn't meant for the likes of them, even if they did have the appropriate lighting fixture. They've bought into the culture's bogus belief that a woman's sexual potential is measured by her appearance and limited by her score on the ever changing eye-candy scale.

It's hard to resist this fiction, surrounded as we are by images of women who have been surgically and digitally enhanced to conform to this season's concept of feminine perfection, however unnatural and distorted it might be. The fakery in these images doesn't diminish their persuasiveness: the cheekbones, eye color, skin tone, noses, hair, breasts, and rear ends are phony, but no matter—the women to whom they're attached have been anointed as sexy, so we yearn to resemble them.

Well, you might wonder, what's wrong with that? What's so bad about trying to look good?

What's bad is pursuing an artificial, faddish, skin-deep aesthetic that denies your true and enduring sexual nature and thwarts its expression. Sexuality isn't something visible about you; it's something you feel within yourself. It's down in there, dark and tangled, funky and wild. It's forged in the mind and enacted by the body; it's not only between your legs, it's also between your ears. If others perceive it, it's not because of what they're seeing but because of what you are feeling and exuding. It's about how you feel and how you think, not about how you look.

But if you believe your sexuality is about your appearance, as so many of us do, you become fixated on superficial characteristics and obsessed with altering them. You increase your bustline, de-crease your eyelids, hoist your bottom, and have your lipo sucked. You go under the knife and over your credit limit. And eventually you learn that no matter how many surgeries and procedures you undergo, you'll never be as flawless, voluptuous, and boldly coquettish as the babes in the Victoria's Secret commercials (nor as skilled at sliding backward, mouth half open and eyes half closed, onto a satin-sheeted bed without banging your head on the night table). Never mind that each of us knows at least one woman who bears not the slightest resemblance to a lingerie model yet is inexplicably, inescapably seductive. You know who I mean: the woman who's not exactly pretty and whose body isn't great, but to whom men are drawn like ants to a fallen scoop of Rocky Road. If we'd take the time to analyze her appeal, we'd see that it has little to do with her exterior and everything to do with what's emanating from within her—but no matter. We still equate sexiness with how we imagine we look to others rather than how we feel inside. So we lower the estimate of our sexual potential along with our expectations.

How did this happen? How did we mature into a generation of women who demand excellence in every area of our lives except for sex? We graduate from top colleges and professional schools; we work construction and fight fires; we sit on the Supreme Court, run for the House and Senate, and stand by our men. Yet when it comes to sex, we're pretty willing to accept what we get, minimize our disappointment, and channel our erotic energies elsewhere. Why?

One reason is that for women, sex is as much about connection as it is about climax, and we tend to conflate the two, settling for the comforts of closeness when we're also wishing the sex would improve. While most women would agree that a toe-curling orgasm goes a long way toward putting things right in their world, they would also say that having an emotional connection with their partner is the best way to ensure they'll have an orgasm in the first place. The emotional intimacy that results from feeling connected to her partner is, for a woman, a prime component of good sex. This means that a woman's sexual identity (the way she perceives her sexuality, revealed by the sorts of people to whom she is erotically attracted) might manifest itself in terms of her relationships rather than her actual sexual behaviors. For that reason, some women may seem to have chronic relationship problems—always falling in love with married men or repeatedly getting involved with guys who mooch off them—and blame their sexual dissatisfaction on the relationship when it is actually their sexual attraction for such men that is the problem.

I also believe we settle for so-so sex because most of us don't know how sexual we could be; we know only how sexual we are. How sexual we are has been shaped by decades of indoctrination by mothers and fathers, sisters and brothers, family and friends, teachers, religious leaders, and romantic partners, not to mention a society that worships a bewildering fusion of childlike sexual innocence and cynical. nihilistic hedonism. If Marilyn Monroe doesn't do it for you, there's always RuPaul. The culture's sexual pulse throbs so lustily for both the sublime and the ridiculous, it's hard to separate the sensible from the absurd, the nutty from the normal.

So what *is* normal?

It all depends on what's normal for *you*. What do *you* need to feel sexually stimulated? What makes *you* feel desire? How do *you* become aroused enough to achieve orgasm? How much sex is enough for you? How often is often enough, and how seldom feels like never? I am reminded of a scene in *Annie Hall* with Woody Allen and his therapist on the right side of the screen and Diane Keaton and her therapist on the left. Allen's therapist asks, "How often do you sleep together?"; then Keaton's asks, "Do you have sex often?" "Hardly ever," Allen says. "Maybe three times a week." Then Keaton says, "Constantly—I'd say three times a week." The scene is funny because of its intrinsic honesty: "hardly ever" to him is "constantly" to her. The thing is, each of them is a reliable witness; both she and he are reporting accurately how frequently they make love. But even though they possess the same information, they interpret it differently. And notice that neither of them is complaining about the quality of the sex—it's the three-times-a-week part that rankles both of them. Neither one of them is happy about it, and they're both right.

But what if hardly ever or even never is just fine—is there something wrong with you? Society says yes, but science says otherwise. According to a Canadian study published a few years ago, about 1 percent of adults are utterly uninterested in sex, or asexual.[3] For this 1 percent, no sex is more than enough. Asexual adults do not engage in sexual activity, nor do they miss it. And there is nothing wrong with them. If you are content living without sex and have always felt that way, no sex is normal because you are probably asexual, and that's what is normal for you.

The contentment factor is significant, as it is one criterion by which doctors determine whether or not a person has a diagnosable sexual disorder. The *Diagnostic and Statistical Manual of Mental Disorders*, fourth edition (*DSM-IV*), published by the American Psychiatric Association, is, at 943 pages, a mother lode of information and the primary reference tool used by American mental health professionals to formulate diagnoses. According to the *DSM-IV,* you don't have a sexual disorder unless distress is one of your symptoms. It follows that if you have never felt sexually attracted to anyone and are not distressed about it, you are most likely asexual, not dysfunctional, and normal, if not average. If you and your partner have sex four or five times a year and both of you are content and neither of you feels deprived, then you most likely don't have a problem, either, because that's normal for you. On the other hand, if you and your partner are having sex four or five times a week but you're left feeling empty, frustrated, and dissatisfied and you *are* distressed about it, that's *not* normal for you, and you might want to do something about it.

The key is becoming aware of yourself, learning what *your* sexual normal is, and raising your expectations to that level—and knowing the difference between what's normal for real human beings and those phony, jazzed-up media femmes fatales. If you don't, you erode your capacity for intimacy and eventually become estranged from both your sensual self and your partner. The erosion is so gradual, you don't realize it's happening until the damage is done and you're shivering at the bottom of a chasm, alone and untouched, wondering how you got there. To climb out, you must become aware of your sexual self. You must become actively conscious of your body (how you inhabit it, not how it looks), your mind, and the galvanic influence each has upon the other. And once the light begins to dawn, you need to speak up—to yourself and your partner—and stop settling for less than you want and need.

What if the light dawned a while ago? What if you're aware that your sex life could use some work but you don't know how to fix it? While awareness is a prerequisite for better sex, it isn't enough on its own. Women who know that the sex could be better often lack the motivation and moxie to make it happen, especially when they can't put their finger on what's wrong. Is the problem with you or your partner? Is it physical or emotional, biological or psychological? Is it that you have an infant and are tired all the time, or are you resentful that no one helps with the housework? Is it the wild hormonal swings after childbirth or your irrational fear that the baby might stop breathing if you don't check him every ten minutes? Or is it all these things happening at once?

Sexual dissatisfaction is not as distinct for a woman as it is for a man: if he's not aroused, he can't get it up; if he can't get it up, he can't have sex; and if he can't have sex, he feels like less of a man. For most guys, this is a crisis and worrisome enough to motivate them to pick up a phone, call a doctor, and get help.

But for women, sexual dissatisfaction is more a disappointment than a crisis. Our fundamental sense of self, our essential womanhood, isn't threatened, so the situation doesn't seem dire. Women's sexual frustrations are more subtle: we can have sex whether we're aroused or not; we just might not enjoy it very much, or at all. Most women tend to be stoic about sexual disappointments: if we feel deflated after an anticlimactic lovemaking session, we might not oooh and ahhh about how great it was, but we're not likely to declare a state of emergency, either.

What if you know it isn't you? Even when a woman has the insight to know that the problem lies with her man's behaviors or technique (or lack of it), she will probably be too concerned about hurting his feelings or losing his affection to say anything—better he should think she's undersexed than a ballbreaker. (For lesbians, the issue is less about fear of damaging their partners' egos than about women's capacity for verbal intimacy and emotional relatedness, which may obviate a lesbian couple's need for sex to achieve closeness.) Rather than rock the boat or bore another hole in a sinking ship, a woman is likely to smooth the waters by reframing the situation and telling herself that she's the one with the problem.

That is, unless the problem is undeniably his.

A few years ago, the only Americans who knew about erectile dysfunction were the men who had it and the physicians who treated them. Now every man, woman, and child in the country is accustomed to seeing foxy middle-aged couples gazing saucily at each other, because for the guy, at least, help is just a tablet (and about thirty minutes) away.

It would be sweet if we too could swallow a pill and banish our sexual woes, but alas, things aren't that simple for us. When Pfizer, maker of the anti-impotence drug Viagra, announced it was abandoning efforts to develop a similar formula for women, it was no small event; the company had studied the effects of sildenafil citrate (which it markets as Viagra) on more than three thousand women and spent more than eight years—and a great deal of money—hoping it could duplicate its colossal success with men. I had firsthand experience with the process, as I helped administer several of the clinical trials here at the University of Virginia.

I was disappointed that Viagra didn't solve our problems, but I wasn't surprised. It's not that the drug doesn't do for us what it does for guys; in fact, it dilates blood vessels in women just as it does in men, collecting blood in the genitals and creating the symptoms of arousal. But while men almost always want to make love when they're aroused, women don't necessarily want to do any such thing. We might be physically able, but that alone isn't enough to get us in the mood. We need something more, and that something is more than robust circulation. Mitra Boolel, head of Pfizer's research team, told *The New York Times*, "There's a disconnect in many women between genital changes and mental changes. This disconnect does not exist in men. Men consistently get erections in the presence of naked women and want to have sex. With women, things depend on a myriad of factors." Dr. Boolel said his researchers were continuing their work but were "changing their focus from a woman's genitals to her head. The brain is the crucial sexual organ in women."[4]

This wasn't exactly breaking news to me, and it might not be to you, either. But it is the crux of the matter: the vast power of a woman's brain—*your* brain—to influence your interest in making love, and to collude with

timing, self-awareness, circumstance, culture, and chemistry to either ig-
nite or extinguish your capacity to take pleasure in it. As every woman
knows, it's seldom a seamless and soaring progression from desire to
arousal to orgasm to cigarettes and sighs of contentment. Woman's libido
rarely launches into orbit unimpeded; instead, it ricochets off the facets of
her several selves (lover, mother, daughter, wife, breadwinner, cook, driver,
housecleaner, social director, dishwasher, volunteer, gatherer of groceries,
clipper of coupons) until it comes spinning back, with or without amorous
intentions. This is a very different dynamic from that which governs man's
sexual urge: when he is aroused, he wants to make love; if the flesh is able,
the spirit is fierce. Man is direct, woman is oblique. For a candid explanation we can thank Mr. Rogers, who was in the right neighborhood when he
sang, "Some are fancy on the outside; some are fancy on the inside." That's
precisely the point: woman's sexuality is almost entirely on the inside, out
of sight (and, all too often, out of mind).

I've treated hundreds of intelligent, highly competent women whose
sexual self-awareness has hardly evolved since their mothers handed them
a box of Modess . . . *because.* Because why? Because woman's sexuality
runs rampant every twenty-eight days, a crimson reminder of what's really
going on underneath all the daintiness we're supposed to be about. We
were handed a dirty little message along with those sanitary unmention-
ables: your teeming womb is the crowning glory of your womanhood—and
you'd better keep every trace of it hidden, or else. It's the *or else* part that
keeps us trembling on the brink of self-awareness, longing for a lover's unstoppable passion to touch us where we dare not touch ourselves. My own
research confirms what I instinctively knew long before I earned a medical
degree: that the sexual nature of woman is a subtle fusion of mind with
body, flesh with feeling, and what we know about it could fit in the backseat of a Miata.

Woman's sexuality is an intricate, interwoven phenomenon—you can't
pull just one thread, unravel the fabric, and reveal the mystery within. It's
a densely textured cloth, woven here and braided there, sometimes elaborate, other times plain. My mission is to direct your gaze toward the tapestry of your sexual self and coax you to both revel in the beauty of its

complexity and recognize the stitches, loops, and imperfections in the weave. I want to pique your curiosity about your sex life, heighten your awareness that it can be better (and could probably be worse), and reassure you that all women—Victoria's Secret models included—experience a dose of agony along with ecstasy when it comes to sex.

One reason for this is that women tend to focus on problems in their sexual lives as if those problems could be isolated from the rest of existence, and the fact is that they cannot. You find little nubs in the weave and think, *Oh, the stitches aren't quite right here—if I snip them out, it will be perfect,* mistaking the nubs for flaws. This misperception is the reason for the little tag on your new dupioni silk suit, which proclaims that the imperfections in the fabric are not blemishes but rather the signature of its natural beauty. The small lumps, known as slubs, result when two silkworms work together on one cocoon, producing strands of varying thicknesses that are then spun together to create dupioni silk cloth. The slubs occur randomly, rendering each swatch of dupioni silk different from every other.

So it is with woman: the myriad threads of biology, sensuality, psychology, and soul entwine to loom a cloth of infinite variation. Your exultations and fears, memories and fantasies, friendships and intimacies, work and obligations, kinks and quirks comprise the pattern, hue, smoothness, and slubs in the tapestry of your sexual self. To view its abundant variety as a flaw is to misconstrue its essential character: the motley nature of the weave is a manifestation of its vigorous, pulsing vitality.

Does this mean that a woman with indisputable intimacy problems is not sexually dysfunctional but merely experiencing a tapestry malfunction? No, of course not. Even the most vibrantly chaotic weaves sometimes unravel, and some women do suffer from sexual dysfunction. But there's a difference between dysfunction and disappointment, and many women don't get it. My patient Holly* was one of them.

Holly was a highly intelligent twenty-year-old premedical student with an A in anatomy but a long way to go toward understanding her own.

---

*The case histories in this book are composite portraits based on patients in my practice, whose names I have changed.

Holly was unable to reach orgasm with her boyfriend and had convinced herself that she was orgasmically dysfunctional. I thought she might be, too, until she let it drop that she had bought a vibrator the previous semester and had been enjoying wildly satisfying climaxes with it ever since. I'll go more into detail about Holly later on, but for now what you need to know is this: if you cannot have an orgasm with your partner but you can have one using a vibrator, your hand, or a handheld photo of Viggo Mortensen, you are not orgasmically dysfunctional. Disappointed perhaps, but not dysfunctional. Holly had dismissed her device-assisted orgasms as somehow less real than the ones she hoped to have with a flesh-and-blood man. Take note: an orgasm is an orgasm is an orgasm. An orgasm you have during intercourse is no more legitimate than one you achieve through less traditional means. An orgasm is rather like a velveteen rabbit—if you have one and you love it, then it's real.[5]

So we do know a thing or two. We do have some facts about how women's bodies respond when aroused, but we don't know how the complex interactions of a particular woman's psyche and sexuality manifest as difficulties, nor how her body conspires with her mind to initiate a warm embrace or turn a cold shoulder.

While we don't yet know as much as we should, we do know that women's sexual disorders fall into four general categories: difficulty feeling desire, difficulty becoming aroused, difficulty achieving orgasm, and experiencing bodily pain during sexual activity. Here are some brief descriptions:

1. **Hypoactive sexual desire disorder.** The prefix *hypo* means "under" or "beneath," so if you have this problem you seldom if ever feel the desire for sex, and you're also distressed about it. (If having a low or nonexistent sex drive doesn't bother you, you do not have a disorder.) A related and less common condition is **sexual aversion disorder,** which is classified as a phobia. If you feel fearful at the prospect of sexual activity, do your best to avoid it, and feel distressed about feeling this way, you may have sexual aversion disorder.

2. **Sexual arousal disorder.** You may have this if you feel the desire for sex but your body isn't producing the signs of arousal (for

example, swelling of the genitals and vaginal lubrication) that enable you to have sex comfortably. If this is the case and you are distressed about it, you may have sexual arousal disorder.

3. **Orgasmic disorder.** If you consistently have difficulty reaching orgasm or are unable to do so after you have been sufficiently aroused, and this situation causes you distress, you may have orgasmic disorder.

4. **Sexual pain disorder.** This disorder has several subcategories, including *dyspareunia* (recurrent pain in the genitals during intercourse); *vaginismus* (spasms in the lower portion of the vagina that impede the ability to grant entry to a penis or other rigid object, and cause pain and distress); and *noncoital sexual pain disorder* (genital discomfort or pain brought on by sexual activity other than intercourse).

I will explore these categories more thoroughly by sharing my patients' case histories throughout this book, and I promise that not all of them will feature tidy, uplifting denouements. Most of my patients leave therapy with more psychological and emotional ballast than when they came in; a few just leave. All physicians want to believe they have been of help to their patients, and most of the time we are. But I know that the degree to which I can help a patient is determined as much by the patient's knowledge of him- or herself—or willingness to seek it—as by my knowledge of psychiatry.

For this reason, I urge you to open yourself to mining the vein of gold that is your sexual self. I want you to broaden your view of your sexuality, much as a wide-angle lens extends the boundaries of a photograph. I want you to focus less tightly on specific symptoms in favor of a panoramic view of your sexual landscape. As your vision expands, I will guide you on a tour of what Natalie Angier aptly called a woman's "intimate geography."[6] I will point out aspects of the terrain that you haven't noticed because they've always been there: an attraction for elusive, disreputable men who reincarnate a long-lost, shiftless father; a thin-lipped conviction that it is repulsive to even think about touching yourself down there; ancient, smoldering resentments that inflame every morning but dampen, via Jack Daniel's, by nightfall; the involuntary recoil as you stand before a dressing room mirror and behold the fleshy, fluorescent body of a full-blown woman and not the whittled, jutting hips of a nine-year-old. When was the last time you emerged from the shower, slick with steam and rosy of cheek, gazed upon your nakedness, and saw that it was good? Or anticipated with pleasure the approach of summer and the prospect of declaring your assets at the pool?

Consider how you feel about your body. Do you love its fullness, its softness, its flow? Do you celebrate its fleshiness or avert your eyes in disgust? Have you ever run into a friend who looked unusually good that day and felt a bolt of envy rip through you? Or heard a friend tell another friend, "Oh, you've lost so much weight! You look great—I hate you!" Or said it yourself?

You don't have to be a sociologist to know that American women are hostile toward their bodies (their own as well as their friends'). We know this as intimately as we know our weight. But what we seldom consider is how dearly we are paying for our folly. If the waters of woman's sexuality run deep, this self-loathing contaminates the well. It taints a woman's perception of her erotic yearnings, clouds her insights into intimate encounters, and confounds the intuitive awareness that would otherwise guide her toward sexual gratification. I have treated young, healthy college students with luminous eyes and gleaming skin who sat before me with one perfect leg thrown over the other and asked if they might be able to reach orgasm with their boyfriends if their bodies were more alluring in some homogenized, fat-free way. Whenever I hear this, I can't help picturing those dimpled, bountiful, Renaissance nudes with attendant seraphs on the walls of the Louvre and wondering what those babes would think if Cupid reached into his quiver, drew out a ThighMaster, and told them to get to work. I suspect they'd give him a swift kick to the wingpits.

Conversely, many contemporary women kick themselves when they are unable to achieve ecstasy in their every erotic encounter. Our competitive, lust-saturated culture has taught us that earth-moving, mind-blowing sex is our birthright, and many young women are too inexperienced to know that their expectations are as preposterous as the Hollywood love scenes that spawned them. It's not a conspiracy, it's common sense: men create the vast majority of film and television programming, and it's logical that they would write about what they know. When it comes to sex, what most men know is a focused, urgent, line-drive surge from desire to arousal to climax to . . . well, what happens next depends on the movie. But those intense, pounding sequences where two sinuous, sweat-slicked bodies grasp, entwine, and shudder in simultaneous, unstoppable, spasmodic release are not realistic portrayals of the way women and men make love (at least not 99 percent of the time). They are, rather, the yearning fantasies of the guys who write the scripts and direct the productions.

I'm not saying that women don't have heart-stopping, frock-flinging, headboard-gripping sex. We do. Nor am I saying that women shouldn't have high expectations for their sex lives—I believe just the opposite, in fact. What I *am* saying is that our expectations should be rooted in visceral, intimate knowledge of ourselves, what is normal for us, and what feels good to us, not what looks good on Angelina Jolie or whomever *Esquire* magazine is touting as the sexiest woman alive. As far as you and your partner are concerned, the sexiest woman alive is *you*.

I'll tell you what I tell my patients: I want you to entertain and eventually own the concept of yourself as every bit as sexual as a sex symbol—indeed, the only person who should symbolize sex for you is you.

The first step toward believing this is not to avert your eyes from yourself but to turn them inward with curiosity, awe, and acceptance. I want you to peer into the dark and scary corners and ask, "What is the one thing I've never told anyone—neither my partner nor my closest friends, not anyone—about this part of me?" and shine the light of self-revelation on what you find there. Don't shrink from it, either—I can offer you a leather-clad guarantee that there's probably nothing shocking or vile about your deepest yearnings, however they might scandalize your inner feminist. Every woman thinks she's the only one with such wicked thoughts, and every woman has them.

As you look inward, self-revealing lamp in hand, I would like you to use your other hand to jot down thoughts and feelings that may come, unbidden and unnamed. This will become a concrete record of the fleeting sensations that animate sexual awareness. Your progress through this book and inward toward yourself may cause a chord of familiarity to vibrate within you or raise prickles of recognition. These twinges, jolts, and emotional echoes might whisper in your ear or shock you with a shiver and be gone before they fully register; yet they hold poignant clues to your sexual self. Part of knowing yourself lies in heightening your awareness of these sensations—the rush of longing when your boyfriend reads your child a bedtime story, or the curdling of desire half an hour later when he consumes without comment the chicken and frisée salad with roasted red peppers, toasted almonds, and manchego you worked so hard on.[7] My research has taught me that if you have to write something down, you have to think about it. It's these seemingly trivial interactions that often spark our deepest feelings, and by jotting down your reactions you'll come to see how they affect the ebb and flow of your sexuality.

That's how I work with my patients, about whom you will read in this book. You will meet fifty-eight-year-old Renata, who had lost all desire for sex and came in for treatment at the urging of her husband. At our first session she spoke brightly about how fortunate she was in her marriage and all she had to be grateful for. Meticulous in dress and self-expression, Renata presented herself as someone who had come in strictly to appease her husband, who, frustrated at their lack of sexual intimacy, was becoming increasingly distant. She attributed her loss of desire to menopause and an antianxiety medication she was taking yet was too fearful about starting hormone replacement therapy (HRT) or stopping the anxiety drug to do either. Renata said she missed the sexual intimacy she used to enjoy with her husband, but not enough to risk leaving the comfort zone of habit and complacency in which she was ensconced. It took nearly a year of talk therapy for her to be able to see that while menopause and medication were part of the problem, what was really killing her desire was a potent stew of rage and resentment she had been repressing for more than twenty years.

You'll also meet Karla, a twenty-four-year-old graduate student who came to see me because of acute anxiety. It turned out her anxiety was caused by the abrupt termination of a romance she was conducting with her professor, who was twice her age and with whom she had shared a house until he informed her, without ceremony or preparation, that she had to vacate it by the end of the week. Everything had been wonderful between them, Karla assured me, including the sex. I helped Karla through this crisis and continued to see her on and off over the next several years, during which time I came to recognize her as a serial triangulator— that is, someone who repeatedly gets involved with people who are already involved with someone else. The sex was great with all the men Karla fell in love with—which was exactly the point: the only way she could have exciting sex was to succumb to the kind of love that left her bereft of the very connectedness and solace she sought.

You might be thinking, *Doesn't Karla have a relationship problem rather than a sex problem?* Well, yes and no. Karla's romantic relationships were indeed troubled, but the problem was not rooted in her inherent capacity to receive love, reciprocate the feeling, and commit. That was all intact. The problem lay in the fact that she was sexually aroused by men who were bound to hurt her. Karla may have been able to enjoy sex, but she still had a sexual problem. And the past tense is apt: Karla had a sexual problem, but she doesn't have it anymore, thanks to an arduous course of self-examination.

The key is knowing yourself—not just your body but everything about you. Most of the therapy I do involves helping women reconstruct their understanding of themselves. By writing this book, I invite you to join them, and me, in this most rewarding inner work. As you read, think, and jot down your thoughts, you will begin to see the myriad physical, emotional, cultural, and medical factors that influence your sexual yearnings and behaviors. If you have diabetes, for example, you must understand how the disease can compromise circulation, diminish sensation, and possibly cause problems with arousal and orgasm—not to mention your self-image. Likewise, if you take an antidepressant, you must be sufficiently in tune with your nonmedicated self to discern how the medication is affecting your libido. And if you're one of those women who feigns ecstasy to spare her lover's feelings, you must accept that faking orgasms makes it unlikely that you ever will have one. Why? Because you're floating outside your body and observing it rather than living inside your body and exulting in it. You're not focusing on what you're feeling; instead, you have intuited your partner's needs and placed them above your own. Your craving for connection trumps your willingness to risk discord. And once again your sweetie drifts off to sleep, sated and snoring, as you lie awake, wishing the sex were better.

• • •

Psychiatry is an intimate practice. Every day I sit and listen as patients tell me things they have never put into words before. Some come in and, even in the first session, say, "I've never told anybody this—" and then tell me. Psychiatrists hear a lot of stories, and after a while you think you've heard everything—but of course, you haven't. Patients really surprise me, not so much by what they say as by how they say it. A woman once came in to be interviewed as a participant in one of our Viagra studies. She said she didn't get aroused anymore and that she was hiding this from her husband of thirty years because she feared he would think she didn't love him anymore or that she didn't find him attractive.

I asked, "Are you distressed about this? Do you feel guilty? Are you worried that your marriage is going to end?"

She just looked at me and said, "Nothing is the same! We're getting old, and it's horrible. Look at me!"

Then she stood up, lifted up her dress, and said, "Look at this! My thighs! My belly! I'm fat, I'm unattractive!" She went on and on as I sat there silently.

My impulse was to say, "What are you doing? Stop it! Put your dress down!" But I'm trained to control my impulses and not to betray my feelings. So I composed my face and listened as she sat down and talked about how she had used to wear fishnet hose with garters, and satin thongs, and then she and her husband would get aroused and make passionate love. She had lost this precious part of her self, and her anguish was so great that lifting her skirt was the only way she could explain it. This woman was not an exhibitionist; she was grieving a loss so profound that its weight crushed the boundaries of propriety. That we barely knew each other was immaterial: she had to make me understand, she had to make me *see*.

And it's not just my patients—people I hardly know expose their hearts and reveal details of their intimate lives because things aren't going very well and they have to talk to someone. Once, a representative for a pharmaceutical firm was driving me to a speaking engagement when he suddenly said, "You know, I'm worried because my wife and I don't even have sex once a month now. We've got three kids, and by the time we get them all in bed she's ready to collapse. I miss her, I miss the physical connection. She says she misses it too, but she just can't make it happen."

My heart went out to this guy, and I told him that this is normal, that it happens to many of us. We're all overstressed and overworked, and women have bought into the ludicrous fiction that we can do it all, have it all, and be all things to all people, all at once. But it just isn't true. When life is pulling you in one direction and pushing you in another and push comes to shove, sex gets shoved aside—and we suffer for it.

This is the book I've always wanted to read but was never able to find. Now, after twenty-two years as a physician, I have written it instead. It's my chance to tell women everywhere: if you're crazy about your man but he doesn't drive you crazy in bed; if your favorite fantasy is too nasty and squalid to ever put into words; if you turned down sex yesterday but can't live without it today; if you yearn for intimacy but all you get is sex (and your partner doesn't see what's wrong with that or what the difference is)—it's okay. Yes—you are normal. No—there is nothing wrong with you. You don't have to crave sex all the time to be sexually healthy. You don't have to make love like a porn star (or look like one) to keep your lover happy. You are not crazy or defective or unfeminine. In fact, you're as feminine as it gets. You're a woman, and when you can look within yourself, become aware of who is really there, and embrace yourself and your essential nature, the sex can only get better.

SEXUAL INVENTORY

What's Normal for You?

1. **What phase of your erotic life are you in?**

2. **Are you just beginning to explore your sexual self, or is your sexual identity familiar territory?** Do you seek sexual adventures with numerous partners, or are you searching for a monogamous relationship? Have you lost all interest in sex in general and with your husband specifically, or might the spark be rekindled if he'd pick up his socks? What role does sex play in your life, or what role do you wish it were playing in your life? Are you making love frequently enough to feel satisfied, or are your erotic encounters so infrequent as to leave you feeling sex-

ually isolated and frustrated? If you are involved in a sexual relationship, is the lovemaking as satisfying to you as it is to your partner? If not, why are you settling for less than he or she is? If you are not involved in a sexual relationship, do you wish you were? If the answer is yes, what is your ideal scenario of how the lovemaking would be?

3. **Are your sexual expectations, if any, higher or lower than they used to be?** If they are higher, what has made you expect more from sex? If they are lower, what has made you settle for less? Do you feel you are less sexually attractive than you used to be? Are you less attracted to your partner than you were before, or is your partner less interested in you? Do you believe you have no business expecting satisfying sex at your phase of life?

4. **Have you ever faked an orgasm, or do you do so routinely?** If the answer is yes, why did you do it, or why do you do it? Are you doing it to spare your partner's feelings? To get the whole sex thing over with? If so, why do you want to get it over with?

5. **If you have faked an orgasm or do so routinely, are you pleased with or frustrated by the results?**
   ■ What do you believe is gained when you pretend to reach a climax?
   ■ What do you think would happen if you were truthful with your partner instead?

6. **Think about the physical and psychological changes you experience when you are sexually aroused and consider:**
   ■ Where are your erogenous zones? (There are more of them than the ones men tend to home in on, so think about your entire body.)
   ■ What kinds of sensations do you find most pleasurable?
   ■ Is there a sexual behavior or practice to which you are attracted but that you have never tried? If so, what excites you about it? If not, what has kept you from trying it?

CHAPTER 2

Whom Do You Love, and Why?

A woman enters my office and sits. She looks about forty, although she could be somewhat younger or quite a bit older. She is dark-haired and attractive, but she could just as easily be blond and plain. She could, in fact, be anyone.

"I've been depressed," she says. "I recently broke up with someone I'd been with for a long time. Things were not good between us at the end, but when he left, I still felt terrible." She pauses.

"It sounds as if you had mixed feelings about him."

"Not until the end. I really loved him. But it didn't work out—it never works out. I try and I try and I try. But no matter who I'm with, it always ends the same way."

"What way is that?"

She is weeping now. I hand her a box of tissues and wait for her to compose herself.

"I fall in love, and I commit, and I give everything I have to the relationship. Everything. There is nothing I won't do to make a relationship work. But they never do."

"Why do you think that is?"

"I don't know. I've tried everything. I've gone out with every kind of guy you can imagine. But it doesn't matter who it is; we get to a certain point, and things fall apart. I don't know what keeps going wrong."

The woman, a mortgage broker, had spent the last year living with a gentle man who loved kids and cared even less about football than she did. When they met, he was working part-time as a substitute high school teacher and looking for a full-time position. He was solicitous of the woman and eager to please her, and although he seldom initiated sex, he was tender and worshipful when they did make love. At forty-two, he was ready to marry and start a family, which they talked about doing as soon as he found permanent employment. But nothing seemed to work out for the guy: he heard about a teaching position in the next county but missed the application deadline; he was offered a job at a new school, but it would mean driving an extra forty miles round-trip. The woman got him a lead on a job at a nearby prep school, but he lost the phone number; by the time he found it, the position had been filled. Another time, she arranged a meeting for him with a representative of the local school board. Afterward, he fretted about how he had conducted himself in the interview and pre-dicted that nothing would come of it (he was right). He began to talk about starting his own business, but when the woman tried to get him to discuss his plans, he could not articulate any. The more he floundered, the harder she tried to create opportunities for him, until she found herself thinking obsessively about his career and neglecting her own.

The woman did all she could for the man, but his prospects didn't im-prove. She wasn't a fool; she could see that he was using his lack of secure employment to continually postpone his commitment to her. As her re-spect for him dwindled, so did her desire. The more she withdrew, the more desperate he became to win back her affection, and the harder he tried to woo her, the more pathetic he seemed. When she suggested he move out, she expected him to break down and ask her for another chance. He did break down but made no requests. In tears, he packed his bags and left.

I asked the woman about her other relationships. Before the teacher there had been a charming, well-spoken actor who had been working in regional theater for fifteen years and whose elderly parents sent him money every month to help make ends meet. Before him there had been an accountant who had been separated from his wife for six years but still had not finalized the divorce. And before him there had been a real estate agent with a wicked sense of humor who lived with his parents because he still hadn't found the perfect house and besides, his mother did his laun-dry.

"You know, as I talk about it, these guys sound like a bunch of losers," the woman said, "but they really weren't. They were all neat guys—smart, nice-looking, good dressers. They treated me well. The sex was good, too, at least at first. But that's as far as it goes: there's a strong attraction, the sex is great, we get close, and it doesn't go anywhere. I give it everything I've got, and I still can't make it work."

If this woman were your friend, you might want to sit her down and say, "Listen to what you just said: *I still can't make it work*—'I,' not 'we.' These men aren't your partners, they're your protégés. You're attracted not to the man but to his potential. There's something about a man's lack of accomplishment that arouses you; you're turned on by the challenge of being his muse, of inspiring him to become his finest, most virile self. You experience these feelings as love for him, but what you're really in love with is the notion of yourself as savior, the one and only person who can prevent your incipient hero from squandering the vast potential that only you can see."

Your friend would probably reject your theory, but you would probably be right. You know this woman well, and you've seen her repeat this pattern over and over again. You've met some of these men and found them all to be decent if not dynamic guys. You've listened over the years as she's told you about the vicissitudes of her love life, and you know what will happen before she does. Yet when you once suggested that she think about why she was sexually attracted to men who were destined to disappoint her, she demurred, saying that she was different from you, she could not embark on a relationship with preconceived notions about how it would turn out; that when it came to love she was a romantic, not a pragmatist, and listened to her heart, not her head. So you held your tongue and settled in for another bout of listening.

So it is with psychiatrists: we listen, sometimes over months and years, as a patient's words weave a fabric of thoughts and emotions that hangs in the air between us, manifesting patterns that coalesce into clues that we have been trained to interpret, much as a radiologist interprets an X-ray. But while a radiologist can point to a spot on the film and say, "See this line? This is the fracture, this is where your leg is broken," and make the patient see the source of the pain, a psychiatrist doesn't have it so easy. We might sense the outline of a broken heart as clearly as a radiologist sees a fractured tibia, but pointing to it directly seldom has a healing effect, because when it comes to the heart, the patient seldom sees what the doctor sees. You can't just say, "Come on, don't you see what you're doing? You're sleeping with a different guy every weekend because you're trying to resurrect the feelings you had with your first love over twenty years ago. All these affairs are about wanting to re-create the feelings you had with your college boyfriend, except with forty-year-old men. What's up with *that*?"

If men and women would take an unflinching look at what ignites their libidos, they'd be less likely to repeat the patterns that guarantee chronic sexual discontent. But all too often, we are blind to what propels us, aglow in a mist of equal parts rationalization and delusion, toward people who are destined to disappoint us.

Why do we do this? Some people get a rush from taking a flying leap into the abyss of risky love, and, like emotional bungee jumpers, trust that the beloved's heartstrings will yank them to safety before they hit rock bottom. But these romantic thrill seekers are relatively rare. More often we pursue people who appear to possess an admirable trait—confidence, compassion, strength of character, or spiritual depth—only to learn that they are presenting a façade that masks a dearth of the very quality we seek.

We've all done this: fallen in love with a man who exuded confidence and self-reliance but couldn't stand up to his parents when they insisted that he spend his birthday with them and leave us behind. Or the guy who got on so well with your kids not because he had a natural feel for parenting but because he needed you to be his mother as much as they did. Or the incurable romantic who wooed you with flowers and cute animated e-cards but who, once he captured your heart, tossed it back as if it were a hot potato. I once treated a woman who had fallen in love with a man she had met at church. She was attracted to the fierceness of his faith and unwavering commitment to walking a righteous path, and envisioned a future where they would grow closer together in their love of God. But after they married, the man's piousness seemed less about embracing the sacred than obeying the rules. He expected his wife to intensify her religious practice to conform to his and was distressed when she resisted. Over time, the woman saw that her husband was using religion not to elevate his spirit but to rein it in, and that while she sought rapture, he relished rigidity. When they met, she saw a man of faith, but what she saw was different from who she got.

And there but for the grace of God go all of us. You luck out and land the greatest lover you've ever had; he knows just how to touch you, and where, and how long and how hard, and can set you aquiver by passing the salt. He's a master of sex, but the buck stops there: ask him how he feels about you, and you'll get a blank stare (assuming he hasn't already hightailed it out of your house).

And so you press on, dazed with delight and desire, attentive to the melting sensation north of your kneecaps and south of your gray matter. All you know is that you see him (or her), you think he's cute, he smiles back, and your ability to reason fades to black. So what if he's married or living with someone, or separated but still not divorced after five years? How can such picayune concerns withstand the redemptive power of love?

You'd be surprised.

Karla: The Triangulator

Karla was referred to me by the campus health center, where she had arrived complaining of acute anxiety resulting in insomnia that had lasted for more than two weeks. All I knew beyond that was that she was twenty-four, single, and pursuing a doctorate in Asian studies.

She arrived at my office in a flurry of activity. Purplish shadows pooled beneath her eyes, which held mine for only a second before focusing on her hands, which were rummaging through a large leather satchel that hung from her shoulder. She couldn't stop moving, even after she sat down; she smoothed her skirt and then her hair, reached back into the satchel, and pulled out a wad of what looked like toilet paper, which she jammed against her nose. When she looked up again, her eyes looked swollen.

"I'm about to lose it," she said. "This person, she's . . . I've had to leave where I've been staying because this woman is coming. It's like I'm losing my home because my boyfriend . . . that sounds funny, because he's much older than I am . . . it's his house but he's got no choice; all of a sudden they're letting her out. He didn't expect this to happen, and now he says it's over and I don't know what to do. I'm supposed to be doing my research, but I can't focus and I'm starting to panic. I can't sleep, I can't work, thoughts keep racing through my head. Why does this have to happen now? Things were going so great, and now she's ruining everything."

I was intrigued: Who was this other woman? Who was letting her out, and from where? How could she ruin everything if it was going so great? How many answers could I get without asking too many questions?

"Tell me more."

"About what? Her? I can't tell you much. I mean, he told me about her, I knew she existed, but he said that she was going to be there for a long time and that this was strictly an arrangement between them. And I don't want him to get in trouble—this isn't his fault. Strictly speaking, we shouldn't be seeing each other, because he's on my dissertation committee. Which is insane. I mean, it's not like I'm an undergraduate away from home for the first time. I was once married, for heaven's sake. We're supposed to be adults. You meet someone and there's a powerful connection and we're supposed to ignore it because he's on faculty? It doesn't make any sense."

Actually, it makes very good sense, but Karla wasn't about to see it that way. I chose to pursue a different angle.

"You said you're losing your home?"

"Yes, kind of. I've been spending a lot of time at Henry's house. But now he says I've got to leave. I kept my apartment, but it still isn't right. Why doesn't he tell her to get her own place? I don't understand why this is happening."

The story began to gel. The other woman was a Chinese political activist named Shan whom Henry had met years earlier when he was doing research in Guangzhou. She had written some inflammatory pamphlets and attracted the interest of local officials, who had confiscated her passport. Now, as a result of some political maneuvering, she had been granted permission to come to the United States. She had seniority over Karla in the household arrangements because she wasn't the other woman at all; she was Henry's wife.

"Oh," I said, careful to act a lot less surprised than I felt. A psychiatrist is not supposed to act in ways that a patient might interpret as judgments.

We are supposed to remain calm and collected, no matter how big a bomb the patient drops.

"They met, they worked together, she wanted to teach here in the States, he felt sorry for her, and he agreed to marry her so she could come. Only, before they could leave, she got arrested. Now they're letting her go and he's kicking me out so she can move in. I just don't get it—he doesn't love her. He just feels responsible for her."

"Is that what he says?"

"No, but I know it's the truth."

The truth was another issue and would require more than a single session to sort out. Karla agreed to come in twice a week.

What does this have to do with sex? Quite a bit, when you consider the pattern of Karla's romantic liaisons. Over the course of our work together, I learned a lot about my patient. She was born to college-educated parents in rural South Carolina. Her mother's family owned a successful rice plantation, which her father now ran with Karla's two older brothers. This was significant; Karla was the only person in her family to pursue a graduate degree in an exotic field rather than return to the familiarity of the family business after graduation.

Karla's childhood was uneventful until she became a teenager, when, in her words, her mother turned on her, finding fault with Karla's choice of friends (too fast), taste in clothes (vulgar), and professional aspirations (too enamored of foreign cultures; what's wrong with American studies?). Her brothers were four and six years older than Karla and away at college by the time the trouble started, so they could offer minimal comfort to their kid sister. Karla retreated to her father's warmth and approval. When Karla quarreled with her mother—which happened frequently—she would wait for her father to return from work and urge him to intercede on her behalf. When he did, the results were usually explosive, with Karla's mother accusing him of favoring his daughter over her and storming off to the bedroom, slamming doors along the way.

Not surprisingly, Karla was jubilant when she was accepted by a college in another state. Shortly after her arrival there, she became romantically involved with a young man in her freshman English class, who, in her words, looked good on paper. The only son of a well-to-do, well-connected family, he lived in a new condo paid for by his parents and enjoyed an unobstructed view of both the Blue Ridge Mountains and his future. He treated Karla with a courtliness and respect that seemed formal to her but were reassuring to her parents. They were married at the end of their junior year; eighteen months later, it was over. Karla had little to say about the young man other than that he was decent but dull; the marriage lacked excitement and pizzazz. After six months, she felt as if she'd been married for sixty years.

Now, two years later, she was enmeshed with Henry, a much older man who had breached the university's code of ethics by conducting an amorous relationship with a student in his department. Interestingly, the adulterous nature of the affair did not faze Karla, who had persuaded herself that all Henry's wife expected from the marriage was a green card. She was shocked and hurt to find herself so swiftly cast out of Henry's house, heart, and bed, especially since she had thought their sex life was so good. She found Henry extremely attractive and said that he was a considerate and virile lover. He was, in fact, the best lover she had ever had, and she thought he felt the same way about her.

I considered the information in my possession. Was Karla turned on by drama? Was the sex exciting because of the illicit nature of the affair and the power Karla implicitly wielded within it? After all, sexual relationships between faculty and students are forbidden, and Henry would be subject to censure, if not worse, were his affair with Karla to become public. But the more I thought about it, the less plausible this seemed. Karla appeared averse to endangering Henry's career: she showed neither an interest in using the affair to manipulate him nor the hostility that would support such sabotage. The thrill of living dangerously may have been part of it, but it didn't feel like the whole thing.

My emerging view was that this was an Oedipal conflict, that Karla was trying to be with her father, and that the dissident wife represented Karla's mother. This scenario made more sense, both rationally and intuitively. I considered how to suggest this approach to Karla; I didn't want to come on too strong lest she reject me as too bound to tradition and out of touch with the complex dynamics of her situation. I decided to start by picking up and following a conspicuous thread: Karla's view of Henry as a beleaguered do-gooder, lured into a marriage of convenience that had become painfully inconvenient for him and his student-turned-sweetheart.

It was slow going; Karla was not eager to acknowledge Henry's complicity in creating the debacle, not to mention her own. But over time, Karla was able to reframe her view of her lover and see him more clearly: as a charismatic figure of fulsome tastes and flawed judgment who had flouted university policy, betrayed the trust of both his student and his wife, and wreaked a good deal of havoc, academic and otherwise, in the process. She eventually acknowledged the Oedipal elements of the relationship and saw that desiring her professor was a way of being with her father and that blaming his wife for the problem paralleled her conflict with her mother.

Before we go any further, let me say one thing: this took time. I did not sit Karla down and, after posing an exquisitely crafted question or two, elicit from her a montage of Technicolor flashbacks that made sudden blinding sense out of the twenty-four years of her life. That happens only in the movies. Real therapy happens in real time, and not every session crackles with revelation and self-discovery. Many sessions ended with Karla in tears and as befuddled about what was driving her as when she first walked into my office. But every once in a while, a shaft of light would penetrate and spark Karla's self-awareness. At these moments, she might not say much, but I would know by the look in her eyes that they had seen something new and rare. That is how we acquire knowledge of ourselves, in blazing slivers of insight. If we accumulate enough of these, we may even grow wise.

Session by session, Karla began to entertain the possibility that Henry's presence in the marriage was a result of choice and not coercion. As it became clear that Shan was not moving out, nor was Henry moving on, she weaned herself away from the vision of a future with this man.

Karla decided to leave graduate school with a master's degree; as her relationship with Henry ebbed, so did her interest in earning a doctorate. She took a job in town, managing the office of a small photography business owned by a couple in their late thirties who specialized in shooting portraits and weddings. Frank and Irene were not married themselves but had been living together for more than a decade when Karla began working for them. A few months after hiring Karla, they invited her over for dinner. After several bottles of chardonnay, Irene said she had an early shoot the next morning and was going to bed. An hour later, Karla found herself naked in the couple's hot tub with Frank and, shortly thereafter, in hot water with Irene. Once again, Karla was persona non grata.

After Karla told me the story, I pointed out that she seemed drawn to men who were quite a bit older than she and entrenched in long-term relationships, and that even though Frank was a wobbly step in the right direction—he was fifteen years younger than his predecessor and not legally married—you could hardly call him available. She responded by saying that, yes, it did look as if she preferred older, unavailable men, but these were the guys she was meeting, after all; it wasn't as if she went out trolling golf courses and Rotary Club picnics for married men. She was twenty-five years old and out in the world; she couldn't help it if all the guys she met were older.

Irene kicked Frank out of the house and refused to come to the studio when Karla was there. Frank started spending nights at Karla's, then told her he had to reduce her hours so Irene could be at the studio when Karla wasn't. Frank, guilty over slashing Karla's income and anguished at the prospect of losing Irene, developed the beginnings of an ulcer and had to cancel several shoots. Within a month, Karla realized that the arrangement was doomed: she quit the job and asked Frank to leave her house. This was progress; rather than waiting to see what would happen, Karla had taken control. She was out of work, but that didn't worry me. Karla was highly competent, and I knew she would soon find a job.

At about that time I left for a two-year stint as a Navy psychiatrist, during which I neither saw Karla nor heard from her. But the story doesn't end there.

I had been back from my Navy assignment less than a week when I ran into Karla in a restaurant. She greeted me warmly, looked cheerful and healthy, and said she was working for a community social work agency and had come a long way in the last two years. So I was surprised when she called a few days later to say she wanted to see me. I had a cancellation that afternoon, and three hours later she was in my office. She wasn't fidgeting as much as when she had come to see me the first time, but the cheer I had seen in her face at the restaurant had been replaced by a forced gaiety. Her mouth was smiling as she spoke, but her eyes looked wary.

"It's Scott, this guy I'm seeing. He's my age, and don't worry—he's single. He's good-looking, he's got a good job and makes plenty of money, drives a new BMW, we go to nice places . . . you know, he looks great on paper."

That's how she had described the young man she had married. My inner antennae pricked up.

"And in reality?"

"Well, he's, I don't know how you'd say it, he's kind of into himself. He's not really selfish, at least not always. But sometimes he pushes me to do stuff even though he knows I don't want to do it. It's nothing horrible, but I sometimes feel I have to do things or he'll get angry and it'll be over between us."

He sounded narcissistic to me. I pressed Karla gently. "What kinds of things does he want you to do?"

"Most of the time it's small stuff, like eating where he wants to eat or doing what he wants to do. Once we were planning a weekend away and I really wanted to go to D.C. to see this art exhibit that was leaving for Chicago, but he really wanted to go to the Outer Banks, so that's what we ended up doing. And it was okay, we had a good time. But there's other stuff, too." She stopped and looked down at her hands, which were busy tracing the threads in her slacks.

"What kind of stuff?" She still had not looked up.

"It's not easy to talk about."

I sat and waited. Finally, Karla spoke in a small voice.

"It's kind of weird, and I don't know if he really means it, but he keeps saying he's always wanted to have a threesome, you know, with another woman."

This didn't shock me; many men fantasize about making love with two women but never venture past the fantasy stage. But I did become concerned when Karla went on to say that Dianne, an old friend from high school, was coming to spend the weekend. This friend was important to her; they had been confidantes for many years. Karla had always been the more adventurous of the two, Dianne the more cautious and traditional.

Now Dianne was coming to visit Karla and meet her new boyfriend, and the plan was for the three of them to cook dinner together at Scott's place on Friday.

Had I been Karla's friend and not her psychiatrist, I would have told her that this plan had disaster written all over it, that she should take Dianne to a restaurant or the movies—*anywhere* that wasn't Scott's place. But I am a psychiatrist and don't tell my patients what to do. (The only time I do give unsolicited advice is when I think a patient needs a lawyer, and then I'll say so.) So I did not say, "You know what, I think you're going to get into a threesome this weekend and it's going to turn out badly." Instead, I asked her what her expectations were for the visit and how she was hoping the dinner might turn out. I wanted to get her to think about the scenario she was creating and what some possible outcomes might be. But Karla's answers were evasive, and because she had not said she was planning a threesome, I could not respond as if she had. Instead, I wished her a pleasant weekend and told her to be sure to call me if things didn't go well.

Things did not go well, and Karla was in my office on Monday. Shaken and teary, she told me that the three of them had started drinking and ended up in bed together. Not surprisingly, the sex was less than ecstatic. When they awoke the next morning, Scott was hungover and aloof, Karla was awash in feelings of jealousy and confusion, and Dianne was humiliated and angry. She accused Karla of inviting her to visit merely to lure her into a freaky sex scene, and when Karla said that wasn't the case, Dianne said it certainly was the case or Karla would have protected her from Scott's advances. Karla pointed out that Dianne hadn't exactly fought him off, at which point Dianne hurled a few choice words in Karla's direction along with a half-eaten Danish and stomped upstairs to pack her bags.

Karla ran to the kitchen, where Scott was drinking a cup of coffee, and begged him to apologize to Dianne and ask her to stay. Scott said something to the effect of "Look, no one forced her to do anything. Stop being so emotional, she'll get over it."

By this time Karla was highly agitated and in tears. She ran after Dianne, who had taken her bags out to the car, and tried to keep her from closing the trunk. But Dianne was adamant; she got into the car and, according to Karla, nearly ran her over as she peeled out of the driveway.

When Karla got back inside, Scott said he thought it would be a good idea if she went back to her own place until she calmed down. This was Saturday morning.

Karla phoned Dianne repeatedly that weekend, but all she got was the answering machine. When Dianne finally picked up the phone on Sunday night, her voice was clipped and professional. The buoyancy of their connection had been replaced by the leaden air of reproach. Feeling the frost in Dianne's voice, Karla felt alone and emotionally unmoored.

During a course of therapy, a patient is sometimes pierced by insight, a shard of self-awareness that slices, like a scalpel, down to the heart of truth. This was such a moment for Karla. No sooner did she acknowledge that she'd helped instigate a love triangle than it dawned on her that she'd been doing it for years—*all* her love affairs, with the exception of her marriage, had been triangles. It was as if after years of digging with a teaspoon in the soil of her self, she had unearthed a map of her interior world. She acknowledged that she was attracted to sexual situations that placed her in competition with another woman, just as she'd competed with her mother for her father's affection. It didn't matter if the woman she vanquished was her lover's wife or girlfriend or her own girlfriend—the adolescent triumph still resonated for Karla, and she sought to revive it repeatedly, if unwittingly, in her adult encounters.

Karla learned the hard way that women were important to her. She also learned that connecting deeply with a man involves more than the electric charge of novel sex, that just because a man wants to make love with you doesn't mean he is *in* love with you.

After two more months of hard work and self-examination, Karla worked up the strength to end her relationship with Scott. (Yes, it took her that long. And if you're sitting there shaking your head and thinking that *you* would have sent him packing a lot sooner, I say to you, don't be so sure. We're very perceptive about other women's boyfriends but blind as bats when it comes to our own.) With some strong hinting from me, Karla decided that her next romance should be with a man her age—twenty-eight at this point—who cared for her, was not otherwise involved, and would agree to let sex wait until they had established an emotional intimacy. These prerequisites would have sent the old Karla into a fit of eye rolling, but to the chastened Karla, they made sense.

For the first time in her adult life, Karla was without a man in her bed or on the horizon. I told her I thought this was a good thing because I believed she ran from man to man for fear of being alone, and it's not so horrible to be alone. It was worse, she discovered, to be aroused by the challenge of winning a man away from someone else, especially when the prize was not the man's love but the satisfaction of wresting him from another woman's arms into her own (talk about a lose-lose-lose proposition).

Some months later, Karla heard about a new job at an agency that needed someone to work with recent immigrants, so she set up an interview. When the people there heard she had a working knowledge of Vietnamese, they hired her on the spot. Karla's work consisted of helping newly arrived families, many of them Asian, to find housing and employment. The satisfaction of helping these people and the gratitude they expressed persuaded Karla that she was doing good in the world, as did the praise of a colleague who made no secret of his interest in her. Martin was thirty-two and had a master's degree in social work and neither a wife nor a live-in partner. Karla described him as not gorgeous but pleasant-looking, intelligent, kind, and in need of some hipper clothes. When he invited Karla out to lunch, she accepted. The next day, she came in for her regular session.

"He's really nice," she said. "He asked me all these questions about myself—where I was born, what my family was like—and acted as if he really cared about what I had to say. He's a good listener—I guess you can tell he's a social worker."

"But here's the thing: I'm not sure I'm attracted to him. I mean, he's sort of cute, in a straight kind of way. But the other guys I've been attracted to . . . it felt different with them."

"Different how?"

"It's hard to describe. More . . . I don't know, more exciting or more challenging, maybe."

"More dangerous?"

"Yes, maybe. You know, riskier, like there was more at stake."

"How does it feel with Martin?"

"Warmer. Safer. Like I know I can trust him. Which I know is good in theory. But I don't know if that translates into sexual excitement for me."

Karla made me a promise: she would give the relationship with Martin a chance to develop before she bailed out. At their next lunch, she told him she needed to move slowly. He said that was fine with him. Lunches eventually progressed to dinners. By the time they did sleep together—which was after at least four months of dating—they were already intimately acquainted with each other. Karla learned that Martin's outward equanimity had been hard won; she heard about his difficult childhood, his mother's suicide, and his struggle to justify his own existence in the aftermath of the tragedy. She came to see that his even temperament betokened not a lack of passion but rather a deliberate attempt to manage it. The man she had feared might not be exciting revealed himself to be a person of deep feeling and compassion, which he lavished on Karla as he came to know her. They eventually married, and Karla's course of therapy came to an end.

I did see Karla once again, a year after the birth of her second child. She had been offered a high-paying job that required a good deal of travel, and she didn't know what to do. She came in, and I said, "Karla, you know yourself; you've thought about this"—and it was true. She did most of the talking; I didn't speak much at all. In one session, she was able to sort out what she wanted to do. Which is not to say she wasn't anxious while she worked things through; Karla's anxiety was what always propelled her into my office. But once she was here, she was able to separate what appealed to her about the offer (challenging work, regular trips to Asia, a lot more money) from what did not appeal to her (guilt about being away from the family, fear that making more money than her husband would offend him and fray the marriage) and make a decision (she took the job). Perhaps the best part of it was that Martin was her greatest champion: he went on a part-time work schedule to help care for the kids and bragged about Karla's new job to anyone who would listen.

Karla's story is one of those that might seem to be more about a woman with relationship problems than one with sexual problems, and it very well could be; it all depends on how you look at things. If you look at Karla's case from the outside—that is, her string of triangular love affairs—the sexual thread doesn't stand out: she came in complaining about anxiety and insomnia, not her sex life, after all. From the outside, Karla might appear to be an intense young woman with a vigorous sex life and rotten luck with men.

But I look at things from the inside out, starting at the sanctum of the psyche, because that is where woman's sexuality is forged. So with Karla, I started with the anxiety—the slub in the surface of her psyche—and followed it deeper into the pattern, where it led inexorably to the essence of her sexuality: a fiercely competitive hunger that had ripened in the hothouse of her parents' blooming and wilting affections. Karla was in early adolescence when her mother started finding fault with her, and the timing was no coincidence. As Karla's sexuality bloomed, so did her mother's anxiety, evolving into what felt to Karla like a relentless denunciation of her intellectual pursuits, her friends, and her efforts at self-expression. When Karla retreated to her father's embrace, she found more than comfort there; she found a way to manipulate her parents into conflict and her mother into another part of the house. Her father rescued her and vanquished her oppressor, and it felt good. It was those feelings of conquest and safety that Karla stored in her body's memory as well as her mind's, and that caused a quickening of desire when, as an adult, she sensed an opportunity to relive her triumph.

The result was that Karla was sexually drawn to older men who were temporarily beguiled by the attentions of a nubile companion but whose erotic energies, like her father's, were already committed elsewhere. She thought she had broken the pattern when she took up with Scott because he was neither older than she nor committed to someone else. Yet he represented a mere variation in the pattern, as his narcissism required Karla to cater to his whims and desires, one of which placed her in sexual competition with another woman—with whom she had deep and long-standing ties, as she had with her mother—and back into the pattern.

Karla didn't think she had a sexual problem, because she enjoyed making love with these men—that is, until their significant others showed up and she got booted out. But Karla did have a sexual problem, even if she had no problem having sex. Her sexuality was sabotaging her primary emotional requirement: a stable, loving alliance with someone devoted to her. By following the thread of her anxiety beneath the surface, she was able to see a pattern: the more exciting her sexual encounters were, the more damage they did to her, body and soul. It was then that she began to know that she was the architect of this pattern, and that it was fully within her power to change it.

Laurel:
Leaping into Infatuation, Fleeing Intimacy

Some people seek connection with others whom they imagine will fill the void of the happy childhood they never had or the big love that didn't work out. They are drawn to these relationships because they promise to right wrongs done to them, whether by the uncaring parents fate foisted upon them or the uncaring lovers they chose for themselves. Sometimes it works out and they elicit from a husband, wife, or partner the unconditional love they didn't receive as a child, or an even bigger love than the one that got away. Yet even when it does work out, deliverance seldom arrives on the first, second, or even third try. They might spend years, if not decades, seeking a person who has adequate reserves of love and will liberate them from their loneliness.

Laurel falls into this category, although I suspect she still doesn't fully realize it. I can't be sure, as I see her only sporadically now. But while she was regularly under my care, I gradually came to see a pattern in the women she was attracted to.

To label Laurel a lesbian would be to oversimplify her experience. She had dated men before she became my patient, which was when she was in her early forties. She even alluded to having been engaged twice, once in her twenties and once in her thirties. She didn't talk about these episodes other than to say that her fiancés had been good guys who deserved better than to end up with someone who didn't love them enough, so she had ended the engagements. At about the time she turned forty, she went to a gallery opening near her condo and struck up a conversation with a woman who suggested they leave and get some dinner. Two hours later, they were back at Laurel's apartment, necking like teenagers. The relationship lasted six months; then the sex began to falter.

When Laurel became my patient, she was still recovering from a dalliance with a colleague named Dawn more than a year before. There had never been a romance but rather a single night of spontaneous, away-on-business, I-can't-believe-we're-doing-this sex, made all the more thrilling by a postcoital phone call from Dawn's husband, Douglas. Laurel said it was one of the most poignant encounters she had ever had, and by far the most freighted with fantasy.

Laurel and Dawn both worked in new product development at a large semiconductor fabrication facility in Richmond and got to know each other when they collaborated on a project. Laurel was smitten with Dawn's intelligence, business savvy, and gentility, which Laurel described as of the steel magnolia variety. Dawn was in turn impressed by Laurel's resourceful and scrappy personality; when Laurel said she would do something, she got it done, and Dawn was soon relying on her. The two developed a good-natured, bantering relationship and felt as if they had known each other for years. Dawn introduced Laurel to her husband and began inviting her to family events. Laurel became particularly fond of Dawn's parents, fourth-generation Richmonders whose affection for their daughter extended to her friend. When they began inviting Laurel to spend Christmas at the family home, they could not have predicted the redemptive power of the gesture.

"My mother wasn't normal," Laurel said at her first session. "She never treated us the way other mothers treated their kids. She would say she loved us, but it was like we knew it intellectually but never felt it. She was never really there emotionally, and then one day she wasn't there at all. She disappeared when I was twelve. One day my brother and I left for school, and when we got home, the house was empty." Outside of a brief visit when their father tracked her down in Chicago, Laurel and her brother never saw their mother again.

Three years later, Laurel's father married a woman he had met at work. Norma was divorced, blond, and no beauty, but attractive in a way that resulted from weekly visits to the hairdresser and faithful reading of fashion magazines. Laurel remembered that she used to wear shiny shoes with no backs on them and little feathers on the toes. She had no children of her own, and while Laurel said she was not unkind to her and her brother, she never really loved them, either. Moreover, Norma's classic girly-girl femininity—to use Laurel's term—seemed to captivate Laurel's father and focus his awareness with increasing dismay on Laurel's dungarees-and-work-shirt style. She had never doubted her father's love, but now she felt the sting of his disapproval. Laurel's brother joined the Army and left home when he was eighteen. Two years later, Laurel won an out-of-state scholarship and left for college.

Now, nearly thirty years later, Laurel had replaced the fractured bonds of her family with the strong, new ties she had woven with Dawn's. The friendship they began at work flourished in an atmosphere of professional respect and personal harmony; they not only got along well but clearly delighted in each other's company. So it was not utterly shocking that, on a business trip a thousand miles away from home and light-years away from real life, the emotional intimacy between the women leapt from virtual to reality. Laurel didn't offer many details other than that the sex had been spontaneous, mutually pleasurable, and, despite its occasional awkwardness, thrilling.

The morning after, Dawn had been unsettled but not freaked-out; she said she didn't know what had come over her; she had never done anything like that before. She hoped that Laurel didn't think their lovemaking betokened a change in the nature of their relationship: their tryst was a wonderful but onetime episode. She wasn't about to leave Douglas, nor would she consider a clandestine affair that could damage her marriage as well as her career. That said, she thought the world of Laurel and hoped everything could continue as before.

For Laurel, it could not; though she wanted to keep Dawn in her life, she could do without the frustration of seeing her every day. Laurel transferred to the purchasing department, a move that would remove her from Dawn's daily orbit and require her to travel two weeks out of every month. Several months later, she met a hairstylist named Judy, and they began to date. The affair began passionately but foundered after a couple of months.

"Judy was very sweet; she had a great body, and it was very intense at first. I'd think about her and couldn't wait to see her, but after a while the sex became kind of dull. And she was so, I don't know, so damned agreeable! It sounds crazy but it really worked my nerves. One of the things I love about Dawn is that she speaks her mind. When she thinks I'm full of it, she says so, and I love that. But with Judy, no matter what I did or said, it was like, 'That's okay, that's fine, whatever you say, I don't care'—it drove me crazy. After a while, I couldn't wait to get out of there."

"It sounds as if you enjoy being with someone who challenges you," I said.

"Doesn't everyone?"

"Not at all. Some people don't like being told they're full of it."

In the year since their fateful night on the road, Laurel and Dawn had remained friends but spent less time together. After breaking up with Judy, Laurel began passing her evenings at home visiting Internet chat rooms. It was through one of these that she had met Sonya, a New York stockbroker.

"We have this strong connection," she said. "We wrote back and forth for a month, sometimes fifteen, twenty times a day. Short stuff—Sonya was at work—but very hot, very intense. So we decided to meet in Washington, D.C., and I drove up there on a Friday afternoon. When I got to the hotel, I walked into the lobby and I saw this woman. And I had this powerful, electric feeling. She wasn't conventionally gorgeous, but she gave off this energy. And I'm thinking—this is so screwed up—I'm thinking, *I have simply got to meet this woman.* And I'm feeling like a jerk because I was there to meet Sonya, and I take one look at this other woman and I'm, like, gaga.

"So I go up and get myself ready. We'd arranged to meet in the lobby at six-thirty and to go to dinner. So I go down in the elevator and I look around, and there she was, the woman I'd seen before. And she walks up to me—I'm standing there like I'm paralyzed—and she says, 'Are you Laurel, by any chance? I'm Sonya.' I almost passed out, I swear."

They went straight up to Laurel's room—no drinks, no dinner, just wild, uninhibited lovemaking, with room service at two in the morning.

The sex had Laurel buzzing for days. She and Sonya began seeing each other on weekends when Laurel wasn't traveling; Laurel would fly up to New York or Sonya would fly down. For a while, it seemed as if Laurel had found her soul mate. But after a few months her ardor seemed to cool. In session, she would spend more time talking about her last trip to China than about her time in New York. When she did talk about Sonya, the narrative was punctuated with sighs. Sonya wanted a commitment and had asked Laurel to move into her apartment on the Upper East Side. But Laurel was balking; she liked her new job and didn't want to move, especially to New York. Besides, Sonya wasn't turning out to be as independent as she'd seemed.

"Emotionally, she's high maintenance," Laurel said. "She's tough all week at work, but on the weekends, she's like, 'Why can't we just take in

Chinese food and be together? Why don't you move in with me?' But when I explain for the umpteenth time why I don't want to move to New York, she gets all hurt and weepy."

"So," I said, "how do you think things will go this weekend?"

"With Sonya, you mean? She's not coming down this weekend."

It turned out that Dawn's parents had invited Laurel to join the family for a few days at their ten-thousand-square-foot river cottage. Dawn was eager for Laurel to come and told her she was welcome to bring a guest. But Laurel thought it would be too distracting to have Sonya around, so she told Sonya she would prefer to introduce her to Dawn's family at another time, on more neutral ground. When Laurel didn't elaborate further, I changed angles.

"How do you feel about spending a weekend with Dawn and her family?"

"I'm really looking forward to it; I feel ready. And as a matter of fact, I was wondering if I could bring Dawn along when I come in next week. I'd really like you to meet her."

They say a picture is worth a thousand words; when it comes to therapy, a live appearance is worth quite a few more. Dawn was about forty-five, tall, blond, and handsome, with a throaty laugh and confidence to spare. I was struck by the force of her personality: she looked me straight in the eye, smiled easily, looked at Laurel with open affection, and, true to her reputation, did not hesitate to tell Laurel when she thought she was full of it. When this happened—and it did, more than once—Laurel would smile and look both abashed and pleased. One thing was clear: Laurel loved it when Dawn stood up to her—something her lovers never seemed to do.

The following weekend, Laurel left a message saying she was still at Sonya's and would have to miss her Monday-morning session. She appeared for her next one looking tired and grim. After thirty seconds of silence, I took the lead.

"How are you?"

"Absolutely fabulous. Sonya calls me every half hour, cries, calls me names, and hangs up. I haven't slept in four days, and last night I went through two pints of Häagen-Dazs in an hour. Outside of that, I'm in great shape."

It had been a tough weekend. Sonya was hurt and angry that Laurel had not taken her to meet Dawn's family and accused her of never having cared for her in the first place. Laurel told Sonya she was overreacting, that they weren't obligated to spend all their time together.

"I care deeply for Sonya," Laurel said. "But lately, all we do is argue. And our sex life—forget it. The last few times we did it, it was like . . ."

Silence.

There are times when you don't want to interrupt a patient, and this was one of them. Laurel's silence was far from empty; she was wrestling with herself, trying to marshal the courage to say what she really felt.

"This sounds terrible, but it was like mercy sex. I don't want to hurt her feelings, so I do it. And then I feel horrible. But that's how things are between us now: everything is about making Sonya feel happy, making Sonya feel safe and protected and loved. It's all about meeting Sonya's needs."

"What about your needs?"

"My needs? I can't even remember what they are."

"So you acknowledge that this relationship isn't meeting your needs?"

Silence again. And then a slow, sad nod.

A pattern had emerged. Each of Laurel's romances would begin with a frenzied infatuation that hurled her into sexual bliss. The attachment would be intense, to use Laurel's word, and the lovemaking would be passionate for a while. But the sex wouldn't last; there was always something that caused the lover to fall from grace, and Laurel's desire would ebb. It was as if she were unable to perceive any flaws in the new relationship until after she and her lover were welded together. Then, with grim insight, she would start to identify every shortcoming and defect in both the lover and their attachment and begin the painful process of prying herself away. As the affair with Sonya ground to a halt, I made a note to myself to pay close attention when Laurel even hinted that she was thinking of getting involved with someone new.

I didn't have long to wait. Within a month, Laurel met Heather, a mother of three who lived in Richmond and had divorced her husband a few years earlier when she realized she was a lesbian. As usual, things happened fast, and, according to Laurel, the sex was hot. Heather was good-looking, Laurel said, with an infectious laugh, a great body, and a solid relationship with her kids—a fifteen-year-old son and two daughters, thirteen and eleven. This was the first time Laurel had had a lover with children, and she took to them with gusto, spending as much time at Heather's place as at her own.

Heather worked part-time in a local branch of a national bookstore, so there were plenty of mysteries lying around—of several varieties, as Laurel came to discover. Heather told Laurel she had been sexually abused by her stepfather as a teenager, and as Laurel spent more time at Heather's place, she noticed that the recycling bin usually contained an empty gin bottle. Their evenings centered around being home with the kids, watching a movie, and drinking: wine for Laurel and martinis for Heather.

Then one night, when she was at her own place, Laurel was awakened by the telephone. It was Kevin, Heather's son, calling to say that his mother had run a stop sign, hit a parked car, and been arrested for drunk driving. Laurel jumped into her car and bailed Heather out. She got Heather into Alcoholics Anonymous, found her a therapist, and focused her energies on getting her lover well.

Then a funny thing happened: the sex began to go. It went from several times a day to once a week and dwindled from there. Laurel came in glum and dejected. Things were falling apart. Heather had gone from being an upbeat, together woman to being a hypersensitive crybaby.

"When I first met Heather, just thinking about her would make me crazy," Laurel said one day. "But now—I feel guilty saying this—thinking about her now makes me feel anxious, not aroused. Emotionally, she's a train wreck. All this stuff coming out in therapy makes her moody. She comes home and collapses on the couch and all she wants to do is rent a movie. So I finally told her I was sick of watching movies and wanted to get out and have some fun. She just stares at me and goes into the other room. Then she comes out and wants to make up, and one thing leads to another, only I don't feel like it, and she gets hurt all over again. It's a nightmare."

Later that week, Laurel called and canceled her next session, saying she was going away on business and would phone to reschedule when she returned. So I was astonished when she called three weeks later and said she wasn't coming back. A lot had changed, she said; she had broken up with Heather, had been promoted at work, would be traveling even more, and felt she needed a break from therapy.

Wait, I wanted to say, you can't stop now. We're making good progress—don't quit! But I didn't say that.

"What brought this on so suddenly?" I asked.

"Actually, I've been thinking about it for a while. I feel I should be able to handle this stuff on my own. But I'd like to stop in and see you from time to time, if that's all right. You've been really good for me; you've helped me see that a lot of the people I get involved with are wrong for me."

Perhaps. But how do I make Laurel see that the reason all her lovers are wrong for her is because they aren't Dawn, whose forthright personality and solid sense of self so closely mirror her own—and who is, not incidentally, not only heterosexual but also married and utterly unavailable? That part of her attraction for Dawn might be her unavailability, which obviates the dependency that intimacy invariably brings? That she chose her subsequent lovers hoping, however unwittingly, that one would duplicate not only the dynamism of her interactions with Dawn but the comforting embrace of Dawn's family? That the loss of Laurel's mother so early in life had shaped her burgeoning sexuality and was still guiding her choice of lovers? That the sexual heat generated early in her attachments cannot help but cool without the constant, simmering warmth of an ongoing intimacy—the kind of day-to-day, high-contact, low-drama intimacy she and Dawn had created when they were working together? That intimacy seems to be exactly what she is trying to avoid, because the sex goes south as soon as emotional vulnerability sets in? And that she won't find someone who's right for her until she understands why she loves whom she loves?

Did I say these things? No, I did not.

First of all, Laurel would not have been receptive to hearing them. Pelting her with my insights, however astute, would hardly have persuaded her to return to therapy. Second, there was always the possibility that Laurel would reject my theories, write me off, and never come back—a far worse outcome, in my view, than having her come in for a session from time to time. So I chose my words carefully. I said that I had enjoyed working with her, felt that we had made solid progress, and hoped she would come back and see me so we could continue the work we had begun.

And that's what happened. Laurel comes to see me about four times a year and the work continues. She says she and Dawn run into each other at work and have dinner together every couple of months; her social life is neither great nor desperate, and she's begun to experience some of the emotional ups and downs of the menopausal transition. She says she is looking for someone; that she wants to have a relationship with someone and is still thinking through the reasons why her relationships thus far have not worked out well.

But Laurel is making progress. She recently became involved with a computer analyst she had met through friends. They saw each other a couple of times a week, and it sounded as if they were developing a relationship, but after about a month and a half Laurel said, "You know, I can see this isn't going to work out"—and she ended it. But here's the best part, at least for me: they had not slept together. They were developing an emotional connection first, and the fog of infatuation hadn't descended and obscured the attachment's shortcomings. Laurel's cool head had prevailed, and she'd ended the relationship before either she or the other woman became too deeply entrenched.

Laurel's story is another one that could be interpreted as more about relationships than about sex; again, it all depends on how you look at things. If you look at Laurel from the outside—an attractive, prosperous, confident person who enjoys sex and has no trouble cultivating erotic encounters—you might see a hot-blooded woman with an unconventional but vibrant sex life and underdeveloped people skills. And you wouldn't be entirely wrong: Laurel's relationships do thrive on lusty sex, at least at the start, and her brash manner makes her an unlikely candidate for the diplomatic corps.

But from the inside, Laurel looks different: a child whose mother could not express her love for her adequately even before she disappeared, who matured into a woman who longs to feel loved yet bonds more readily through sex than through emotional intimacy. She seems to choose lovers on the basis of sexual chemistry without considering other factors, such as their maturity and stability; indeed, during the time she was my patient, she chose several lovers whose fervid sexual energies belied their emotional neediness. The rush of a fresh sexual encounter would propel

Laurel into a state of manic pleasure that insulated her from the reality of the relationship. When the physical frenzy began to ebb—as it must in all mature attachments—and feelings would flow in to fill the space, Laurel would retreat. When she realized that she had chosen someone who could not fulfill her needs yet was demanding that Laurel meet hers, Laurel's desire would cool, and the sexual component of the relationship would fade.

What is the answer for Laurel? I believe that Dawn, the person she was most strongly drawn to, is the one with whom she was most evenly matched and the one with whom she shared and continues to share the most balanced connection. Of course, the fact that Dawn is straight, married, and unavailable makes her less than an inspired choice. Did Laurel allow herself to grow close to Dawn precisely because Dawn was unavailable? Perhaps; I can't say. But I believe that when Laurel meets a gay, unattached woman to whom she is as well suited as she is to Dawn and allows herself to open to that woman, she will have a real chance at finding lasting love and the sexual satisfaction that can come with it.

If you were to ask Laurel and Karla to tell you what kind of person they tended to fall in love with, you would get wildly different answers; if you asked them why, you'd probably get no answer at all. But they had a lot in common: when it came to sex, both women were more comfortable taking physical rather than emotional risks and reveled in explosive physical encounters that burned brightly in bed but withered under the light of intimacy. Karla was aroused by men who posed no threat to her heart; Laurel was turned on by women with strong sexual needs but lost interest when their other needs became evident. Both women sought exciting sexual encounters as a form of reassurance, because at bottom, they both had the sense that they were unlovable. The symptoms of their discontent were different, but what they shared was a reluctance to reveal themselves to their lovers and an attraction to those kinds of people who either would not or could not demand that they do it. Had Karla and Laurel understood the essence of both the people they loved and why they loved them, they might have saved themselves and their lovers a world of heartache and hastened the arrival in their lives of real intimacy.

Your Patterns of Intimacy

1. Is physical intimacy connected to emotional intimacy for you?

- If so, which comes first? In other words, do you tend to become sexually intimate with someone before you become emotionally close with him (or her)? Or do you tend to let sexual intimacy grow out of emotional closeness? If so, why do you think this happens? Have you always been this way?

- If not, or not always, what satisfaction do you derive from physical intimacy? From emotional intimacy? How much intimacy do you need, and how often do you need it? Can you see a pattern?

2. Think about the kind(s) of people to whom you are attracted

- physically: Is there a kind of face, build, or voice that renders you helpless in its presence, no matter to whom it belongs? Is there someone in your past with whom you associate this characteristic?

- emotionally: Is there a kind of person with whom you tend to fall in love because he makes you feel a certain way? Can you articulate what the feeling is? Does he make you feel sexy, smart, safe? Again, is there someone in your past with whom you associate these feelings?

- intellectually: Are you ever aroused by a person's mind, his way of thinking, the vigor of a sparkling intellect? Do these characteristics remind you of anyone in your past?

3. Think about your three most recent relationships.

- What, if anything, do they have in common? Were the people you were involved with similar in any of the ways described above? Can you see a pattern in the way the relationships played out? Were there ways of behaving that you consistently practiced or avoided?

■ Did you come together because of sex or in spite of it?

~ Did sex bring you together?

~ Did sex keep you together?

~ Did sex—or lack of it—drive you apart? If so, why could you not or did you not surmount the problem?

4. **When, and with whom, have you enjoyed the best sex?** The worst sex? What made the best sex so good, and the worst sex so bad (for example, your partner, the timing, the situation, or the stage you were at in your life)?

5. **Have you ever been powerfully and inexplicably attracted to someone?** If you fantasize about that person, what do you picture happening between you? What does the fantasy tell you about your sexual self?

CHAPTER 3

To Risk or Not to Risk
Our Uneasy Relationship with the Truth

> Risk! Risk anything! Care no more for the opinion
> of others, for those voices. Do the hardest thing on
> earth for you. Act for yourself. Face the truth.
> —KATHERINE MANSFIELD[1]

What would you be willing to risk to have great sex? What would it be worth to you to feel fairly certain that you would have an orgasm whenever you made love? What would you lay on the line to come home to a lover who knew your body as well as his own, whose knowing, masterful touch would haunt you by day and bring your flesh to lusty life at night?

I suspect you would say you'd do anything: there's no mountain high enough, river wide enough, or foundation garment torturous enough to keep you from that dream lover—nothing, that is, except perhaps letting that lover get close enough to really know you and what you need to be satisfied in bed.

It should be an organic part of a relationship, letting your partner know what turns you on, what doesn't, and what he might do to hasten you toward ecstasy. It's not realistic to expect a new lover to know your erotic hot spots and intuit your fantasies, and clueing him in would be the least you might do to ensure that you get the pleasure you want and he gets the pleasure of pleasuring you.

It seems an essential part of an intimate relationship, but in many cases, it isn't. I cannot count the women who have come to me wondering what's wrong with them because they can't seem to enjoy sex, reach orgasm, or maintain an erotically charged connection with their partners. They think it might be a medical matter; a hormonal imbalance, perhaps; or a deep-seated psychiatric problem manifesting itself after years of dormancy. And sometimes it is. But far more often the problem is directly related to a woman's willingness to tell the truth and risk allowing her boyfriend, husband, or lover to know who she really is and how she experiences their lovemaking.

Why should this be so difficult? Why are so many women reluctant to reveal themselves to their partners? And why do so many of us prefer to live with sexual frustration rather than practice self-disclosure?

Because when it comes to romance and sex, we're very touchy about what we're willing to risk. One woman is willing to risk her health, not to mention her life, pursuing intense, urgent, unprotected sex with strangers but is loath to share emotional intimacy. Another woman is afraid to risk her husband's disapproval by telling him what really turns her on, so she represses her urges and grows frustrated enough to consider having an affair. Still another woman doesn't know about her body's capacity for pleasure because she is afraid she'd be committing a sin if she masturbated. And then there's the college student I mentioned earlier who couldn't have an orgasm with her boyfriend and figured there had to be something wrong with her.

Holly: Afraid to Ask for Satisfaction

I was organizing a study on women with orgasmic disorder, and a twenty-year-old college junior answered a call for volunteers. The young woman before me was lovely—attractive, energetic, and quick on the uptake. Her eyes were lively and intelligent, her face animated. She seemed fully present and full of life and had no trouble making eye contact when I asked her why she thought she'd be a good candidate for the study.

"I've been dating this guy, Rich, for about"—her eyes rolled up, and she cocked her head to the side—"about eight months. He's a physics major, and he's really cute in a goofy sort of way."

"Goofy how?"

"Well, he's really smart and he's really funny, and he's got these small eyes so he looks a little, I don't know, sort of Neanderthal, if you know what I mean. And he has these really hip glasses that kind of don't go with the rest of him. It's hard to explain, but it's really sexy to me that he looks sort of like a caveman but he's actually really smart."

"So you're attracted to him."

"Oh, absolutely. I get very turned on when we, you know, fool around, and so does he. Everything goes great, if you know what I mean. And it's not just physical. I really like him; sometimes I think I'm in love with him. And he likes me, too. So I know that's not the problem."

"What problem do you mean?"

"Well, I can't seem to climax when we have sex. And it's really upsetting because I know he wants me to, and I want to. He's pretty good about stimulating my clitoris, and I get all aroused and I'm jumping out of my skin, but it doesn't happen."

"Does he know it isn't happening?"

"I don't know. I mean, he knows I'm turned on. But I don't know if he knows I'm not having an orgasm."

"Are you pretending to have one?"

"Not exactly. I mean, I don't playact it or anything."

"Have you said anything to him?"

"No, I haven't, because I don't want to upset him or make him think I'm not happy with him. So I thought maybe I could be in the study and find out what's going on."

Holly wasn't the first student who had come to see me because she couldn't have an orgasm. Typically, I ask these young women if they've ever had one, either with a partner or through self-stimulation. And I often get a wide-eyed, almost indignant response, at least to the latter option. I looked at Holly and took the plunge.

"You said that Rich takes care to stimulate you, so you obviously know where your clitoris is. Have you ever been able to climax with anyone else, or by yourself?" She looked at me with wide eyes.

"Oh, sure, all the time, with my vibrator. It's fantastic. I've taken physiology, so you're right, I have a pretty good idea of where everything is. I've learned exactly what I need to do to climax; I don't think I've ever *not* climaxed when I use it."

This was good news for Holly, if not for my research. It meant I had lost a candidate for my study, but it also meant that Holly definitely did not have orgasmic disorder.

What she did have was an invitation, a year earlier, to a gathering at a friend's house where a young saleswoman had unpacked a trunk of what used to be called marital aids and spent two hours displaying, and in some cases demonstrating, everything from scented lotions to slinky sleepwear to battery-operated, impressively animated, multitasking phalluses (think Tupperware party with peals of laughter). Holly had forked over thirty dollars for a Wascally Wabbit* and had been using it with unabashed pleasure ever since. Not only that: she had told her four housemates about it, whereupon they had all gone out and ordered their own, and had been using them regularly—even though they had boyfriends. I was astonished: here was a young woman who was comfortable enough with her sexuality to not only tell her friends she was using a vibrator but sell them on the idea of using one themselves.

Holly's uninhibited household aside, I've always been amazed at how many young women are discomfited by the notion of masturbation; at least two thirds of the students I've treated swear they would never do it—even the ones who have had sex with fifteen or twenty different men. There's a dichotomy with this generation in that they believe it's morally acceptable to have sex, even with multiple partners, but it's not morally acceptable to pleasure yourself. To these young women, it is better to have intercourse than to engage in oral sex or manual stimulation or any other erotic act, especially masturbation. Even though they aren't married, they rationalize intercourse as an act of communion—they are connecting with another person—whereas to masturbate would mean they were self-indulgent by pleasuring only themselves.

Another reason why I believe masturbation isn't more common is that a woman has to be motivated to pleasure herself, which she need not be to have sex. For a woman to masturbate, not only must she feel horny, she must make a conscious decision to stop whatever else she is doing, find a private place with a lock on the door, and do something about it. In other words, she must own up to wanting to have an orgasm and take responsi-

---

* Its real name. Go check the Internet if you don't believe me.

bility for making it happen. To have sex, however, a woman need not own up to wanting, desiring, or craving it at all; if there's an interested man around, all she's got to do is not resist. Afterward, she can tell herself that it was all his doing—"I never wanted to have sex; he seduced me." It's a subtle angle that bears some scrutiny because, psychologically speaking, succumbing to a guy's sexual advances is a more passive—and socially acceptable—way to get satisfaction than locking yourself in the bathroom, firing up the Wabbit, and taking care of business. In this scenario, you don't need a man, and it's bad to not need a man because our society is ordered around the concept of couples—man-and-woman couples, that is—and sexual intercourse is the apotheosis of the concept.

It's all tied up in a belief that there's a certain way that sex is supposed to be, that *real* sex, *real* intimacy is between one man and one woman in missionary-position intercourse, and that everything else is either second best, bogus, or perverse. We buy into it as a *should:* this is what society expects of us, not necessarily what we want for ourselves. Part of it is the idea that there's much more emotional intimacy when you're having intercourse compared to oral sex or some other erotic act. And there is some truth there: during intercourse, the most vulnerable, sensitive part of his body is *inside* the most mysterious, life-giving part of yours; you can feel the force of his passion as he thrusts within you; and if your up-close vision is still good, you might even be able to gaze into each other's eyes.

But missionary-position intercourse doesn't guarantee greater intimacy for all couples. If a guy knows that you don't have an orgasm during intercourse and he's willing (let alone eager) to perform oral sex because he wants to pleasure you, that's a more caring guy and a more emotionally intimate encounter than when you have missionary-position intercourse without climaxing and the guy says, "You didn't come? But you were so hot and wet—what's wrong with you?" or "You didn't come? But you were so turned on—what's wrong with *me*?" There are many ways to make love and be emotionally intimate, none of them more real or right than the others. Does it really matter what you and your lover do to have an orgasm as long as both of you are adults, acting of your own free will, and not hurting anyone? In my book the answer is no: if pure physical release is your goal, it doesn't matter how you have an orgasm or whether you have it with or without a partner.

So I was encouraged to learn that Holly was a seasoned practitioner of self-stimulation; at least her body was responding normally to sexual stimulation. The question was why she wasn't responding as well with a living, breathing man. The answer soon emerged: Holly was the first real girlfriend Rich had ever had. He was nineteen, his hormones were in a frenzy, and he was racing through the delicious, arousal-enhancing first course to get to intercourse as quickly as possible. Then, not surprisingly, he would ejaculate well before Holly was aroused enough to climax.

I asked if they had oral sex and learned that they did but that it served as a prelude to intercourse, not as an end in itself for Holly's satisfaction. I then asked if they ever made love more than once an evening, which might have enabled Rich to maintain an erection long enough on the second try to bring Holly to orgasm. But Holly shook her head and said they would have one brief, intense sexual encounter that left Rich limp with exhaustion and Holly quivering with frustration.

The interesting thing was, Holly had the know-how to recognize that Rich was ejaculating—and losing his erection—too soon to provide enough clitoral stimulation for her to climax during intercourse. She was also savvy enough to know that you have much less control—and stimulation— when you make love with a person than when you masturbate: a vibrator is much easier to master than a guy, who, if he's young and inexperienced, might have minimal mastery over the timing of his orgasm. And she knew how and where to touch herself to consistently have orgasms with her vibrator. So why did she not tell her boyfriend how and where and how long to touch her to achieve the same results? And considering she was a premed major and knowledgeable about the workings of the body, how could she think she had orgasmic disorder when she was able to bring herself to climax with a vibrator?

I think Holly believed the problem was hers because, like most women, she was loath to disrupt the stability of the relationship by admitting she hadn't quite made it to ecstasy, let alone been driven there. Every woman fantasizes a lover whose potent sex appeal and polished technique cause her to melt, gasping and lubricating, at his touch, and Holly was no exception. But, like many of us, she found herself involved with someone whose sexual technique needed some work.

Does she tell him this? No, of course not. Not only doesn't she want him to see himself as a failure; *she* doesn't want to see him as a failure: after all, she may be in love with this young man and contemplating a future with him. Instead, she idealizes him: he's a great guy; he's smart, good-looking in a goofy kind of way. She doesn't want to think that he's an inexperienced lover (why couldn't she attract an older, more discerning man?), a lousy lover (how can she contemplate a future with a loser?), or a selfish lover (she's too much a feminist to be with someone who doesn't care about her pleasure). To do so would be to see that he's not perfect, and she's still too infatuated with him to acknowledge his flaws. Holly was not willing to risk seeing Rich in the cold, stark light of day because she would see things that needed changing, and making the changes might hurt or offend him. And hurting or offending him might make him leave.

For Holly and millions of other women, keeping a relationship intact is more important than risking its demise by suggesting some bedroom improvements. We wish the sex were better, but the idea of saying so makes us so uncomfortable that we let things slide for weeks, months, or even longer. I have treated women who have been married for twenty-five years and never expressed their sexual needs to their husbands. It's a matter of being willing to risk displeasing your partner for the sake of increasing your pleasure (and ultimately improving the relationship)—a risk that most women seem unwilling to take.

It is important to understand that while Holly knew she was sexually frustrated, at no point did she consciously decide that telling Rich the truth was too risky and that diagnosing herself with a sexual disorder was the way to go. Something deep within her, half instinct and half cultural mandate, told her it was both practical and right to place Rich's needs before her own. It's worth looking at this phenomenon because, while women have long put up with disappointing sex to spare their lovers' feelings, they probably don't know that their silence decreases the likelihood that they will enjoy sex in the future.

Holly was able to think she had orgasmic disorder even though she was climaxing on her own because she believed that some orgasms were more equal than others and that "real" ones occurred with a man during intercourse. Like millions of women, she had bought into the cinematic sex scenes that are, for the most part, idealized fantasies of the guys who write them: the woman is swooning with desire before the fellow even gets near her, and, once he does, she gasps, collapses, and hurtles headlong into orgasm in twenty seconds, tops. Just the other night my husband was channel surfing and came across a movie starring the ubiquitous Ms. Jolie, the reigning sex goddess of the moment. She and this guy are hot for each other, and he slams her up against the wall, and his pants are on and she's in her bathrobe, but no matter; they manage to have intercourse right there, up against the wall. And she's moaning and squirming and acting as if she's having multiple orgasms. And I looked at my husband and he looked at me and we just shook our heads. How easy is that to do, even, when he's still got his pants on?! I was sitting there thinking, *Give me a break—this is ridiculous.* Yet we accept this preposterous display and believe that this is the way it's supposed to be: you and your man are so wild with desire at precisely the same moment that he hurls you down on the bed or the floor or up against the wall and is able, in defiance of the laws of physics and anatomy, to drive you swiftly to ecstasy. (If you notice, these cinema sex symbols never have their periods, either; there's nothing like a tampon-tugging sequence to douse love's savage flame.)

Because cinema sex scenes leave more vivid impressions than anatomy lectures do, Holly was convinced that a sexually healthy woman who was attracted to her lover should be able to respond to his body and overcome his technical difficulties with enough heat to have an orgasm, no matter what he did (or didn't do) in bed. Rather than ask her boyfriend to own his half of their lovemaking, she found it more comfortable to accept, however inappropriately, full responsibility for the quality of their sex life. It's not just her: women take an excessive amount of responsibility. We're trained that way, and we do it; we can't help ourselves. There are probably genetic reasons for this in terms of mothering; if women weren't excessively responsible, the home fires might burn out, babies might languish cold and unfed, and the race might perish. The same sense of excessive responsibility that tells a woman she's a bad wife and mother if there's no milk in the house also tells her she's a bad woman and lover if she tells her partner there's not enough spark in the sack. She's a bitch, a ballbreaker, a nymphomaniac, a man-eater—or so the culture tells her—so she doesn't tell him.

Another thing she doesn't tell him is that she's having orgasms with a vibrator. I told Holly that I was treating some older couples who had incorporated a vibrator into their lovemaking and asked if she and Rich had tried that. Oh, no, she said; Rich didn't know anything about her vibrator, and she didn't want him to know because he would be hurt that she could have an orgasm with a ridiculously named battery-operated phallus but not with his. Moreover, she said she was concerned that he would think she was an oversexed, superficial sex glutton who cared more about her own pleasure than about their intimacy. No, there was no way she was going to bring the vibrator into bed with them.

What is striking about this case is its ordinariness: hundreds of women, young and not so young, have sat in my office and said yes, they are capable of having an orgasm; no, they are not having any with their current partner; and yes, they are ignoring it or faking it so they don't hurt their lover's feelings.

Women have been faking it for years, and it's just as crazy an idea as it's always been. Why in the world would a woman do it?

If you're faking an orgasm, you have already decided you're not going to have one. Why? Because when you're faking a climax, your mind is occupied with counterfeiting the surrender you could be experiencing for real. Instead of focusing on what you're feeling, you're thinking about what your face should look like and how you should move and what sounds you should make to persuade your lover that you're as aroused as he is. You're hovering overhead, directing the scene, preoccupied with the technique of portraying ecstasy instead of feeling it. How can your body surrender to sensation when your mind is staging a charade? Trust me: you cannot give in to arousal when you're thinking so much, and giving in to arousal is the only way to have an orgasm.

This is a peculiar thing that women do; I have never heard of a man faking an orgasm. And it's not because having an orgasm is a foregone conclusion for a man; it isn't, especially if he is taking medication. Many drugs that treat hypertension (high blood pressure), heart disease, depression, and anxiety can cause anorgasmia in men. But if a man is taking medication and is unable to have an orgasm, nine times out of ten, he'll attribute it to the drug, even if the drug isn't the problem. He won't worry that he's hurting his partner's ego and fake an orgasm to spare her (or his) feelings; he'll probably say, "Sorry, I don't think I can do this because of the medication I'm taking; let's stop." In his mind, it's not him; it's the drug. There's no risk of losing the relationship if he tells the truth; he figures, correctly, that if this person can't understand and accommodate his medical situation and its sexual side effects, there's not much of a relationship to lose.

Which is what I want you to take away from Holly's story: you have got to summon your courage, take a deep breath, and talk to your partner, because what you think is a sexual problem may actually be a communication problem. You have got to be able to say, "These are my needs; here is what I would like to happen *for me, for my pleasure,*" even if you fear he'll be insulted, get angry, or leave. The quality of your relationship—the entire relationship, not just the sexual aspect—depends on it. And it's not just common sense; research bears me out. A recent study of seventy-four college students involved in ongoing heterosexual relationships revealed that students who communicated with their partners about their sexual likes and dislikes tended to be happier with their relationships, and that those who were happier with their relationships also tended to be happier with the sex. Not only that (and this is juicy), *women who told their partners about their likes and dislikes—both sexual and nonsexual—said that such self-disclosure led to greater emotional intimacy, which led to better sex.* But for men, *there was no evidence of a connection between sexual self-disclosure and sexual satisfaction.*[2] In other words, a woman who tells her boyfriend not only what she likes to do in bed but what her favorite bedtime story was as a kid is likely to have better sex with him than if she didn't tell him. Her boyfriend, on the other hand, can tell her what he likes in bed or not tell her—he's either going to enjoy the sex or not, and talking has nothing to do with it.

So if you're waiting for your guy to talk about his sexual feelings and ask you to share yours, forget about it; it's not going to happen. Tell him what turns you off, what turns you on, and what he can do to make you crazy—and let the chips fall where they may. Quite simply, it's a risk you must be willing to take. Not because your fear is unfounded; sometimes women tell their partners what they want, and sometimes men do feel hurt, become ticked off, or bolt; these men are not ready for the kind of commitment that empowers women to demand sexual satisfaction. Even so, if you find yourself wishing the sex were better, you owe it to yourself to tell your partner.

That said, it's worth mentioning that this kind of conversation is seldom easy to initiate. Even if you know that your husband won't divorce you for broaching the subject, it doesn't mean he'll send flowers (although he just might, when the sex gets better). And even if you're reasonably certain that your boyfriend is secure enough in himself and fond enough of you to want to hear what you have to say, it doesn't mean it will be easy for you to say it. But say it you must. Eventually, it will get easier to talk about these things, and when it does, the whole relationship will improve because you will have been honest with each other, which will bring you closer together, which will make the sex better.

And that's the goal, isn't it? A close relationship with someone who loves and cherishes you and wants nothing more than to know you intimately and let you know him? That is, unless living in true, partnered intimacy poses a greater risk than living without it.

Monica: Afraid to Risk Emotional Intimacy

"I wanted to see you," my new patient was saying, "because I'm getting married in eight months and I'm giving myself a thorough medical overhaul. This time I'm doing it right."

"Doing it right—what do you mean?" I said.

"I mean I don't want to wait until after I'm married to deal with problems that I can handle now. I'm doing everything in my power to make it work this time."

"You've been married before?"

"You could say that. Three husbands, three divorces. But you know what they say—fourth time lucky."

"You're young to have been married three times."

"I'm older than I look. And my marriages tend not to last very long. The last one was the longest, nearly six years."

"And why do you think you need to see a psychiatrist?"

"I want this marriage to work," she said. "Carl is a great guy, and I don't want to screw things up. I'm fifty-four"—she shot me a meaningful look—"and I don't have much time left. This could be my last chance, and I'm committed to seeing it through."

Monica wasn't the first woman who had come to me seeking treatment for prewedding ambivalence, but her grim determination set her apart.

She interested me: I see more women who are unable to find a husband than I do those who manage to find a new one every few years. She did look younger than her age, largely because she was unusually fit; her arms were tanned and sinewy, and she looked as if she wore a size two. She had just taken a new job running the mountaineering program at a popular resort in the Blue Ridge Mountains and looked as if she could clamber up the rockiest slopes with ease. She seemed sure of herself, the kind of person who likes to be in control of her life and leave as little as possible to chance. Yet here she was, taking another chance on marriage.

Monica began by talking about her parents. Her mother was emotionally distant and her father was, according to Monica, a petty criminal of sorts; she had memories of arguments about a job he'd once had selling televisions that had "fallen off a truck." Her father's emotions were as volatile as her mother's were remote; at one point he had started knocking Monica's mother around when they fought, which was often. Monica said she felt loved when she pleased them and rejected when she didn't; she described them as masters of conditional love and, although she was still in touch with them, saw them no more than once or twice a year.

Monica said her first marriage had been an unmitigated disaster, albeit with a very nice guy. She had met Brett at an art fair where he was exhibiting his paintings; Monica owned a sporting goods store, and Sunday was her day off. They were both in their late twenties, and Monica said he was the most gorgeous guy she'd ever met, so much so that she initially distrusted his interest in her. He was bright and serious about his work, and anointed Monica his muse. He was the most emotionally available man she had ever known, and Monica thrived in the warmth of his affection. The only thing amiss was their lovemaking: about half the time, Brett had trouble getting an erection; on the occasions when he did, he would either lose it quickly or be unable to achieve orgasm. Monica attributed the problem to prewedding jitters and figured things would improve after the ceremony.

But Brett's sexual ardor only diminished after the wedding. He began working late at the studio but would often find Monica awake when he returned home, sometimes at dawn; she had begun dreaming about having lesbian sex, and it disturbed her so much, she'd stay up all night. One night she went out with friends and picked up a guy at a bar; Wayne struck her as a shady character, but she went home with him anyway. The sex was on the rough side but exciting, and Monica started seeing him on the sly. She said she felt a little bad about sneaking around but wouldn't have done it if Brett hadn't been leaving her alone all night.

One morning Brett came home and started weeping. After two hours of tears and self-recrimination, he told Monica he couldn't go on with the marriage any longer because he was gay. He said he had in fact been attracted to men when they had met but had been hoping his feelings for Monica would change him. Sadly, they hadn't. Monica wasn't shocked; in fact, she believed her lesbian dreams indicated that, on some level, she suspected Brett was gay. Monica began divorce proceedings and continued seeing Wayne until she noticed that money was disappearing from her wallet. When her Visa bill arrived with eight hundred dollars' worth of charges from a phone sex line, she reported the fraud and turned Wayne in. Feeling alone and humiliated, Monica withdrew from her friends and spent a good six months working late, expanding her business into the store next door, and riding out her funk until she could be sociable again.

Thus began a pattern of brief marriages to good guys punctuated by even briefer affairs with bad ones that would lead, inevitably, to divorce and bouts of depression. After Brett, Monica married Anthony, and after Anthony, she married Paul. Both men were in love with Monica and, according to her, devoted husbands and ardent lovers. In both cases, she fell in love, got married, and declared that this one was it. But then some cute guy would inevitably come into the store or approach Monica when she was out with friends. He'd flirt and ask for her number; Monica would take his instead, wait a week, and then call. They'd meet for lunch, end up back at his place, and start a clandestine affair that would distract Monica from her marriage. The men she'd take up with—a part-time drug dealer during her marriage to Anthony and a former car thief while she was married to Paul—sounded reminiscent of her father: small-time hoods with big-time sex appeal. Monica would withdraw from her husband and become less and less available emotionally and physically. Eventually, the husband would confront Monica about the increasing distance between them. She would then accuse him of being insecure, meddling in her friendships, and stifling her independence. She would storm out of the house, he would stew inside it, and the marriage would disintegrate. She would ask for a separation, and the husband, hurt, bewildered, but willing to cooperate, would agree. Within months, she would file for divorce, citing irreconcilable differences, but maintain the outside affair until she realized she was sleeping with someone who was at best a cad and at worst a criminal. She would then end the affair and sink into a depression from which she would emerge several months later, aching for connection and searching for love.

Now Monica was engaged to Carl, a high school principal in his late fifties, and determined to make things work. She had sold the sporting goods business for close to a million dollars, taken the resort job, and was in the process of relocating from her apartment to Carl's house.

"Tell me about Carl," I said.

"Well, he's older than I am, for once," Monica said, "and he's very good to me. He isn't insecure or demanding, and he gives me plenty of space."

"Are you comfortable in your sexual relationship?"

"Well . . ." Monica sighed and looked away. "Not exactly. It doesn't always work. In fact, it doesn't work most of the time."

"What seems to be the problem?"

"Well, it's like he comes right away, once he's inside me. Not all the time, but a lot. It's over so fast, I don't feel much of anything."

"Have you talked about it? What does Carl say?"

"He doesn't say anything."

"And are you saying anything?"

"It's not something I feel I can bring up with him. He's very insecure about—some things. It would really hurt his feelings."

"Monica," I said, "this isn't about Carl's feelings; it's about your upcoming marriage. And the problem may not be what you think it is."

Monica thought Carl was having premature ejaculations, but it was much more likely that he had erectile dysfunction, which is not unusual in middle-aged men. When he penetrated her for intercourse, he would lose the erection and, while Monica thought he was ejaculating then, it's a hard thing to judge. Carl could solve the mystery by telling her, of course, but he wasn't talking and she wasn't asking. Which is, again, something that women do: she didn't want to cause him to feel bad by making sex an issue. But sex was important to Monica, and here she was, planning to marry a man with whom she had a dismal sex life. She had already been through three divorces; why was she willing to risk a fourth?

Because Monica is more frightened of marriage than she is of divorce. I think Monica is afraid of emotional closeness, which is why she has consistently embarked on affairs with bad guys while married to a good one. What is interesting is that she chooses good, decent men to marry, but when they try to get close to her, she flees to the arms of a bad guy who provides sex without intimacy. If you ask her to compare sex with her good-guy husbands to sex with her bad-guy lovers, she'll say that the sex is good both ways, but different: with the bad guys the sex focuses on physical sensation, while with her husbands there's a move toward emotional vulnerability that frightens her. When she makes love with a husband, it is as if she is afraid that he will dump her when he finds out who she really is, so she leaves him before he can leave her.

The irony of Monica's case is that her greatest fear is of being abandoned by those she loves, so she abandons them instead. I see a clear connection between this behavior and her troubled relationship with her parents, especially her father, whose bad-guy persona and elusive affection are re-created in the men with whom she has affairs. In this way, Monica remains in control: she escapes her husbands' desire for intimacy by having sex with dangerous strangers, yet she feels she can leave these affairs when she wants to—which she does, once the affair has served its purpose and scuttled the marriage. The outcome leaves Monica bereft of both love and sex, but at least she didn't risk letting anyone get close enough to see her true self, a self she believes, deep down, to be unlovable.

This pattern is not unusual, nor are fathers the only culprits. I often see these behaviors in women whose mothers' lack of warmth and approval have left them feeling unworthy of the unconditional love they yearn for in a lover and are sometimes fortunate enough to find. Or the culprit could be someone else who was important to a woman when she was younger, someone whose love and approval she needed but whose favor was seldom forthcoming. In Monica's case, both parents were cold, albeit in different ways: her father expressed his emotions, which were often negative and sometimes violent, while her mother kept much of her emotional warmth in reserve. When a child grows up with parents whose love turns on and off, she may be left with emotional scars such as Monica had. She was attractive, confident, and professionally successful, but underneath, her fear of intimacy rendered her incapable of trusting anyone to truly love her. To allow any man—even a faithful husband—near enough to know her was too great a risk for her to take.

Monica is still my patient. Our work focuses on helping her next marriage succeed by considering why her other ones didn't. We talk about why she is willing to risk bodily harm, not to mention her health, by sleeping with dishonorable men, but unable to risk intimacy with trustworthy men who love her. We also talk about her fiancé, whom I persuaded, through Monica, to see a urologist. After all, Carl's sexual difficulty could be rooted in psychology, but it could also be a medical problem—one that could be easily corrected. A new marriage is challenging enough, what with the myriad adjustments both husband and wife must make. Why complicate matters by allowing a sexual problem to go undiscussed and undiagnosed?

Intimacy and old age have something in common: neither one is for sissies. Allowing another person to really know you is scary stuff; all of us have skeletons rattling in our secret closets. Yet each of us yearns for someone to unlock the closet door, confront the skeleton, and say, "Big deal! Rattle all you want—I love you anyway!" If you want that to happen, though, you have to hand over the key and trust that the person will still want you when he sees what's in there.

The point is that partnership is an intimate alliance that carries a certain amount of risk—risk that each person weighs differently. Monica's affection for her first husband may have flourished not despite his homosexual vibe but because of it; the ambivalence of his longing was no match for her defenses, and she felt safe. Her second and third husbands, however, were heterosexual and their yearning more urgent. The risk they posed to her guarded self was too great, so she disengaged from the marriages by cultivating less demanding partnerships.

Whether you're married or not, a committed relationship is strongest when it comprises both emotional and physical intimacy. That is what most of us have been taught to want, expect, and work toward. But more and more young people are delaying commitment and marriage until they are older and their careers have taken off. They still want to have sex but aren't necessarily looking for anything more—at least that's what they tell themselves.

Hooking Up

So what do twenty- and thirtysomething singles do when they want to have sex?

Some of them hook up with someone they know or sort of know or virtually know, maybe a friend of a friend, someone they met at a party, or a person they find on an Internet dating site. They meet for a drink, make sure they like what they see, and go off and have sex. When it's over, they might hang out until morning or get dressed and go home (especially if they have to get up for work the next day). There's neither the expectation of another rendezvous nor the need to shell out money for a date. There's nothing romantic about it; it's just straightforward sex, no-frills thrills. Depending on who you are and how you've been brought up, you might find it refreshingly liberating or depressingly cynical.

As I see it, the biggest thing hooking up has going for it is its honesty: the participants have similar (if not lofty) expectations. Both woman and man are in it for the sex and come together more as equals than they do when romance is in the air. From the man's point of view, it's a bargain: he doesn't have to pick up the tab for dinner and a movie; he doesn't even have to pick up the woman, who will probably meet him somewhere for a drink that she is just as likely to pay for as he is. For the woman, it's a welcome gust of freedom: if she sleeps with the guy, it's because she wants to, not because she feels obligated to because he spent more than a hundred bucks on dinner and another two hundred on Springsteen tickets. For the price of a drink or two, max, she can size up the situation and say either yes or no, free of guilt and obligation.

Hooking up also offers a kind of personal homeland security, if you will, which is particularly beneficial to women. When you hook up, there's a built-in screening process. It could be a guy you met at a party whose body turned you on but whose brain you wouldn't want to marry, or your girlfriend's boyfriend's college roommate who's a nice guy, in town for the weekend, and sounds like your type. Or it could be someone you've been corresponding with online, which means you'll probably know something about him and have an idea of his language skills and whether or not he could sustain a conversation over cocktails. While there's no guarantee that any of these guys would win a citizenship award, at least you'll still know more about them than you'd know about a stranger you picked up in a bar.

So compared to going home with someone you've just met in a smoky, deafening singles bar while under the influence of too many overpriced drinks, hooking up has several things going for it: honesty, equality, and a modicum of security. A woman can initiate an encounter as comfortably as a man, so she need not wait to be chosen; for once, she can do the choosing herself. Both parties know why they're there and so can dispense with the tiresome game playing that can make dating so cumbersome. And neither party expects a hookup to ripen into a romance, so no one is disappointed, right?

Well, yes and no; it's all a matter of expectations. If you expect nothing from the encounter except an hour or two of physical exertion and release, you might not be disappointed. You might be relieved to dispense with the ritual of spending the night, sharing an awkward breakfast the next morning, and pretending you're going to see each other again when you know you aren't. And you won't have that rotten feeling you get when you've been dating a guy for a while, fending off his advances, and then, after you finally sleep with him, realizing you're never going to hear from him again; when you hook up, you're using each other, and both of you know it. The question is, are you comfortable being with someone explicitly for sex and knowing that he is with you for the same reason?

You know yourself better than anyone; you know if you can separate sex from love and liberate your body from your soul. Most men can and routinely do; for most guys, sex and love are two different things. There's a poignant scene in the film *Shirley Valentine* wherein a middle-aged British woman, played by Pauline Collins, leaves behind her sour, disagreeable husband and goes off to the Aegean on holiday. There she meets a handsome Greek, played by Tom Conti, who invites her out on his brother's fishing boat. She hesitates, worried that accepting will imply that she is willing to sleep with him. He grasps what's going on and gazes mournfully into her eyes. "You afraid," he says, in clumsy, unadorned English. "You afraid I want make fuck with you. Of course I want make fuck with you—you are a beautiful woman; man would be crazy not want make fuck with you. But I don't ask you to fuck. I ask you to come on brother boat. Different thing: boat is boat; fuck is fuck."

The candor of his words is both touching and hilarious, and their crudeness emphasizes the innocence of his meaning: Don't confuse sex with sailing, lady; they're two different things. (As you might have guessed, Shirley ends up with both different things and is none the worse for it.)

But are sex and love two different things for you? That's the key: What feels right for *you?*—not for your friends, the person you're with, or the you you'd like to be; but for the real, essential you? Are you able to sleep with someone without becoming even a wee bit attached? Can you be vulnerable enough to enjoy sex without feeling used afterward? Are you stoic enough to hook up with someone and have great sex with him the first time, all the while knowing it could be the last time?

If your answer is a resounding yes, then you might be able to hook up from time to time without suffering too many ill effects. But if you're the type of person for whom sex is inextricably bound up with feeling—and many, if not most, women are—you might not have the stomach for it. You might, in fact, be well advised to masturbate instead.

As I see it, you can derive pretty much the same benefit from masturbating as you can from hooking up, with zero risk. When you masturbate, you don't have to worry about catching a disease or ending up in bed with someone who suddenly strikes you as weird, distasteful, or dangerous. (Nor must you resist the urge to bond with a proficient lover; if the sex is good, you have only yourself to thank.) With masturbation, there's no possibility of romance, of course, but a prearranged session of emotionally detached sexual intercourse doesn't inspire much swooning, either. When you hook up, you run the risk of realizing you don't even like the person you're with, whereas with masturbation, at least it's sex with someone you love.[3] And while hooking up saves you from squandering time and energy on a relationship that doesn't go anywhere, it also denies you the exhilaration of investing yourself in one that could go on forever.

That's a big risk of hooking up: it diminishes your motivation to go out and find someone who can give you more than sex. If you are satisfying your bodily urges by bedding down with a willing partner every so often, you dull the ache to truly connect and mask the urge to take a chance on something deeper and longer lasting. It takes nerve to go out with different people and put yourself on the line, and you could easily get out of practice (just ask anyone who ends up back on the dating market after being married for a while). As a short-term measure, hooking up may permit you to shelter your heart, but in the long run, it discourages you from disclosing your true self to another person and lessens your chances of getting more than an efficient, vacuum-packed roll in the hay.

Janelle: Hooking Up, for Better and for Worse

Janelle became my patient four years ago, when she came in seeking treatment for anxiety. She complained of worrying all the time about things that didn't seem to bother anyone else: oversleeping (she kept two alarm clocks at her bedside), forgetting appointments (she had an elaborate web of sticky notes affixed to her furniture, dashboard, and makeup mirror), and offending people (she had once spent three hundred dollars on a dress she disliked because the saleswoman said she looked great in it and Janelle didn't want to hurt her feelings). I diagnosed her as having generalized anxiety disorder (a condition in which people find themselves beset with worries they know are unreasonable and excessive yet are incapable of dispelling) and prescribed a low dosage of an antianxiety medication. Now in her late twenties, she manages the condition by taking the medication and coming for therapy.

Janelle is slender and attractive but feels anxious in social situations and often avoids them, so she hooks up with single men via the Internet. If a guy sounds interesting, she meets him for a drink and, if she's attracted to him and reasonably sure he isn't dangerous, sleeps with him once, maybe twice, before the e-mails grow sparse and stop coming. Then she'll go back online and start the process again. Thus far, none of Janelle's hookups have been heartthrobs, although two of them did pique her interest and occupied her imagination after the initial encounter. As it became clear that return engagements were not going to happen in either case, though, Janelle endured a bout of melancholy before she felt confident enough to put herself online once more and try again. As thirty looms on the horizon, Janelle finds herself craving sex and love and is increasingly fearful about not finding someone with whom to share her life. But hooking up has become her primary form of sexual contact, and she is beginning to show signs of battle fatigue.

From the outside, most people would think Janelle leads a charmed life. The eldest daughter of a prominent family, she grew up in a stately house, slept in a canopy bed, and attended exclusive private schools. She holds a master's degree in marketing, works for a high-end women's retailer, and lives in a luxury two-bedroom apartment paid for by her parents.

But Janelle's life is not as rosy as it seems. Her younger sister has cerebral palsy and lives at home with their parents. At twenty-four, Emily is unable to hold down a job or care for herself, and Janelle says she cannot remember a time when Emily's needs did not dominate everyone else's. This was especially hard for Janelle during her sophomore year away at college, when she was date-raped by an upperclassman she had been seeing. She declined to press charges, went for counseling, and, after some time, was able to resume dating. But she never told her parents about the incident, believing they had enough to worry about without her adding to their burden. It was after the rape that Janelle developed her anxiety symptoms, which she has mentioned to her parents without remarking on their severity.

Some months ago, Janelle took a bold step and accompanied a friend on a two-week vacation to Italy. Upon her return, she came to see me in a state of blissful agitation: she had met someone in Florence, also on vacation, and it was, well, fantastic. He lived in Belgium but had emigrated with his family from Pakistan; Sami was good-looking, a few years younger than she, and incredibly sexy. They could barely keep their hands off each other, and Janelle said the sex was unbelievably exciting. Best of all, she said, was the way Sami looked at her: he called her his "golden-haired goddess," and for the first time in her life, Janelle felt adored. They'd had only three days together before her return flight home, but Janelle said they were in touch via e-mail and were planning to meet in Paris in a few months' time. When I asked Janelle what she expected from this relationship, she said she didn't really know and, at this point, didn't really care: the sex was great, and that's all she was thinking about. She shyly alluded to trying some "new stuff" at Sami's request; he had asked her to shave off her pubic hair, and she said she might do it for the Paris rendezvous: did I think it was too kinky? I told her it didn't sound terribly kinky to me, although it could be itchy when it started to grow back.

"Do you think this is someone you could really care about?" I said.

"I do care about him," Janelle said.

"Yes, but I mean in the context of a committed relationship." Janelle thought for a moment.

"We're from very different backgrounds," she said. "His family is Muslim, and I don't know if I should invite him home for Christmas." She giggled. "But that doesn't need to happen right away. That's why we're meeting in Paris—neutral territory."

Janelle came in for a session two days before she left. She was somewhat anxious about possibly missing her plane connections but was otherwise in high spirits. She left my office with an appointment to come in right after she returned.

Ten days later, Janelle sat facing me, crumpled in a chair. The trip had felt off from the start. Janelle arrived at the hotel trembling with exhaustion and anticipation to find Sami's suitcase on the bed with a note that he'd gone out exploring. When he sauntered in three hours later, Janelle was tearful, but he took her in his arms and all was forgiven. They made love for hours, Janelle said, and things felt great again.

But the idyll didn't last. Little, petty things came up: Sami would be impatient waiting for Janelle to get ready in the morning; he teased her for not speaking a foreign language (he knew English, French, Dutch, and Urdu) and made a cutting remark about materialistic Americans one night when she offered to pay for dinner so they could eat at a better restaurant. Then one morning Sami was leafing through Janelle's passport when he looked up, shocked. He hadn't realized she was twenty-eight, he said; he was only twenty-two and felt that Janelle had misled him into thinking she was younger than she was. They quarreled; Janelle cried, Sami apologized, and they fell into bed. But the spell was broken. Janelle said the sex was still okay, but the intimacy stopped there; the emotional connection she had felt with Sami was ruptured, her feelings blocked. They limped through the remainder of the week and separated at the airport; Janelle had not heard from Sami since she'd returned home.

Janelle's experience was not surprising: if you spend seven sexually charged days and nights in close quarters with someone you don't really know, it's likely you'll get on each other's nerves. Likewise, if you're expecting the sex to blossom into a love affair, you're likely to be disappointed. And so it went with Janelle; she returned crestfallen but hopeful that she would soon hear from Sami. When two days passed without a message, she e-mailed him, ostensibly to make sure he had gotten home safely. He did not respond, and now she was on the brink of despair.

Janelle swore that she hadn't been envisioning a grand future with Sami when she had left for Paris, and I believe her, to a point—the point at which many women tend to blur the line between lust and love. Because this is one of the biggest risks for women when they hook up: imbuing an episode of bodice-ripping sex with an emotional undercurrent that isn't there (at least not for the guy).

And why wouldn't you? It seems perfectly logical that a session of passionate lovemaking would cause you to feel something, if only the yearning for it to happen again. For me, this isn't a feminist issue but a biological one. Women have a very different position in sex because we're the ones who get pregnant, carry the babies, birth the babies, feed the babies, protect the babies—not to mention *love* the babies—and keep them alive. It's been that way throughout history, and it's still that way. That's what makes it harder for women to detach sex from emotion: our innate emotional attachment to our babies—who are, after all, the natural consequence of sex and our best guarantee that our bloodlines and the race will continue.

So, biologically speaking, it's hard to separate emotion from sex if you're female, and there's nothing wrong with that. It's not something you have to work on or correct or overcome. In fact, it's a very valuable trait—unless you want to hook up a lot and emerge untouched by it all.

Which is what Janelle has been trying to do, and cannot do, because she is fundamentally ill suited to estranging her soul from her sexuality. It just isn't her. She wants sex and enjoys sex and can hook up with a guy, fully aware that he's not likely to be the man of her dreams.

But like most of us, she still has those dreams, so she ends up developing a fantasy that this will be a relationship, not a mere hookup. And the risk is that she is almost certainly going to be disappointed, if not flung into despair. Because when the sex is good, you get sucked into the idea that it's because you and the guy have connected emotionally and that there's a potential relationship there. And then when there isn't, you castigate yourself: What did I do wrong? Say wrong? I know the feelings were there, so how could he walk away from this? What is wrong with *me*?

Most of the time, what's wrong is not you but your expectations. Your mind inhabits a dichotomy: you either hook up with someone sexually and then think you are going to have a relationship that never happens, or you have a relationship with someone you like who doesn't arouse you sexually. Your body wants sex and your mind wants love, so you're intent on integrating the two, even when it's not meant to be.

When you are young, in your twenties and even in your thirties, it is harder to establish a good relationship than it is to have good sex. So if your primary mode of human connection is sexual, the odds are implicitly lower that your connections will evolve into something more. It follows, then, that if you want to have an emotionally fulfilling relationship with satisfying sex, you raise your chances of finding one by starting with a good relationship.

That is what I told Janelle. Today she is working on establishing a relationship with a good man who lives on this side of the Atlantic. She jokes about it sometimes, the temptation she feels to have a fling when she is a long way from home, but so far, she hasn't strayed from her time zone. She still hooks up with men on the Internet but limits her potential contacts to those who live within a hundred miles of her home. She also arranges to have at least two telephone conversations with a man before she agrees to meet him, because she has found she can learn a lot about a guy by the way he conducts himself on the phone. She has become more selective about who she goes to bed with; when she meets a man she thinks she could care for, she postpones having sex with him until she knows him better. She is rediscovering the pleasures of friendship and intimacies that do not include sex. And when she is not involved with a lover, she is learning to reframe these interludes as time spent in solitude rather than loneliness.

While I would disagree with those who believe that hooking up presages the fall of Western civilization, I can't see myself recommending it to my daughter ("Sweetie, if you're horny, why don't you sleep with that nice boy you met at the picnic last week? He seemed harmless!"—I don't think so). Sure, it scratches an itch, but it may aggravate an even bigger one. And while you may not be risking a short-term heartbreak, you could be letting yourself in for long-term heartache by condemning yourself to years of demoralizing encounters or contracting an incurable (if not fatal) disease. Perhaps worst of all, you might squander your youth in shallow sexual affairs until, when you find someone to share your life with, you learn you are no longer fertile and cannot conceive the child you never thought you would want and now want more than anything.

So before you go any further, look within yourself and ask: Who am I? When it comes to sex, what matters most? What am I willing to risk to get it? Whose voices am I hearing in my head, besides my own, and why do I care what they are saying? What will it take to get the sex I want, and do I have the courage to do it?

SEXUAL INVENTORY

What Will You Risk for Sexual Pleasure?

1. **Are you now or have you ever been in the habit of expressing your sexual likes and dislikes to your partner?**
   - If not, why not?
   - If so, how did your partner(s) respond?
     - ~ Did your candor improve or damage the relationship(s)?
     - ~ Did you become more or less forthcoming as a result of your partner's reaction?

2. **Are you involved in a committed, monogamous relationship?** If so:
   - How satisfied are you with the relationship in general? How has this changed over time?
   - How satisfied are you with the sex specifically? Again, how has this changed over time?

~ If you are less than satisfied with the sex,

- is it because your partner doesn't know how to please you or doesn't care about pleasing you?
- have you told your partner that you are unsatisfied? If not, is it because
  - you are too self-conscious to talk about sex with your partner?
  - you are afraid your partner will think you are overly focused on sex?
  - you are afraid of angering, offending, or hurting your partner? What is the worst that could happen if you were to tell your partner the truth?
- Are you pretending to enjoy sex by either saying you've had an orgasm or faking an orgasm?
- Are you turning away from your partner after sex so he won't see your face and infer the truth?
- Are you avoiding sex so you won't have to admit the truth to either yourself or to your partner?

3. What emotional or physical risks have you taken in a sexual relationship, such as:

- telling your partner about an erotic fantasy of yours and inviting him to enact it with you?
- trying new erotic activities?
- experimenting with different positions?
- using an arousal-enhancing product such as a vibrator or erotic lingerie?

4. If you have taken emotional or physical risks in a past relationship but not in your current one, what prompted you to become more cautious?

5. Have you avoided taking emotional or physical risks in either current or past relationships?

- Do you shy away from risk taking in general, or are you particularly shy about sex?
- Are you more shy with some partners than with others? Do you know why?

6. Do your sexual encounters typically consist of hookups rather than grow out of relationships? If so:

- How do these encounters feel, both individually and cumulatively?

  ~ Are they physically satisfying or disappointing?

  ~ Are they emotionally fulfilling or disappointing?

- What effect do these hookups typically have on you?

- Have you had any hookups that were memorable because they were exciting, disappointing, or disastrous?

- Have you had any hookups that were hurtful to you? If so, did the experience cause you to stop hooking up or change the way you hook up?

- What are you looking for in a hookup? Do you simply want physical release, or are you trying to assuage deeper feelings of loneliness?

CHAPTER 4

Unsexy Sex
The Egg and the I

Biological possibility and desire are not the same as biological need. Women have childbearing equipment. For them to choose not to use the equipment is no more blocking what is instinctive than it is for a man who, muscles or no, chooses not to be a weightlifter.

—BETTY ROLLIN[1]

With few exceptions, girls grow up believing that having a baby is the pinnacle of womanly fulfillment, a noble goal to which they ought to aspire. Motherhood is portrayed to a girl as simultaneously sacred and within her grasp, a vocation transcending barriers of money, education, and class. By the time she is grown, a girl has been inculcated with the belief that, even if she discovers the cure for cancer or AIDS, being a mom is the most important work she can do. Even if her mother was a rocket scientist and her father stayed at home with the kids, a young woman will still feel pressured to have children as her friends pair off and start families, relatives ask indelicate questions, and the media bombard her with images of what she is missing.

Consider the women in home pregnancy test commercials. They glow and wait for the plastic wand to manifest its magic: are they pregnant, or aren't they? Their complexions range from dark to light, their hair from flaxen to frizzy; together, they define diversity. Sometimes there is a man in the background, clasping a woman's hand so their wedding bands gleam for the camera; make no mistake, these people are married, and they want this baby. And then there's usually another woman, an athletic type, whose wand comes up with nothing in the window, signifying that she is not pregnant after all. But that's fine with her: it is clear from her discreet smile that she did not want to have a baby, at least not now.

What is wrong with this picture? First of all, there's no sex: you can't even imagine these people getting down and doing it. Don't let the cozy, domestic settings fool you: these ads aren't about pregnancy, or living with a man and sharing your bed with him, or what really happens when the two of you become three or four or more. These ads are about the *idea* of having a baby, the bliss we are taught we will feel when we find out that we are pregnant, and the abundant rewards that await us as mothers. The sex is conveniently cropped out of the picture. The man stuff—the drive, the sweat, the urgency, the bigger, hairier, heavier body, the—whoops, never mind, that's not part of the motherhood myth. Just wave your magic wand—or watch it, either way—and the dark and grunty portion of the program dissolves to maternal serenity and pastel-tinted décor, and everything is sweet and soft and feminine. The sex part? Forget it—these women are occupied with higher matters.

But who are these women? They certainly aren't the ones I know and treat. For one thing, every woman in these commercials is content with her results; pregnant or not, she's a happy gal. Each of them knows where she stands on the pregnancy issue and gets what she wants. But wait; where is the working mother who starts trembling with panic when she learns she is pregnant with another baby she can neither care for nor afford? Or the high school sophomore who runs away from home because she fears her parents will beat her when they find out she isn't a virgin, let alone is pregnant? Or the wife so desperate to conceive that she crumples in despair when her test comes up negative yet again?

Those women are out there, living real lives. They are our sisters and our daughters, our colleagues and our friends. They are also my patients, who come for help because their reproductive lives are beyond their control: they are carrying a child they do not want, longing for a child they cannot have, or emotionally estranged from the men with whom they are trying so desperately to make love. They don't understand why they cannot get pregnant when they want to so badly and are doing everything right. They are mystified when their passion to conceive douses the desire that brought them together. Or, if they do get pregnant, they are unsettled by the fog of ambivalence that clouds the baby-blue horizon. They have heard every lecture, read every book, and bought every product promising to confer parenting perfection, yet it still isn't working.

It isn't working because they have also bought into the cult of mythical motherhood, where, deep down, every woman is meant to be a mom, wants to be a mom, and gets to be a mom. Where a couple's longing for a child deepens their passion and brings them closer together. Where not a flicker of ambivalence or worry, let alone distress, panic, or despair, disfigures a woman's serenity.

How could it? Motherhood is something every woman thinks about, daydreams about, even obsesses about, from the day she starts toddling around the house, dragging her doll baby with her. How can she not know how she feels about it? It isn't as if you can be a girl in America and escape the message that the secret of life is to have a drop-dead gorgeous face and body so you can attract hordes of men, choose the perfect one, marry him, and have sex with him so you will get pregnant and have babies (thereby wrecking the gorgeous body you worked so hard to create in the first place, but that's another story).

The fact is that many women really don't know how they feel about having a baby, even when they are sure they do. A woman's sexuality is a living, pulsing entity, and her attitude toward herself as a bearer of children both profoundly affects and is profoundly affected by her sexuality. You cannot separate one from the other without creating an artificial division between body and mind. And pummeling both is society's insistence that, if you're a woman, there's something not quite right with you if you don't have kids (and something very wrong with you if you don't want them).

The notion that motherhood is woman's highest calling is programmed into us from early on, so much so that when Grandma Dora and Uncle Joe have the gall to remind us that we've shirked our procreational duties, we feel obliged to explain that it's not that we don't want children, we're just waiting until the time is right. That's what I did when the eighty-seven-year-old patriarch of my husband's family said to my husband, in front of me, "When are you two going to have a baby? You've got to chain her to the bed!" Never mind that I was deeply invested in my budding career and that my husband had three children from a previous marriage, the eldest of whom was entering adolescence and living at home with us. And never mind either that this otherwise chivalrous man had proudly squired me around to his club and his church group, bragging that I was a doctor in the Navy. To him, it was unimaginable that a woman would not make motherhood the priority of her life. If a woman didn't have a baby, it was either because she couldn't have one or because she didn't realize what she was missing. It was inconceivable that she didn't want one. (For the record, not only did I want one, but I eventually had two, a son and a daughter, when the time was right.)

Today this attitude seems quaintly benighted. We know we have options; we can get married and have children in our twenties or wait until we are older; we can even have children without getting married at all. Or we can choose not to have children and devote ourselves to our careers, our partners, or ourselves.

Yet freedom of choice does not necessarily confer peace of mind. In fact, having multiple choices can make your life more complicated by burdening you with more options to research and offering fewer excuses for choosing the wrong one. Likewise, a woman may know she wants to have children and be vexed by the seeming freedom she has to choose when she wants to have them, how many, and with whom. She may have a good husband but bad credit and want to wait until they are out of debt before starting a family, yet worry about waiting too long. Or she may have a great job and plenty of cash but a partner who doesn't want to share her with a baby just yet. Or she and her husband already have a child but he wants another and she isn't sure. Or maybe she is forty and single and doesn't know if she should try to get pregnant, adopt a child, or wait a little longer and try to meet someone to have a child with.

On the other side of the issue is the woman who yearns for a child and is so obsessed with conceiving one that sex becomes a chore freighted with purpose and grimly eros-free. She has studied the literature and knows her stuff: precisely when she will ovulate, how long the egg will be viable, and exactly when her chosen mate has to hop to it and supply the semen to effectuate the miracle of life. It is as if the act of lovemaking were not the engine of conception but a time-wasting inconvenience, and the man not her beloved but a sperm donor. These women don't see that the love they are lavishing on their idea of a child is vanishing from their own, very real relationship.

And what of the woman who wants children—or may already have children—and can't reconcile fulfilling her own needs with meeting those of her family? Having a child changes your life utterly and forever, and a degree of ambivalence is normal. Yet many women feel guilty if they have mixed feelings about becoming pregnant and won't admit the feelings to either their partners or themselves. Instead, they tamp them down where they don't have to see them, not realizing they'll surface again during sex. For a woman, the connection between sex and childbearing is bred in the bone and set in the psyche, and not subject to banishment by birth control. It remains there, like it or not, lurking beneath her consciousness and the bedclothes, coloring her sexuality whether she knows it or not.

Samantha:
"I Can't Have This Baby—I Can't Handle It"

"No offense, but I don't think you can help me," the young woman said. She was twenty-seven but looked older. Her only jewelry was a thin gold band on the ring finger of her left hand and tiny hoops in her ears. She wore no makeup, and her hair was pulled straight back in a ponytail secured by a plain elastic band.

"The only reason I'm here is because the OB said I should come. But there's nothing wrong with my head except I can't sleep, and maybe you could give me something for that. But I shouldn't be here taking up your time, because I don't need a psychiatrist. I need an abortion."

"You seem to feel very strongly about this," I said.

"Yes! I don't want this, okay? I can't go through with this. I can't. I can't." She started to sob, and I passed her a box of tissues.

"I'm sorry," she said. "But I cannot go through with this pregnancy. Not after the last time. It was so horrible, I swear I thought I was going to die. And I swore I wouldn't do it again. So they gave me a new diaphragm, and I used it, I swear. But it didn't work.

"I've already got two kids. How am I going to do everything? How am I going to get to the hospital on time? Who's going to take care of the kids? I can't have this baby. I can't handle it. You've got to help me take care of this."

Samantha's obstetrician had referred her to me because he was concerned about her state of mind. She had gone to his office the previous week asking for an abortion and had become distraught when he declined the request. Samantha was halfway through her sixth month, and a doctor won't perform an abortion when a pregnancy is that far along and both mother and fetus are healthy. Samantha's psychological health wasn't great, but a dread of childbirth isn't sufficient reason to end a pregnancy that is more than halfway to term. There are ways to ease the pain of labor and childbirth, after all, and many mothers who are apprehensive about it are overjoyed once they have their babies. Samantha was upset but far from psychotic: she was lucid, able to express herself coherently, and had a fairly accurate if somewhat pessimistic view of reality.

"Samantha, I think I can help you," I said, "but I need to know more. Tell me about why you can't sleep."

"By the time I get the kids in bed and clean up from dinner, I'm totally wiped. But when I get into bed, I start thinking about last time, and then I start panicking about what's going to happen this time, and my heart starts pounding, and forget it—the sun comes up and I'm still awake sometimes."

"What happened last time?"

"It was . . . it's hard to describe. I mean, I love Brittany, I'd never want not to have her, but it was the worst experience of my life. And the funny thing is, the first time was so much easier. With Maddy, there was plenty of time, I had an epidural, my mother and sister and Greg were there, it was okay. But last time they didn't give me anything, and it was horrible, just horrible."

This was the first time Samantha had mentioned Greg, whom I inferred was her husband. He had been conspicuously absent from her vocabulary until now.

"Greg is your husband?"

"Yes."

"How does he feel about the pregnancy?"

"I don't really know how he feels. He isn't around much."

"Where is he?"

"He drives a truck, and he's on the road a lot. I . . . we . . . we haven't been real close lately."

"What about after the first baby? Were you close then?"

"Yes, I guess we were. He was home more then."

"And now?"

"Now? He goes away. He comes home. Then he goes away again."

"How is your sexual relationship?"

"It used to be great. Now it's, like, over."

"What about after the first baby? Did you make love then?"

"After a while, sure. But not this time. I'm too tired. I'm not in the mood. I just don't want it anymore."

Samantha and her husband were still in their twenties and, according to her, used to make love several times a week, even after Maddy was born. But after the second baby, her desire diminished drastically. She began avoiding sex by either going to bed early and feigning sleep, or busying herself in the bathroom until Greg dozed off. Months passed, and Greg began taking long-distance jobs, staying out of town for weeks at a time. Samantha noticed that when he did come home he wasn't clamoring for sex, and she began worrying that he was having an affair. Then Greg came home on his birthday bearing gifts for the girls and flowers for Samantha. She was overwhelmed with tenderness for him and they made love. That was nearly six months before.

"I found out I was pregnant, and since then, it's been a disaster," she said. "I don't know what he does when he's on the road, and at this point I don't really care. All I know is, I can't go through this again. At least last time we lived in town. Now we're way out in the country, thirty minutes from the hospital, and I don't know if I'll get there in time. I worry that I'll have the baby in the car or at home and something bad will happen. I have all these horrible thoughts, all the time. It's driving me crazy."

Samantha's state of mind was troubled, and so was her marriage. Not only was she physically exhausted, she was emotionally depleted from isolating herself from her husband. She had just admitted she did not care if he had sex outside the marriage—not a good sign—and could be perceived as having pushed him in that direction. She had convinced herself that a geographical inconvenience was an insurmountable obstacle that she was powerless to overcome. Her anxiety had taken over her life, compromising her ability to cope with her considerable responsibilities, not to mention her health (and that of her unborn child).

The first priority was to help Samantha stop worrying so much, so I suggested she consider taking an antianxiety medication. As it happened, she had used one during her last pregnancy and tolerated it well, so I prescribed a low dosage. She was disappointed that abortion wasn't an option, but I promised that if she would work with me, I would help her develop a plan for getting through the rest of the pregnancy, the birth, and afterward. She agreed to come in once a week.

Since then, Samantha and I have been working to eradicate her anxiety by tracing it back to its source, which seems to be her sense of isolation. She feels cut off from civilization in general and her family specifically because of living out in the country. Even though her mother and sister live only ten miles away, the distance seems vast to Samantha in the context of going into labor and needing them to come right away, get her to the hospital, and watch the kids. So we are working out a plan for her mother and sister to alternate spending the night at Samantha's house as her due date approaches.

Her greatest anxiety, however, seems rooted in her alienation from her husband, which springs from her fear of childbirth and resulting aversion to sex. All Samantha told me about Brittany's birth was that it was very fast (six hours), excruciatingly painful (there was no time for an epidural anesthetic), and the worst experience of her life (she doesn't want to go through that again, ever). And while a difficult six-hour labor may not be as excruciating as a difficult twenty-hour labor—and plenty of women have the twenty-hour kind—it wasn't going to help Samantha to tell her that. For her, that childbirth was a trauma, and that was that.

Many women experience a diminishment of desire after having children, but Samantha's libido wasn't the problem; she was actively avoiding sex due to her dread of enduring another traumatic labor. Her sex life had resumed after the first child was born, but not after the second; to me, that was significant. Nor had she said anything about wanting to limit her family to two children or being unhappy with the children she had. She was a full-time mother who loved her children and enjoyed caring for them, yet was desperate not to have another one. She seldom mentioned her husband, revealing her sense of aloneness, an aloneness she had cultivated by spurning him sexually. Without sex to bond them, Samantha and Greg were spinning in their own orbits, rarely intersecting. Samantha's anxiety about the upcoming birth was magnified by her estrangement from Greg: any encouragement and comfort he might have provided were swallowed by the space between them.

What we learn from Samantha's case is that a woman's attitude toward motherhood can have a powerful effect not only on her desire for sex but on how she negotiates her marriage, and that that attitude depends on the woman in question and where she is in her life. Samantha wanted children, had children, and loved being a mother. But she did not love her second labor and childbirth, and that had changed her view of herself as a mother and a wife. Samantha did not set out to erode her marriage after Brittany was born, yet she did just that by avoiding sex with her husband. The irony is that people typically have children to enrich and strengthen a marriage. All too often, however, they learn that parenthood has emphasized their differences and weakened their bonds, especially the sexual one. When the sex goes, the connection frays, and the fabric of the marriage wears out. And while some people are better off divorced than married to each other, children are usually better off if their parents can resolve their problems and keep the family together.

My work with Samantha focuses on restoring her confidence in her ability to be the mother she always has been and an active partner in her marriage. She is learning to control her free-floating anxieties by anchoring them to concrete solutions. She has assembled a roster of friends and family members who carry cell phones or beepers and are prepared to spring into action the moment she goes into labor. Greg's supervisor has agreed not to dispatch him on long-distance assignments as Samantha's due date approaches. And the couple has worked out a birthing plan with Samantha's obstetrician that calls for her to receive an epidural anesthetic during labor and a tubal ligation after the birth to ensure that she doesn't become pregnant again. This minor surgical procedure, which consists of tying off the fallopian tubes to prevent the descent and fertilization of an egg, is minimally invasive and 99 percent effective in preventing pregnancy. I hope that Samantha's sex life will improve once she has had the procedure and is no longer fearful about conceiving another child.

Why did Samantha need a psychiatrist to prescribe such over-the-counter remedies? Because she was too anxious and agitated to identify the source of her worry and therefore could not dismantle it. She thought she had lost her sex drive, but what she really wanted was to prevent a pregnancy. She thought she wanted an abortion, but what she really wanted was to avoid another agonizing delivery.

Kendra: Ambivalent About a Second Child

Kendra might have needed a psychiatrist, but she sure didn't want one.

"I know your gynecologist sent you here for issues concerning fertility," I said, "but otherwise I don't have much information about you. Can you tell me a bit about what you see as the problem, and how I might be able to help you?"

"The problem is that I had a baby two and a half years ago, but now I can't seem to get pregnant again. And I apologize for saying this, but I don't see how you can help me at all." At least she was honest.

"Do you know why your doctor suggested you see me?" I said.

"She thinks I'm suffering from anxiety and that it could be compromising my fertility. But I've always been this way, and I was certainly this way when I got pregnant with Ruby. So I really don't think that has anything to do with it."

She had a point. Research suggests that women who have infertility problems develop depression and anxiety disorders, as opposed to depression and anxiety causing infertility, which is what people used to think. But just because you don't conceive right away doesn't mean you are infertile.

"According to your records," I said, looking at her file, "you and your husband have both undergone fertility testing—"

"And they can't find anything wrong with either of us. That's the point; there's got to be something they're missing. I got pregnant with Ruby right away. And I'm only twenty-nine, so it can't be my age."

"How long have you been trying to conceive?"

"Eight and a half months."

This was odd. A couple doesn't usually undergo a fertility workup unless they have been trying to conceive for at least a year. This woman wasn't even thirty but was behaving as if her childbearing years were nearly over. The intensity of Kendra's distress was out of proportion to the direness of her situation.

"From the look of it," I said, "there isn't anything medical preventing a pregnancy. So something else might be going on, and it could be related to the anxiety. If it is, we can deal with that."

"You mean with medication?"

"Medication is one possibility."

Kendra shook her head. "No, that's out. I don't want to take anything because if I get pregnant, it could affect the baby, and I don't want to take any chances." I knew of several antianxiety medications that were safe for pregnant women but decided not to push the issue.

"What else can you tell me about yourself?" Kendra glanced at her cell phone.

"There's not much to tell. I'm home with Ruby full-time. I used to work as an environmental engineer, but it was too hard after Ruby was born. We would be spending more on child care than I was bringing in, and we didn't want a stranger raising our daughter anyway. So I quit. They let me telecommute one day a week, writing grant proposals. It isn't much, but it's better than nothing."

"Do you enjoy the work?"

"Actually, no, I don't enjoy it. It's deadly dull. But I'm good at it and I can do it at home, so I do it. But no, I don't like it. In fact, I hate it." Kendra's eyes glittered, and her voice sounded choked.

"What would you rather be doing?"

"I would rather be doing what I used to do. I would rather be working with adults and talking with adults and thinking about something besides what a two-year-old thinks about. I used to go to conferences and give talks and make good money. I used to do work that mattered. Now the highlight of my day is if Ruby makes it to the potty on time.

"I feel so out of control. I used to be so organized, so in charge of every-thing. Now everything is a mess. The minute I start doing something, I have to stop and help Ruby do something or make sure she isn't getting into something dangerous. Then Forrest gets home and he asks me what I did today, and I don't have anything to say." Once again, Kendra looked at her cell phone.

"Are you expecting a call?" I said.

"Not exactly. Ruby's with a sitter, and I'm not used to leaving her. My mother usually takes her, but she couldn't do it today. So she's with this woman. But she's into everything and you've got to watch her really closely. You hear such crazy stories." She was holding the phone now.

"Do you want to call home and check on her?" Kendra shook her head.

"No, I probably shouldn't. This is when Ruby takes her nap, so if I call now I might wake her up. And Forrest said he'd call, so I probably don't have to."

"How is your relationship with Forrest?"

"Forrest is completely supportive. He wants this baby, and he's doing everything he's supposed to." Interesting; I had asked Kendra about her marriage and she had responded by talking about the child she hoped to conceive.

Kendra explained their sexual routine. She kept careful track of her menstrual cycle and took her temperature each morning before getting out of bed. As her ovulation date approached, she would take her temperature several times a day so she would know precisely when it rose, indicating that an egg would soon be released. Then she would call Forrest into the bedroom—or at work on his cell phone—and he would come home immediately so they could have sex.

"What about at other times, when you aren't monitoring your temperature?" I said.

"We pretty much stick to a schedule. I know exactly when I'm going to ovulate, and I don't want anything to interfere with that."

"Not even sex?"

"No, not even sex, I guess. Right now I'm focused on getting pregnant. If it's the wrong time of the month for that to happen, there's not much of a point."

I felt as if Kendra had just handed me the key to her sexual psyche. This young woman was doing everything in her power to conceive a child—everything, that is, except making love with her husband. They may have been having sex, but they weren't making love. Sex had ceased to be an act of intimacy and communion. Instead, it had become a procedure.

This happens frequently among couples who are trying to conceive: their focus shifts away from the concrete reality of each other to the fantasy of the child they hope to have. It is usually the woman who unwittingly initiates the shift, for it is she who is keeping track of when she is fertile and able to conceive. She may become grimly efficient, keeping detailed notes about her body's readiness to receive and make the most of her husband's sperm, perhaps shunning sex unless she knows she is ovulating. The man usually goes along with the program, bowing to the woman's superior knowledge of her body and, often, her more urgent desire for a child.

But when you focus on the product rather than the process of sex, it pulls the woman away from her partner and toward herself as the vessel of the longed-for child. The idea of a baby replaces the flesh-and-blood couple as the core of the partnership, and the woman's body acquires an aura of sacred purpose while the man becomes little more than a sperm donor. Sex becomes a procedure: like taking blood or giving a urine sample, it is something to soldier through rather than enjoy for its own sake. Stripped of intimacy, passion, and spontaneity, sex becomes about managing the body rather than surrendering to it.

This can seriously alter both the couple's intimate life and the rest of the relationship. If the woman does not conceive within the first few months, she may grow discouraged. Discouragement may deepen into depression, at which point she may turn inward, away from the man and toward herself, losing her interest in sex. The man, on the other hand, is not depressed; he still wants sex and intimacy but is being rebuffed. He wants to be sensitive to the woman's needs and supportive of her wishes but is unsure of how to proceed. Is he allowed to initiate sex when the woman isn't fertile? Is his need for sex and intimacy as important as their mutual desire for a child? How do his needs stack up against hers? Where does sexuality fit into their lives after their quest for a child is resolved?

Further, it seems that when a couple becomes fixated on having a baby, they may actually diminish their ability to conceive. It's a fairly common story: a couple tries in vain to have a child, sometimes for a decade or more. Eventually, they come to terms with the situation, decide to adopt, and, within months of bringing a child into their home, find out they are expecting. We don't know exactly why this happens, but we do know that anxiety and stress can affect hormone levels, which in turn can reduce fertility. When the couple stops trying to conceive a child, their stress levels diminish, and sometimes their fertility improves.

It starts in the brain, in the hypothalamus and pituitary gland, which dispatch messages to promote production of follicle-stimulating hormone, which sets in motion the process by which an egg is released from the ovary and causes estrogen and progesterone levels to rise. If a woman is unusually anxious, these levels may not rise and she may miss a period. This phenomenon, known as functional amenorrhea, obstructs ovulation as well as menstruation, rendering the woman infertile for that cycle. And it cuts two ways: sometimes a woman does not want to get pregnant and is so worried that she will that her hormone levels are flung into disarray, she misses a period, and her anxiety escalates because she thinks she *is* pregnant. Either way, a woman's psychological state can have a powerful effect on her reproductive ability.

A case from Japan comes to mind. A forty-five-year-old woman was newly married and eager to have a child without delay, so she and her husband decided to pursue in vitro fertilization (IVF), a physically and emotionally (and financially) draining process. Over the next three and a half years, the woman underwent two separate attempts to implant multiple fertilized embryos in her uterus. Sadly, none of the implantations was successful, and the couple, emotionally and financially depleted, discontinued IVF treatments. Then, eighteen months later, the woman reappeared at the clinic—fifty years old and pregnant.

Why did this happen? The woman's doctors think it had a lot to do with her psychological state. Beset by anxiety, depression, and fatigue during the lengthy IVF regimen and alternately soaring with hope that a baby might develop and stricken with grief when it didn't, the woman was emotionally overwrought for nearly four years. After she abandoned IVF, the emotional tumult subsided, along with its adverse effects on the woman's energy and general well-being. Once she and her husband stopped investing physical and psychic energy into conceiving a child, she recovered some measure of harmony among body, mind, and spirit, and became pregnant without benefit of any technology—at the age of fifty, no less.[2]

I recognized elements of the Japanese woman's situation in my own patient's, even though she wasn't undergoing IVF. Kendra's flare of temper when I asked about her career was significant. Many women are reluctant to express anger because they have been taught it isn't ladylike, so they repress it, sometimes for years. The tension of hiding the anger often fosters an underlying fear that it will surface, causing the woman to live in a constant state of free-floating, nonspecific worry. She starts fretting about issues of minimal importance and minuscule likelihood, such as whether she will interrupt her child's nap by phoning home or endanger her by leaving her with a babysitter. Everything becomes a source of stress and worry, regardless of the actual odds of something going awry.

When a patient is besieged by relentless, irrational worrying, she or he is usually suffering from generalized anxiety disorder, as Kendra was. The first priority was to ease her symptoms. Because medication was out and she really didn't want psychotherapy (or even think it would help), I suggested light therapy, an unorthodox approach. Typically prescribed for people with seasonal affective disorder, or SAD (a mood disorder characterized by depression brought on by the reduced hours of daylight in autumn and winter), light therapy calls for the patient to sit in front of a special lamp that approximates the spectrum and intensity of sunlight. While light therapy has traditionally been used to counteract depression, recent studies were showing that it sometimes relieves anxiety symptoms, so I was hopeful it would help Kendra.

Three weeks later she was back in my office. Light therapy had not worked, so we embarked on a course of weekly psychotherapy. As our work deepened, it emerged that Kendra was wracked with conflict between her vision of what her life should be and the reality of what her life was. She had planned everything out: career, marriage, kids, financial security, personal fulfillment, the works. She thought of herself as a career woman who would take some time off to have a family, as we say (as if you could stop having a family when you'd had enough of it), and then return to the professional world. Kendra had done what a lot of us do: she had bought into the delusion that we can have it all and do it all.

Well, you can't have it all and you can't do it all. It is not humanly possible to nurture a marriage or domestic partnership, manage a career, raise children, run a household, maintain your health and emotional equanimity, and have everything go the way you want it to. You cannot be a high-powered career woman and be with your children all the time or even most of the time. Nor can you be a full-time mother and also enjoy the rewards of having a career and being well paid for it. You cannot expect to raise a family, work outside the home, maintain order within it, and still have energy to make passionate love every night.

The truth is, of course, that you don't have to have it all to have a richly rewarding life. You don't have to be beautiful and rich and famous and sleeping with a gorgeous hunk to be happy; if that were the case, movie stars would stay married forever and never end up in rehab. You don't have to excel at everything to live in a nice place, luxuriate in the love of friends and family, and enjoy rollicking good sex. Things don't have to turn out precisely as planned to be fine and right and good. There are limits to what we can plan and execute, and no matter how competent, efficient, intelligent, and well organized you are, there are certain things you just can't control. And if you try, as Kendra did, you are in for a rude jolt, not to mention some psychological distress.

Kendra came in every week for about three months. She even agreed to try taking antianxiety medication and derived some relief from her worrying. She and Forrest tried several times to conceive a child and were disappointed. Even so, Kendra was adamant about sticking to the sexual regimen she had established: they could have relations while she was ovulating, but otherwise she would just as soon abstain. One day Forrest joined Kendra in session. He missed Kendra, he said; there were times when he desperately needed intimacy and wanted to make love, but she would shoo him away, ostensibly to space out their sexual encounters and conserve the potency of his sperm. Outside of Kendra's fertile days each month, their lovemaking had dwindled to nearly nothing.

Anxious people are in acute pain, and they want the doctor to end it. They also tend to be more sensitive to medication's side effects, suffering severe discomfort when others might be only mildly affected. The bottom line is, they are in pain, they want it to stop, and they don't want to endure any more suffering than they already have to deal with it, so it wasn't a complete surprise when Kendra started missing appointments. At first she would reschedule; after a while she missed the makeup sessions, and eventually she stopped coming altogether. My staff left messages on her answering machine, but she would not return the calls.

The last time I saw Kendra was about six years after our last session, when she appeared at the reception desk, tearful and agitated, demanding copies of her records. When the clerk said it would take a few days for the records to be photocopied, her distress escalated; she left after the clerk promised to have the records available the following afternoon. I never saw Kendra again. I don't know why she needed the records so urgently, but I am haunted by the memory of her distress and imagine she may have needed them for child custody proceedings related to divorce. To this day, I hope I am mistaken.

Kendra's case is a classic example of how a woman's desire for and ambivalence about having a child can lead her to corrupt her primary relationship with her husband. Kendra was referred for psychiatric treatment because she could not become pregnant, but that was not the point. The point was that the process of trying to become pregnant, coupled with Kendra's ambivalence about having a second child, had leached the romance and pleasure from sex, which in turn alienated her husband from her and she from him. By focusing on the product of sex rather than the process of sex, they eroded the essential erotic bond that is, at its heart, both the source of new life and the foundation of the couple's life together.

When it comes to having a baby, people tend to lose perspective. They can become so tightly focused on the fantasy of the longed-for child that everything else is crowded out of the picture: friends, family, partner, even themselves. It is as if nothing matters or exists except the pursuit of parenthood. The danger is that if something goes wrong, there is nothing left to hold on to.

Maritza's story is a classic illustration. She came to me because she was having trouble controlling her anger, which was related to her intense desire to have a child. She was in her early thirties, worked as a bank teller, and felt that motherhood was being withheld from her because her insurance company would not pay for in vitro treatments.

In vitro ("in glass") fertilization is a process by which eggs are removed from a woman's body, fertilized in a laboratory using donated sperm (donated ideally by the woman's husband), and implanted in her uterus, where it is hoped they will attach successfully and develop into fetuses. As I mentioned earlier, it is an arduous process, especially for the woman. She must inject herself with hormones to stimulate the ovaries to form multiple egg follicles, which can cause her mood to vacillate wildly. Then she must submit to an ultrasound every two days to count the eggs and, when there are enough, undergo sedation so the eggs may be collected. At the same time, her husband is in an adjacent room, working up a sperm sample, which is then combined with the eggs, usually in a glass petri dish. The couple then goes home and waits a few days to see how many eggs have been fertilized. If some have been, the woman returns and undergoes sedation again while the embryos are implanted into her uterus. Then the couple waits to see if any of the embryos flourish, develop into a fetus, and result in a pregnancy. Maritza had decided that in vitro fertilization was her ticket to motherhood.

"It isn't fair," she would say. "I want a baby and there's a way for me to have one, but they won't let me do it. It isn't right." Or "If people can help someone have a baby, they should do it. You shouldn't have to be rich." I explained that insurance plans rarely cover in vitro fertilization because it costs upward of ten thousand dollars and is an elective procedure. Still, Maritza felt cheated. To her mind, she was entitled to have a baby: as long as the technology existed, there was no reason it should be denied to her.

One day Maritza arrived in a state of high excitement: her church had raised enough money for her to have in vitro treatments, which she was starting immediately. Two months later, she was pregnant with twins. "I told you," she said. "Now I can have my family." It struck me that Maritza spoke only of "I" and "me," never of "we." I knew she was married, yet she seldom mentioned her husband. When I asked about their intimate life, Maritza said that she was not going to have relations until after the babies were born because she was afraid that having intercourse might harm them. She had also asked her husband to sleep on the couch because the bed was getting too crowded as her belly swelled. It was as if her fixation on having a child had so narrowed her field of vision that there was no room left for her husband, literally and figuratively.

One night several months later I received an urgent call: Maritza had been admitted to the hospital. She had had a miscarriage; it was the beginning of her fifth month. She was distraught; hysterical and agitated, she interpreted the loss as a punishment for some crime she must have committed. She said she did not want to go on living and was admitted to the psychiatric ward, where she remained for several weeks before returning home.

Adjusting to a miscarriage is difficult in any case, and particularly wrenching when it occurs halfway through a longed-for in vitro pregnancy. By then, hormones have reformatted the woman's emotional circuits and primed her for motherhood; she is a different person, both physically and psychologically, than she was before. For Maritza, the blow was especially severe because of her obsessive focus on the pregnancy and the distance it had put between her and her husband. He was not sure how to help her or even how to be with her. He was disappointed; she was in despair. He wanted to be close, but she shrank from his touch. When it was safe for them to make love, they still remained celibate, he afraid to hurt her, she unable to invite intimacy. In fact, it took months for them to resume sleeping in the same bed. Now, seven months after the miscarriage, Maritza and her husband are slowly resuming sexual relations. She has been taking an antidepressant and hopes to discontinue it soon. Then, she says, perhaps they will try again.

Maritza's case is not typical, yet it has much to teach us, namely this: once the focus of sex becomes making a baby rather than making a connection, it pulls you away from your partner and erodes the structural integrity of the relationship. If it goes on too long, the marriage may collapse, taking the family along with it. Recovering from the miscarriage would have been difficult in any case, but by having made the babies her whole world, Maritza lost everything when she lost them (or so she thought). Because sex was irrelevant to the in vitro process, Maritza banished her husband from their bed. In doing so, she severed the connection they had once had that would have provided a safe haven in which to recover.

When Pregnancy Is Not an Option

Even when a woman knows she will not have children, whether due to medical necessity or personal choice, her attitude about wanting or not wanting children will affect her sexuality.

There are many kinds of birth defects and chromosomal abnormalities that render a woman unable to have children but do not affect her ability to enjoy sex. These cases are not uncommon—you would be shocked at the percentage of women who have some sort of abnormality. A woman born without a uterus may learn while still in her teens that she will never be pregnant, yet she still has to work through her attitudes about sex and motherhood. If she is involved romantically with a man, how will it affect their intimate life? At what point (if ever) should she tell him she cannot have children? If she is very religious and believes that sex is meant primarily for procreation, what role can sex play in her life? If she wants children, should she adopt, engage a surrogate to bear a child for her, or remain childless and overindulge her nieces and nephews?

A woman's attitude toward pregnancy and sex may be even more complex if she was exposed to diethylstilbestrol, or DES, before she was born. DES, a synthetic hormone similar to estrogen, was thought to prevent miscarriage and widely prescribed for pregnant women in the 1950s and early 1960s. By the mid-1960s, it became apparent that the drug was ineffective and it fell out of favor. Years later, however, as the daughters of these women matured, an unusually high percentage of them developed serious problems, including cancer of the cervix and vagina, deformities of the uterus, infertility, premature labor, and other problems in pregnancy.[3] (Male children whose pregnant mothers took DES seem not to have been affected by the drug.) The psychological struggles of DES daughters (so named by the U.S. Department of Health and Human Services Centers for Disease Control and Prevention) are compounded by the devastating irony that, in being exposed to a drug that allegedly enhanced their own chances of being born, they were rendered unable to have children of their own. (For a case study of a DES daughter, see Chapter 8.)

Sometimes a woman's attitude toward pregnancy is complicated only by the attitudes of others. A woman in the bloom of reproductive health may be absolutely, positively sure she does not want to have children, yet she too must consider her views on motherhood and be able to articulate them, especially at family gatherings. I know a successful career woman whose very happy marriage has been predicated on the decision not to have children. She and her husband have been married for seventeen years and enjoy a level of intimacy and commitment most couples would envy. Yet she still has to contend with the occasional clueless relative or acquaintance who corrals her in the ladies' room and says, "You two are so happy together—you should have kids!" Whereupon the woman explains that the reason she and her husband are so happy together is because they *don't* have kids.

Having children and raising a family is an inexpressibly powerful and gratifying experience—that is, if it doesn't kill you. It's not for everyone, and there is no reason to think it should be. Not every woman wants kids, and not every woman should have them. Only you can decide if having children is right for you. There are many ways to find Truth, Beauty, Love, and Fulfillment in life without having children. And it's a lot harder to have great sex when you do have children, as we'll see in Chapter 5.

SEXUAL INVENTORY

How Do You Feel About Having a Child?

1. **Imagine that no one could ever know how you will answer this question.** Now identify at least three emotions you feel about the idea of having children.

2. **If you have been pregnant before, can you recall moments of doubt, fear, or a desire not to have the child?** (If your answer is no, you may want to think again, because nearly every woman has them.)

3. **How has the decision to have, or not have, children, been made in your relationship?**

4. **Where does your partner fit into your view of yourself as a mother or mother-to-be?**

5. **If you do want children, how do you decide when the time is right?** Is the decision related to
   - the relationship?
   - your age?
   - your career?
   - your social situation?

- your friends having children?
- what your family or culture expects of you?

6. How important is having children to you?

- Why do you think this is?
- Were children highly valued in your family?
- Do you see children as validating your existence? Or do you perceive them as a burden?
- What are you willing to do, give up, or lose in order to have them?

CHAPTER 5

From Teddies to Teddy Bears

Sex During Pregnancy and Beyond

Have you ever wondered why someone who wouldn't dream of touching a female acquaintance's stomach will think nothing of giving it a good going-over when it's bulging under a maternity blouse?

"Ooh, it's soooooo adorable!" she says (it is usually a she, although not always), patting the impossibly solid and protuberant belly, whose owner stands patiently, waiting for the moment to pass.

Why does this happen? Because a flat stomach is considered an erogenous zone, whereas a pregnant woman's stomach—or any other part of her, for that matter—is considered anything but erogenous. She is no longer a sexual being whose flesh, blood, bone, and breath conspired in an act of bodily delight, whose skin prickled with pleasure, who thrust her breasts against her lover's—

Whoa! Stop right there. Banish that image from your dirty mind. This is a pregnant woman we're talking about. A goddess. An exalted being. The embodiment of selflessness, goodness, and sacrifice. Sex? *Her?* Perish the thought.

But why? What makes pregnancy seem so incompatible with sex, when it's sex that gets you pregnant in the first place? Why does it feel so wrong—blasphemous, even—to imagine a pregnant woman in the throes of passion? Think about it: can you think of even one movie sex scene in which the woman is noticeably pregnant, let alone resplendent in her third trimester, with a rotunda-like belly? I cannot. In fact, the only place you are likely to see depictions of pregnant women in sexual situations is on a pornography Web site.

The dearth of pregnant sex symbols is rooted in our culture's taboo against being a mother and a sexual being at the same time. When *Vanity Fair* magazine plastered a photograph of naked, seven-months-pregnant, twenty-nine-year-old Demi Moore on its cover in 1991, people could not stop talking about it. By today's standards, the photo was relatively discreet, featuring the actress standing in profile, gazing into the distance with her left arm cradling her belly and obscuring her breasts. Still, it had a pungent whiff of scandal about it and inspired giddy conversation in employee lounges across the nation.

Why is the juxtaposition of pregnancy and sexiness so provocative? Because of the unspoken belief that once a woman goes through pregnancy and childbirth, her sexuality is irrevocably changed, muted, civilized. No longer may she abandon herself to the pleasures of the flesh, for if she loses control and goes berserk, who will take care of the baby? Mythology has it that woman is secretive, changeable, essentially unknowable; if she gives way to the passions that roil her, she might languish forever in lustful limbo, out of her husband's reach and control. How will he know if she has been faithful? Even more crucial, how can he be sure that the child she is carrying is his? It's the classic, superstitious view of woman's sexuality: dark and mysterious, a black cat in the road, an alchemy of equal parts allure and apprehension, reverence and fear.

You can see where this view comes from: woman's sexuality *is* more hidden and less direct than man's, and women *are* changed by pregnancy and childbirth. I have yet to meet a woman who didn't say her life was altered forever the day she had kids. Motherhood hits a woman like a tornado, hurling her life heavenward for a brief and blissful moment before returning it unceremoniously to the ground in fragments she may or may not recognize. The pieces are all there, more or less. It's just that when you put them back together, everything looks different than it did before.

It starts the moment you learn you're pregnant. Your estrogen and progesterone levels increase more than a hundredfold. You get much more fluid in your system, and your liver and kidneys start eliminating toxins much faster. The weight you put on in the beginning is mostly fluids that enter the bloodstream; eventually, the fluids ooze out into the tissues, which is why hands and ankles sometimes swell. Everything is pulsing, growing, changing: your breasts, your hair, your midsection, your appetite, all acquire new dimension and significance as you relinquish your dominion over your body and watch it do what it has to do.

Your body is no longer yours alone, and everything you do to it merits mindful consideration: a demitasse of espresso, a goblet of wine, an antihistamine tablet, a dip in the hot tub—what will it do to the baby? What are the risks? Is it okay to exercise? And how about sex? What if the lovemaking is vigorous—can his thrusts hurt the baby? Dislodge it, even? Cause a miscarriage? And what if I have an orgasm? Will the contractions put me into labor? Is it safe? Is it recommended? Is it worth it?

And so begins the inevitable drift away from yourself as a sexual being. Your image of the essential you recedes into the distance as you evolve into an exalted, admired, and untouchable entity, a Mom. Instead of seeing yourself as a woman, or as sensual or hedonistic or wild, you see yourself almost exclusively as a mother, a selfless creature of pristine instinct, one who nourishes and protects her unborn child and reliably places its needs (along with everyone else's) ahead of her own.

Part of it is that you know there's a life inside you and you turn inward, the better to know and nurture it. Whereas before you focused on yourself and your husband, your lover, your partner, now you direct your gaze inward, toward the impossibly unique and unknowable entity that is you and your baby. As you focus on this unit, you redefine yourself, and the new definition includes both you and the growing life within. So even after the baby is born and you're not gazing inward anymore but outward, besotted with love and dulled by fatigue, you see the child not as an extension of yourself so much as a flesh-and-blood emanation *from* yourself. This redirects your gaze away from you and toward the infant, and helps you redefine yourself as a mother.

Women who adopt are not immune to this, by the way. It is not pregnancy so much as the knowledge of impending motherhood that redirects the gaze from self to child, and women who adopt are as vulnerable to the syndrome as their pregnant sisters. A woman who adopts will almost certainly be less fatigued when her child arrives and will be spared the burdens of expanding bulk, unprecedented weight gain, and the ordeal of shopping for wildly overpriced maternity clothes. But not going through pregnancy also puts the adoptive mother at a disadvantage, for she hasn't had nine months of bodily changes to prepare her for what's to come. She (and her partner) may have had months or even years of interviews, paperwork, and fantasies of who their child will be and when it will join them. But when the child does arrive, the physical reality is abrupt: one minute the woman's arms are empty, the next she is holding her daughter or son. Psychologically, it's a bit of a shock—an exhilarating, ecstatic, life-affirming one, perhaps, but a shock nonetheless, and her focus on the child she has adopted may be even more obsessive than that of a woman on a baby to whom she has given birth.

The point is, it's not how a woman becomes a mother but *becoming* a mother that drives her to redefine herself. And when we start to see ourselves as mothers first and women second, we tend to kick sex down lower on our lengthening list of priorities.

That's what happened to Ingrid, a highly intelligent twenty-nine-year-old whom I have been treating for a number of years. She first came in when she was a senior in college and had developed chronic, low-level anxiety, so I put her on medication, which she continues to take to keep the symptoms under control.

Nothing daunted Ingrid; setting her sights on a career as a biochemist, she enrolled in a top-notch doctoral program, married her longtime fiancé, got pregnant, was back in class two weeks after the birth, completed her research, and began writing her dissertation. When her daughter was ten months old, she learned she was pregnant again.

It is now a year and a half since Ingrid's second child was born. She has not finished her dissertation, nor does she mention it. She talks about the children almost exclusively, and when I ask about her husband, Jeff, she says he's not home much because he's working longer hours. She comes in once a month now, and sometimes Jeff comes with her. He worries about money and fears that his bookstore manager's salary won't be enough to support the family. He wants Ingrid to finish her dissertation and get her doctorate, but she shrugs him off, saying she is not about to put the children in day care, nor is she ready to take on the stress of writing a thesis and defending it before a faculty committee. Jeff retorts that both his parents and Ingrid's have offered to help out with child care, but Ingrid says that's not the point; she is their mother and the one who should be with them. As for Jeff and Ingrid's sex life, it has all but evaporated. Jeff says Ingrid spoils the kids, giving them her endless and eternal attention and letting them stay up so late that when she finally comes to bed, she falls asleep in her clothes. Ingrid thinks Jeff is jealous of the kids, that he should understand that they are her first priority and not make sexual demands on her when she is doing so much already. Jeff in turn feels abandoned by Ingrid and betrayed by her refusal to pursue her career; he says they desperately need to move into a larger place but can't get a big enough mortgage on his salary alone.

What happened to this couple happens to many couples when they have children: the woman drifts away from her essential self and becomes that generic entity, a Mother. Not incidentally, the essential self she drifts away from is the person her partner fell in love with, and he is likely to miss her more than she does. Let me be clear: I am not castigating Ingrid for paying attention to her children. It is natural for a woman to attend to her children's well-being. But if she shifts her focus obsessively toward the children, the resulting flight from the self may not serve her well. This was clearly the case with Ingrid: the longer she delayed writing her thesis, the more daunting it seemed and the less confident she felt about returning to the rigors of academia. As she turned further away from her husband, the more resentful he became, and the more he withdrew.

We don't do this intentionally; I have never known any woman, patient or friend, who intentionally demoted sex to a lowly status, but more women than you would expect find themselves alienated from their sexual selves once they become pregnant and have children. And while some women become more sexual during their pregnancies, most women are less desirous of sex as they grow larger, if for no other reason than they have a large, bulky belly that is ill suited to the missionary position—and many others as well. Studies show that during pregnancy, and especially in the last trimester, a woman's sex drive and her ability to experience pleasure and reach orgasm are markedly diminished.[1] The one thing that increases is lubrication, which probably results from rising hormone levels, increased blood flow, or both.[2]

While there are always exceptions, it's safe to say that most women are not eager for sex in the last trimester of pregnancy, which sometimes causes their partners to become frustrated at the lack of bodily intimacy and fearful that it will never return. Whereas some couples become sexually inactive, others become creative. I know some women who, once the baby is born, enjoy the novelty of lactation and invite their partners to enjoy it with them. While it may not be for everyone, I don't see anything wrong with it as long as both partners get something out of it. Some women can shoot milk across the room by squeezing their breasts, and some couples incorporate this newfound talent into sex games. Once again, it may not be your cup of tea, as it were, but people make love in unconventional ways, and there's nothing wrong with it if both of you enjoy it.

Another thing that happens is that your body starts to pack on pounds. Some of this is necessary and healthy for the baby, of course, but too much additional weight tends to stay where it is even after the baby has left the compound—in some cases, for college. (There are many women who never manage to lose the weight they put on during pregnancy, and, just like the child they bore, it's with them for life.) Not all women mutiny against their newfound bounty; many whose maidenly breasts were of apricot-like proportions marvel at the breadfruit-like dimensions they attain during pregnancy (and beyond, if they nurse). That said, when a woman puts on a substantial amount of weight during pregnancy—and many, many do—her expanded contours often oppress her vision of herself as sexually desirable and weigh heavily against her sexual self-esteem.

Add to that the sense of being underrested, overwhelmed, and riddled with responsibility, and cavorting in the bedroom seems about as reasonable as, say, signing up for tango lessons: it would be fun to do, but who has the time or the energy? When you're pregnant, everything you've got is given over to doing what you have to do: going to work, paying bills, tending the family. You have to put gas in the car and you have to buy food and you have to pay the electric bill, but you don't have to have sex, so the sex has to wait.

Meanwhile, you are deeply fatigued because you can't do everything. There's this crazy idea that we can, and we punish ourselves because, try as we may, we can't seem to do it all. Well, I am here to tell you that no one can do everything—*no one*—despite the mothering mavens out there who would have us believe otherwise. Take Alpha Mom TV, an all-day, all-night cable channel founded by a former high-powered Wall Street executive who had a baby and became a turbo-powered mothering magnate. The channel's target audience, she says, is "the new breed of 'go to' moms who are constantly looking to be ahead of the curve and 'in the know' on the newest innovations, hippest trends, and research breakthroughs."[3] I don't know about you, but being hip and ahead of the curve was not high on my hit parade when I was a new mother; managing to get a shower before dinner was. And while I think it's good to provide women with information, I don't think it's good to engender competition among them by suggesting that rearing children is a type of Olympic event that you can win by being the smartest, fastest, hippest, happeningest—not to mention wealthiest—mom in the playgroup. One thing a new mother or mother-to-be does not need is pressure to do more and do it better. She's already doing plenty just by getting out of bed and into those gargantuan garments women get to wear when they are with child. And let's face it: it's not easy to feel sexy when your underpants could rig the mast of a frigate, which is what you might feel like muttering every morning as you hoist them over your poop rail.

So there you are, larger than you've ever been in your life, feeling fatigued physically and emotionally because there is more to do each day than you can accomplish. Much of this is chemically induced: as our hormones change—and they change dramatically during pregnancy—they affect our moods, for better and for worse. There's a belief that women are always euphoric when they are pregnant, but it's not true. Yes, there are rhapsodic interludes when we meditate blissfully on the miracle of creating new life, but we are also subject to fearful ruminations about it. When a woman is pregnant, grotesque thoughts snake through her mind that she's not likely to mention at her baby shower: *Oh my god, what have I done? What if I hurt the baby? I don't want this baby. I'm afraid of what will happen to this baby. What if it drowns in the tub? I wish it wouldn't be born. I wish this had never happened to me.* . . . And there's more where those came from. A college professor tells about her recurring pregnancy dream of going out to dinner, remembering she left the baby in a box in the closet, and deciding to leave it there rather than rush home and cut short her evening. I know of another woman who, while nursing her newborn in the kitchen, homed in on all the lethal weapons it contained—knives, shears, peelers, corkscrews—and what might happen if she were one day to lose her mind while mincing shallots and harm the baby. Neither of these women would ever do anything to harm her child, but these sorts of fantasies are no more rational than, say, the one you have about running away with Bruce Springsteen. They just claw their way up to the surface of your consciousness and float there, leering, no matter how absurd they may be. As monstrous as they seem, these thoughts are very common, quite normal, and nothing to be alarmed about, even if they do make you shudder a bit. Women seldom mention them because they think they're the only ones with such evil, perverse ideas, but in truth, these thoughts are merely anxiety made manifest, and they would frighten us less if we'd talk about them more.

Blooming as you are within this hothouse of prenatal ecstasy and apprehension, physically and emotionally drained, how can your sexuality not be affected? Your partner may find you as attractive as ever—perhaps even more so, given your newly abundant proportions—yet you don't quite believe him. How can he want you when you're so different than you were? Does he want to make love because of your new shape or in spite of it? The truth is, it is hard to trust his attraction for you because *you* don't feel attractive yourself.

Moreover, you may be anxious about how making love might affect the baby. Many couples worry about this, and the anxiety may be keener if the couple has had infertility problems and struggled to conceive. The fact is that there are no data to indicate that even vigorous lovemaking could cause miscarriage in an otherwise healthy pregnancy. (Of course, there are situations where a miscarriage follows a sexual encounter, vigorous or otherwise, but there is every reason to believe that such a miscarriage would have occurred in any case.)

Sexual anxieties abound: many women worry that, if they have an orgasm, the ensuing contractions will cause a spontaneous abortion (they won't) or cause them to deliver early (they won't do that, either). Some women are concerned about having to change the logistics of lovemaking, especially if their men prefer the missionary position. There are quite a few women whose growing bellies make this position extremely uncomfortable, if not impossible, and whose husbands are equally uncomfortable with the notion of making love any other way. Such women sometimes choose to avoid sex with their husbands rather than work through the discomfort they both are feeling, going to bed earlier than the men and feigning sleep when they enter the bedroom, or staying up late and going to bed only after the men have fallen asleep. Or they may routinely turn away from their husbands' erotic overtures until the men weary of the rejection and stop trying. In some cases, men are unreasonable in their demands and give their wives little recourse but to avoid them. But in other cases, women are just as reluctant as their partners to shake up the routine and suggest other positions, and they choose to avoid rather than confront the issue. Ultimately, avoidance alienates the woman emotionally and physically from her husband when she needs him most and can continue to strain the couple's sexual relationship well after the baby is born.

Last and far from least, you have begun to become not only a mom but the maternal archetype, a Mother, and we are not supposed to have sex with our mothers. What if your partner starts seeing you that way? What if you arouse in him an ancient sense memory that starts him thinking, however unconsciously, *Oooh, I don't know about this* . . . After all, a man is bound to see a woman differently as her pregnancy progresses, and he may view her as unattractive. If she puts on sixty pounds, he may begin to see her as matronly. Perhaps he was careful to marry someone who is not like his mother, and suddenly, there's his wife, looking more and more like—don't even go there! It can horrify a man if his wife or lover evokes his mother, because that would be incest, a deeply ingrained taboo. And a woman need not resemble her mother-in-law in appearance or behavior to summon her into her husband's consciousness; the fact that the wife is pregnant may be enough to plant a seed of incest anxiety in both his mind and their bedroom.

Another source of anxiety for some men is uncertainty about who's the real father of the child his wife is carrying. This is an ancient source of male insecurity and, I believe, the reason that men have historically tried to exert control over women's reproductive rights. If you think those days are over, think again: recently, the women's health chief at the U.S. Food and Drug Administration resigned in protest of the agency's refusal to approve the morning-after emergency contraceptive pill, even though FDA scientific advisers overwhelmingly ruled it safe and effective and recommended it be sold over the counter to all ages.[4] You can legislate all you like, but at the end of the day, a woman is the only one who knows who the daddy is, and that makes a lot of men uneasy.

And there are more men than you'd think who have real reason to worry: a radio quiz show recently asked contestants what percentage of men have reason to be concerned about the paternity of their babies. The answer was 6 percent, which means that one out of seventeen men is partnered with a woman whose fidelity he has real reason to doubt. Add in those who are going to worry even if they have no reason to, and with more than four million babies born in the United States each year, you have more than a quarter of a million men whose sexual dynamic, along with their partners', is likely to experience turbulence as they await the birth of their child.

Childbirth can alter the landscape of a couple's intimate relationship. The gusts of emotion and waves of discomfort; the galvanizing pain, replete with promise; its throbbing, bloody, primal physicality, so raw, so violent, so quintessentially female, yet so unlike anything you have ever known. It can forever change the way you feel about sex and your partner, and you may never get over it. And it's hard on the woman, too.

It's no joke: some men emerge from the delivery room more shell-shocked than their wives. And while women will openly discuss the travails of labor with the gusto of soldiers who have survived a fierce battle, men tend to keep their scars covered. A psychiatrist recently wrote in *The New York Times* about several patients who have said they wish they had remained at the head of the bed while their wives were in labor, so disturbed were they by what they saw. Some men reported symptoms similar to those of posttraumatic stress disorder, which a person may develop after experiencing or witnessing a deeply upsetting event. Indeed, some men said they had never recovered the erotic attraction they had for their wives before watching them deliver children. One man who had been married for twelve years put it this way: "I think one of the main reasons I don't feel attracted to my wife is that I saw her give birth three times. It's like I know too much about that part of her."[5]

These men are not cowards, nor are they maladjusted, closeted misogynists. They are men who love their women and have been buffeted by the gale-force emotions that roar through a guy when someone he loves is going through an ordeal—an ordeal, as it happens, that he played a part in preordaining and whose torments he is helpless to relieve. It is only during the last thirty or forty years that men have even been allowed, let alone encouraged, to be present and participate when women labor and deliver their children. Before then, husbands were routinely sequestered well away from the birthing area, where they would pace nervously and wait for news. That seems absurdly old-fashioned now, and I do not advocate returning to the dubiously good old days when childbirth was a private affair to be conducted between a woman and her (male) doctor. But any discussion of postpartum sexuality would be both naïve and incomplete if it did not mention the risks a man takes when he watches the woman he loves go through childbirth. Some intensely moving experiences can also be intensely disturbing, and childbirth is one of them.

If labor and childbirth can be intense for a man, they are particularly so for a woman. Whether a labor lasts for forty hours or four, you can be sure it will be memorable for the woman going through it. Some labors go on for days, progress smoothly, and result in textbook-case deliveries; others take three hours, beginning to end, and are terrifying in their urgency. No two childbirths are alike because no two women are alike. Some women tough it out and go through labor and childbirth without taking so much as a Tylenol; others request an epidural anesthetic when they reach three centimeters; still others schedule cesarean sections because they are fearful of going through labor. Whichever sort of birth a woman has, vaginal or C-section, it will have powerful and in some cases lingering effects on various aspects of her life, including her sexuality.

This is especially true when the labor is a long one. There are some babies who just don't want to come out, and a woman may labor for hours without being able to squeeze the baby's head out far enough for the doctor or midwife to grasp and ease the infant into the world. When this is the case (and neither baby nor mother is in distress), the practitioner and mother have several options to choose from: forceps, a larger version of salad tongs, which are used for gripping the baby's head and utilized less frequently today than they used to be; or a vacuum extractor, which works just as its name implies (a caplike device is affixed, via suction, to coax the baby's head out of the vagina). There is also the option of a cesarean section, but obstetricians are reluctant to perform surgery when less invasive alternatives exist (midwives, of course, are not licensed to perform surgery). So most physicians will try to ease out the baby's head without subjecting the mother to the trauma of major surgery. Most of the time, this works out well, and the baby comes squalling into the world in fine shape. The mother's body, however, might not be so lucky.

Carole: "What Have We Done?"

Carole, a thirty-three-year-old biology professor, came in about a month after the birth of her first child. She and her husband had been about to start infertility treatments when she learned she was pregnant, and they had anticipated the arrival of this baby with great joy. Carole's pregnancy had been complicated by nausea and migraine headaches; between these symptoms and her teaching workload, it was all Carole could do to teach her classes and keep her research going. As she described it, she would come home, collapse on the couch, prepare the next day's lectures while her husband, Gene, cooked dinner, and fall into bed right afterward. Carole said she had felt little or no desire while she was pregnant, and lacked the energy it would take to help Gene satisfy his. Moreover, she had gained thirty pounds during the pregnancy, which worried her, if not her doctor.

As her due date approached, Carole had begun to feel anxious about the birth. She feared she would be quickly overwhelmed by the exertions of labor and require pain relief but knew of several women who had ended up with C-sections after receiving epidurals too early in labor (if too much anesthetic is administered, it can prevent the woman from feeling the contractions, inhibit her ability to push efficiently, and stall the labor), and she didn't want that to happen to her. In the end, Carole and Gene drew up a birthing plan that called for Carole to labor as long as she possibly could before considering an epidural in the hope of avoiding a C-section—assuming neither mother nor child was in distress, of course. Their obstetrician signed off on it, and they were good to go.

Carole went into labor a week past her due date. Everything went according to plan until she dilated to eight centimeters; then the ferocity of the contractions persuaded her that natural childbirth was overrated, and she requested an epidural. After twenty hours of labor and nearly four hours of pushing, Carole was exhausted and her nether regions resembled an inflamed catcher's mitt. Her obstetrician called for the vacuum extractor and performed an episiotomy (a surgical incision into the vagina and perineum, the region between the vagina and the rectum) to widen the vaginal opening, then delivered the baby's head and, after some heavy maneuvering, its shoulders and the rest of it. The good news was that the baby was fine. The not-so-good news was that the baby's head and shoulders stretched Carole's episiotomy beyond its limits, causing a third-degree tear down to her anal sphincter.

Now, I would not recommend a third-degree tear to anyone. It must be stitched shut, takes several weeks to heal, occupies a high-traffic area on the body, causes psychological stress and anxiety when you have to defecate, and hurts. It can also diminish bowel control while the wound is healing and cause some leakage of stool for a few weeks beyond that. Large tears are painful, awkward, messy, and unpleasant. That said, in the context of what can go wrong during labor and delivery, large tears are not tragic; they do heal, and they are easier to recover from than a C-section.

This was cold comfort for Carole as she sat, depressed and morose, in my office. It was nearly a month since the birth, and she was not back to normal (nobody is back to normal a month after her first baby, but she did not want to hear that); she was still bleeding a bit from the birth, the tear was not fully healed, and small amounts of stool were still leaking out. Gene was concerned about her; it was at his urging that she had come for therapy. According to Carole, he was alarmed about some of the things she was saying. Here is more or less what she said to me:

"It's not as if we didn't want a baby. We did. And now that we have one, it feels like the biggest mistake I've ever made in my life. We didn't rush into this; we tried for over a year, so we had plenty of time to think about it. We even signed up for infertility treatments. We were supposed to start on a Thursday, and that Tuesday, I found out I was pregnant. It was like a miracle, although neither of us believes in that kind of thing.

"The first four months were hard, although compared to now, it wasn't so bad. I was sick a lot; I threw up, and my migraines got worse. Gene was great: he took over a lot of the household chores, and he taught my class a few times when I was too sick to go in. He was really understanding about, you know, when things started changing. He never pushed me, never made a big deal when our sex life kind of . . . self-destructed. We knew it was temporary, that it would take some time. It's not as if we didn't know our lives would change.

"But this, this I wasn't ready for. I knew it would hurt, I knew I'd have to heal. But this is horrible, it's a nightmare. It's a month later, and I'm still bleeding. And I'm still—how did she say it?—'experiencing episodes of incidental incontinence.' In other words, I'm leaking shit all over myself. I didn't need a doctor to tell me that. It's lovely, let me tell you. 'Oh, everything's looking fine!' she says. This is fine? Fine for her, maybe; she's not walking around smelling like a cesspool. I'm afraid to go anywhere because I'm worried someone's going to look up and say, 'Where's that smell coming from?' It's the most disgusting, humiliating thing.

"What gets me is that it didn't have to be this way. Why didn't she do a C-section? Why did she let it go on so long? 'You wanted a vaginal birth,' she says. 'You didn't want surgery, the baby wasn't in distress, and we agreed to follow your birthing plan.' We? Who's we? Does she think I wanted to walk around like this? I'm a biologist, not an obstetrician—it's not my job to know what to do. That was her job, and she blew it.

"How am I going to go back to work? I can't think straight; how am I supposed to teach? I'm up for tenure next year; I can't not get my research done.

"What have we done? I have this terrible feeling that we've made a horrible mistake, that we should never have had this baby. He cries all the time, and I don't know what to do for him. I should never have become a mother. I'm lousy at it. Everyone says, 'When the time comes, you'll know what to do.' But you don't—at least I don't. I swear, Gene is better at it than I am.

"He thinks I've lost it, you know. The other day he was saying that he missed me, the way things used to be. And I said maybe we had made a mistake, and maybe—not that we should, or even that I wanted to—but that maybe we should think about putting the baby up for adoption. He looked at me as if I had lost my mind. And you know what? Hearing myself tell the story, I think he's right."

It's common for women to feel ambivalent after having a baby. The great majority of women—70 to 80 percent—experience the baby blues, feelings of melancholy, anxiety, and guilt for a few days after giving birth, and it's easy to see why. You are severely sleep-deprived, your hormones are in a frenzy, a tiny being that used to float silently inside you now shrilly demands your constant attention (or so it seems), you can't go to the toilet without someone howling or needing you for something, and nothing—*nothing*—about your world is the same as it was. You may have had the unsettling experience of roaming the supermarket, babe in cart, or running a meeting at work and suddenly being overcome by an episode of weeping. It perplexes the heck out of you, but when you think about it, it makes sense that you would need some time to adjust to the change in your circumstances.

For 10 to 15 percent of new mothers, however, the blues deepen into postpartum depression, a far more serious disorder that seldom goes away without treatment. With more than four million babies born in America every year, we're talking about 400,000 to 600,000 women who struggle with this burden, and Carole was one of them.

Postpartum depression is not a benign funk from which you can rescue yourself via bootstraps and pep talks. It is a real and serious psychological disorder that many women have and for which they need treatment right away. Postpartum depression can profoundly diminish a woman's abilities, including her sexual functioning and her capacity to take care of the baby and other children at home. It was postpartum depression that made Carole have intrusive thoughts about giving up her baby, when what she actually wanted was to regain control of her life—her marriage, her career, her body, her intellect—a control she felt had eluded her since the baby was born. A big part of what she felt was missing was sexual intimacy with her husband, which had fallen by the wayside as she focused all her energies on the baby. It's that drift I mentioned earlier, that irresistible emotional pull away from your partner and toward your child. It becomes a self-perpetuating problem: the more you drift away from sex with your husband, the less you crave that intimate connection with him and the easier it is to let it go. The more you let it go, of course, the more you drift apart.

Carole's story is a hopeful one. Within two weeks of starting therapy she was taking an antidepressant that worked well for her and she was feeling much better. By the end of the summer, the tear had healed and Carole and Gene were back to having sex once every week to ten days, which is not bad for a couple with an infant. A slot opened up in the campus day care center, and Carole returned to teaching that fall. She was a bit frazzled at first but divided up child care and housework duties with Gene and hired a cleaning crew to come in twice a month and do the rest. She was in my care for eight months overall, which is not very long for treating depression. I believe one reason she improved so rapidly was that she came in for treatment within several weeks of developing symptoms. When it comes to depression, the sooner you get help, the better you'll respond to treatment.

Maureen: "I'm Just Not a Very Good Mother"

"I had a really bad depression after Molly was born. I stopped functioning and ended up in the hospital. I don't ever want to go through that again. So I thought I should come in because I'm pregnant again and I've stopped taking medication for the duration. I don't want another postpartum depression."

I couldn't ask for a more proactive patient than Maureen, I thought. She was thirty years old and sufficiently self-aware to know that another postpartum depression was not only possible but likely. Maureen had a history of dysthymia, a long-term, low-grade depression that doesn't disable you so much as cast a pall over your general view of things. It's like having a chronic case of the blues, and Maureen had first developed it in her early twenties. She had been treated on and off with antidepressants but had stopped taking them during her first pregnancy and had subsequently fallen into a profound depression several weeks after the birth. She eventually got help and went back on medication, which she said had helped her mood but wrecked her sex drive. Her daughter was now two and a half and a pupil at the preschool where Maureen taught part-time. Maureen said she was in pretty good health but tired; Molly kept her very busy 24/7.

"It's ironic, isn't it?" Maureen said. "I love kids, I work with kids. But when it comes to your own, it's different. I can't just tell Molly no the way I do my kids at St. Agnes, even when I know I should. I just don't have the heart.

"Part of it is that I'm exhausted. I'm in the middle of my first trimester, and I'm tired all the time. Molly's not a great sleeper; she's up several times a night, wandering around and coming into our room. Before I got pregnant I'd take her back to bed, but now I just let her climb in because that way I can sometimes fall back asleep. But there's not enough room for all of us and Ted sleeps like a rock, so I end up awake half the night a lot of the time. Then I'm a wreck the next day, and the mornings that I teach—forget it. Just getting Molly dressed and out of the house is a major deal. She's okay once we get there, but getting her up and moving is really hard because we're both tired and cranky and it's just really, really hard." Maureen averted her eyes, blinking rapidly. I nudged the box of tissues in her direction.

"I want to be a good mother," she said, dabbing her eyes. "I want to be all smiley and happy and contented and normal. But that's not the kind of person I am. I get frustrated. I get angry. I don't have the patience a mother should have with her child. I'm just not a very good mother. The medication helps, when I'm taking it. It helps me be more patient, and it makes me less moody, more even. Ted says there's a big difference in the way I am, and he's right; I like myself more when I'm on it.

"But there's a downside, too. My sex drive is, like, dead. I take this pill and it makes me feel better and my husband starts liking me again and he wants to have sex, but most of the time, I'm just not interested. I'm so tired at night, I can barely move. I just lie there and let him do what he wants. It's a miracle I'm pregnant again. And my weight doesn't help. I never lost the weight from when I had Molly, and I'm putting on more every day. If I were a guy, I wouldn't want to sleep with me.

"So that's why I'm here. I want this pregnancy to be different. I want to be a better mother. I don't want this baby to miss out the way Molly did."

"What did Molly miss out on?" I said.

"A natural birth, for one thing, and everything that goes along with it. It was my decision; I agreed to the C-section; nobody forced me. At the time, thirty hours felt like enough, the doctor thought that's what we should do, and I went along with it. It's not what I wanted, but that's what they said was best, and that's what we did.

"But this time I want to do it naturally, no matter what. I really want that experience, and I want it for the baby, too. I know they say it's hard to have a vaginal birth after a C-section, but I want to do it. And I'm going to breast-feed this time. I've always regretted not doing that for Molly. I tried, but she wouldn't latch on right and it hurt like crazy and it was just too hard and I gave up. Looking back, I shouldn't have had the C-section. I should have tried harder. I should have tried harder on everything, for her sake."

I've learned that whenever there's a flurry of *should*s, guilt isn't far behind, and Maureen's was palpable. It turned out that a close friend of hers was a fierce advocate of drug-free childbirth and had urged Maureen to go natural all the way. Maureen was torn between what she thought she should do (go through labor without any anesthesia whatsoever) and what she wanted to do (get through labor as quickly and comfortably as possible). This is not uncommon; the politics of labor and childbirth exert considerable pressure on women to reject pain medication in favor of an allegedly more authentic—and assuredly more painful—experience. My opinion as a physician and someone who has been through childbirth twice is this: as soon as you can safely have the epidural, get it. I don't see the point of suffering, especially if you have a very long labor. It's fine to go without anesthesia if you have a fast labor and deliver in a few hours, and some women do. But no one should make a woman feel guilty for getting pain relief during a long labor.

Or for not breast-feeding. There is no question that breast-feeding is the best way to nourish a newborn, and it's good for the mother, too. I encourage new mothers to breast-feed for at least three months, and for a year if they can. That said, some women have trouble with it, especially if they are depressed. Of the patients I've treated with postpartum depression, very few of them, if any, were able to breast-feed. The mothers try and try, but the babies don't latch on right so they don't get fed, and the mothers feel like failures because they have to switch to bottle-feeding. The depression seems to impose a layer of literal and figurative attachment problems. We aren't sure why this happens; it is as if depression sours the taste of the milk and discourages the baby from nursing. This is a big issue among women with postpartum depression and adds to their worry during subsequent pregnancies.

The first priority was to help Maureen get some sleep. I prescribed a low dosage of a sleep aid that was safe during pregnancy. I also suggested that she place a sleeping bag and pillow on the floor next to her bed and instruct Molly to slide in there during her nocturnal ramblings without awakening her mother. I've known several parents who have done this, and it works: the kids still come in, but the sleeping bag is not very comfortable and they soon decide to stay in their beds.

I began seeing Maureen every week. We worked on easing her guilt and bolstering her opinion of her mothering skills. In fact, Maureen was a fine mother; she loved her daughter and kept her clean, fed, and safe. If she erred anywhere, it was in being too permissive and allowing Molly to run her ragged. So we worked on teaching Maureen to set limits and say no to her child; with another one on the way, she needed the practice.

Maureen also needed to adjust her focus to include her husband. Her guilt over having a C-section and abandoning breast-feeding had caused her to view Molly as a deprived child deserving of her unswerving attention. By pouring all her energy into her child, Maureen had little left for her husband. She felt righteous about making Molly her priority, not realizing that by putting her husband in second place, she was placing the marriage there as well and, by extension, her own well-being. With another child on the way, it was only a matter of time before Ted would be bumped down to third place, leaving their sex life to limp along in fourth place, along with Maureen.

Maureen was due to deliver at the end of November. She came in right before Thanksgiving for a session, and as she was leaving, I gave her a prescription for an antidepressant. "Maureen," I said, "you fill this prescription on your way home, put the pills in your purse, and as soon as that baby pops out, you pop a pill in." Maureen took the prescription and said she would keep in touch.

She didn't, though. A few months went by, and then a few more. After a year passed with no word from Maureen, I closed her chart.

One day, out of the blue, I got a message that Maureen had called and wanted to come in as soon as possible, so I squeezed her in the next afternoon. I almost didn't recognize her; she looked even more tired than before, and her eyes were bloodshot. I asked how the baby was, and she said he was fine; Casey was fifteen months old and healthy, although she had required a second C-section and had once again been unable to breast-feed. Molly was four now and would still sometimes not sleep through the night.

Then Maureen broke down in tears. Her world was collapsing; she was horribly depressed and afraid she would end up in the hospital. She was riddled with anxiety and felt utterly overwhelmed. She was up at least once and sometimes twice a night to feed the baby. During the day, she worried obsessively about the children and felt compelled to check on them every five minutes, even when they were napping. She was increasingly unable to make decisions and found herself indulging in compulsive behaviors, such as washing the baby's bottles in a certain order and vacuuming the rugs so the fibers ran in the same direction. So great was her fatigue, she was becoming afraid to drive and feared she would soon be housebound with two young children. She and Ted were little more than roommates; they had not made love in more than six months.

Worst of all, Maureen had been staggering around, depressed and increasingly desperate, since the baby was four months old, and she had never filled the prescription for the antidepressant. That meant she had been severely depressed and without medication *for nearly a year.* I was vexed. Maureen was an intelligent person who knew that she had a propensity to postpartum depression. She had even come in for treatment as a preventive measure because her first depression had been so severe. Why had she not filled the prescription I gave her? Why had she waited so long to get help?

At first all she said was that she had wanted to tough it out without drugs, but there was more to it. The friend who had argued against epidurals was equally hostile to antidepressants, telling Maureen they got into breast milk and could harm the baby, and urging her to take vitamins instead. Now, I have nothing against vitamins; in fact, I think they're a good thing. But no matter how good they are, vitamins cannot cure depression. And while it is true that most antidepressants do find their way into breast milk, there is no evidence that they cause any harm to the infants who ingest it. Even more to the point, Maureen had not been able to breast-feed, so the argument was not only flawed but moot. Still, peer pressure can pack a wallop well past middle school; Maureen had been persuaded that good mothers don't take drugs, and she was determined to be a good mother. Never mind that she already was a good mother. All that mattered was her perception of herself, and she perceived herself as lacking in the parenting department. So she struggled along until she could sink no lower and then called my office.

Maureen and I worked together over the next nine months. I gave her two prescriptions, one for an antidepressant and a less conventional one directing her not to feed the baby in the middle of the night anymore. I wrote down on a prescription pad that she was to let the baby cry himself back to sleep. If she could do this, I assured her, in two nights he'd be sleeping through until morning. Struggling with a baby who won't sleep through the night is a common problem, especially among women with postpartum depression. It's hard enough to listen to a baby scream for two hours if you're not depressed; if you are, it can drive you to distraction—or at least to the kitchen to get a bottle. Once you do, the screaming stops and you go back to sleep, but that baby's no fool—it's learned that screaming pays off. So it screams in the middle of the night, every night, until it stops getting what it wants. It's hard to listen to your baby wail and not rush to its side, and it helps if the father is involved and can keep the mother from going to the baby (or vice versa, if the father is the softie), which is why I write it out as a prescription. I wanted to impress upon Maureen the importance of getting that baby to sleep through the night so she could, too.

As for the antidepressant, it elevated Maureen's mood but decimated her sex drive. No matter how we adjusted the dosage, she still complained of diminished desire and began to talk about stopping the drug. I reminded her that she was prone to depression and needed medication; she reminded me that she had gotten through pregnancy and well beyond without it.

Maureen began missing sessions, and soon afterward, she stopped coming altogether. I left several messages for her, but she did not return the calls. Perhaps she will return after a long silence, as she did once before. I may never know why she abandoned our work, but I believe it's because she didn't want to acknowledge the fact that she had a chronic illness, that it required treatment, and that a positive mental attitude wasn't enough to fix it. Many people feel bad about themselves when they suffer from a psychological disorder, especially if they have friends or relatives who tell them that they don't need medicine and should buck up instead. Maureen wanted to be happy and normal—whatever *that* is—and seeing a psychiatrist every week didn't conform to her idea of what happy, normal people do.

No one is happy all the time, of course; and as for normal, let's just say that when it comes to sex after childbirth, there's a wide range of normal and the vast majority of people fall within its limits. I had a patient who fretted about being dysfunctional because she had given birth to her first child four months earlier and couldn't yet bring herself to have intercourse. I told her that while research indicated that about 90 percent of women resume intercourse four months after delivering a baby, there were still 10 percent who chose to wait longer, and she was among them.[6] Was she average? Perhaps not. Normal? Absolutely. And the delay might not be due to the woman's diminished desire. The man may be thinking, *She's the mother of my children—we're not allowed to do this.* Or he may be afraid of hurting her. Or perhaps she had a C-section or a bad tear and either she or he or both are reluctant to expose that portion of her anatomy to too much activity.

And let's not underestimate the psychological shock of beholding your new body. If you've been pregnant, you know that your belly doesn't shrink back to prepregnancy proportions once the baby is out. Instead you've got all this stretched-out skin, hanging like a deployed parachute from the vicinity of where your waist used to be. Amid all the joy you're supposed to feel when you've had a baby, you may find yourself grieving for your lost maidenly body after pregnancy has forever widened your hips, expanded your rib cage, and reupholstered your stomach in pinch pleats. Some of these alterations are for keeps: there was a dress I used to wear that my mother wore before she married my father, and I can't get into it now, not because my waist is bigger but because my ribs grew wider apart when I was pregnant. But other bodily changes are exaggerated right after pregnancy and subside with time. If you were a 34A before pregnancy, a 36B in your second trimester, and a 36DD when you were nursing, you may very well go back to an A cup someday but remain a 36. And your stomach will firm up if you exercise and watch what you eat, although it may never regain its taut, concave contours once you've had a child.

The question is, does your sexuality reside in your stomach? Your abs? Your proud, pouting breasts? (Just for once, I'd like someone to show me how breasts can pout. Or be proud, for that matter.) The media besiege us with messages that equate woman's sexuality with unnatural and even grotesque images of alleged bodily perfection, and we buy into them at our peril. I cannot count the women who have wept in my office after having children because they are convinced that their husbands no longer desire them. They aren't having sex because their bodies are fat and ugly, and who would want them anymore? Then I ask them to bring their husbands in, and the men sit there and say, "No, I love my wife, I *am* attracted to her, I *do* want to make love with her, but she won't let me near her. She's obsessed with her weight, but so what? When I tell her she's beautiful and sexy, she doesn't believe me." And the women sit there in disbelief because their sexuality is tied into what they imagine they look like rather than an unshakable knowledge of who they are.

I have met relatively few men who would qualify as cads when it comes to postpartum sex. The vast majority of my patients' partners love the women in their lives and are far less put off by female fleshiness than the women themselves. To cultivate real intimacy, we must not only accept but embrace ourselves so we can open ourselves to our partners. And when it comes to accepting ourselves, we are often our own worst enemies.

Reclaiming Your Erotic Relationship

Every couple has to find its own way back to intimacy after having a baby, and there are no guidelines for how and when it should be done. I know from my own experience that once you have children, your marriage and intimate relationship will require more care and feeding. I know of hardly anyone who has a baby and then says, "Oh, our sex life is better than it ever was!" (If I do hear this, I have to assume they have a matronly live-in nanny and a bedroom at the opposite end of the house from their children's.) As a parent, you have to work harder at creating the intimate moments that used to seize you unawares; you can't, after all, fall into passionate lovemaking on the kitchen floor with a toddler running about. Which is not to say you can't have spontaneous sex anymore; you just have to plan it.

How do you plan spontaneity?

First of all, you must install a lock on your bedroom door if it doesn't already have one. You'd be surprised to hear how many parents have problems in the bedroom because they fear their children will come barging in when they are making love. Children have an uncanny ability to sense when their parents are getting it on, waking out of a deep sleep to stop sex dead in its tracks. You and your man might be feeling frisky for the first time in weeks or even months, frolicking on the bed amid the unfolded laundry, when this apparition appears in the doorway, whimpering that it can't sleep and catapulting you into a tableau suggesting a couple in the throes of electroshock therapy. Take my advice and get thee to a hardware store—installing a lock is a lot more expedient than sex counseling, and cheaper, too.

When you have kids, you plan for the unexpected. You carefully set things up so that if a romantic spark is struck, you are free to fan it. You must deliberately set time aside for romance and sex; you can't just wait and see what happens (sex seldom just happens when you have children). Some couples hire a babysitter one night a week, no matter what, so they can go out to dinner at a quiet place, look at each other without interruption, and talk. If they aren't hungry, they might go to the mall or take a long walk, anything that enables them to be together and partake of a coherent, adult exchange. If you do this, try to stay out late enough to ensure that the kids are asleep before you get home, or they'll come charging to the door when they hear you return, and any sexy spark between you and your mate will fizzle before you get your coats off.

Some couples work out arrangements with other parents to host each other's children for a weekend now and then, which works especially well if your kids are friends with children whose behavior you find at least tolerable, if not uplifting. This means that sometimes you'll have to handle twice as many kids as usual, which is why you should make sure you like the kids you're offering to host (good table manners and a pronounced deference to adults are prerequisites). But other times you'll have no kids at all and an empty house to yourselves.

Other couples take vacations without their children, finding it easier to relax and rekindle romance when they are away from the house. This works best if you have family members or close friends whom you can trust to take the kids for several days at a time, because you don't want to be away on vacation worrying about the children's well-being (or how much the babysitter is going to cost). Family vacations can be fun, but there's something to be said for getting away with your partner and leaving the kids and household chores behind.

You also have to deal with the fatigue issue. If you tended to make love at bedtime before you had kids—and many, if not most, couples do—you are likely to find yourself too tired to do anything but pass out once you hit the sack. Studies show that women still do far more housework and child care activities than men, even if they work outside the home. So as the night wears on, a woman is likely to be more tired than her mate and less inclined to feel like having sex. In such a situation, which is extremely common, a man may be doomed to serial rejections if a woman doesn't communicate her wishes clearly or if he isn't adroit at reading her signals.

We could learn a thing or two from primates in this department. When a female ape is in estrus (the point in her cycle when she is able to conceive), she gets up and displays her buttocks to a male. He just sits there; he's not convinced. She parades about, presenting her rear end to him over and over and over again until he figures, *Okay, she must really mean it,* and only then does he approach her and have sex with her. He doesn't jump up when she first comes around, let alone pursue her. He waits until her intentions are clear, because if he misinterprets her gestures he gets jumped by the other females, who shriek and pummel him as if to say, Whoa, fella—that's not what she was saying at all! She doesn't want to have sex with you; she was just doing her stretching exercises. Scram!

I have a theory that we are not all that different from our simian counterparts. Picture a woman at the sink doing the dinner dishes. Her back is facing out into the kitchen along with her rear end, which is vibrating as she scrubs baked-on lasagna from a casserole dish. Her mate looks up from across the room, likes what he sees, and starts getting ideas. He goes over and embraces her, caressing her buttocks or her hips or her breasts, and he's thinking, *Come on, honey, let's get it on.* And she feels his hands on her and she's thinking, *Oh, for crying out loud—I'm in the middle of doing dishes! What's the matter with you? You want something else from me right now?* Had this poor guy been thinking like an ape, he would have waited to learn if his female's posterior was actually issuing an invitation before RSVPing. I've said this to many patients, couples, husbands, partners, and colleagues at conferences: If you're really smart, here's what you do. You come over, you do not touch any sexual body part, and you say, "Honey, let me do the dishes—I'll join you upstairs in a few minutes." And, peeling those glamorous latex gloves from her hands, you reach for the scrubby pad and get to work. Believe me—if men would do this, they'd be much more likely to get sex after dinner.

Sleep Sharing

Some couples cultivate a more inclusive form of intimacy by sleeping in a family bed, parents and children together. The practice, also known as sleep sharing, is based on the belief that it is both natural and nurturing for a baby to sleep close to its parents. For one, the mother can nurse the baby with minimal disturbance to her sleep. Second, proponents of the practice say that babies were never meant to sleep away from their parents and that requiring them to do so deprives them of the immediate parental response they were meant to have. From an evolutionary standpoint, this is probably true; when we were nomadic peoples, mothers probably did sleep with their babies curled up next to them. And newborn infants are accustomed to feeling the vibration of their mothers' heartbeats, so it makes sense that they would feel comforted by bodily closeness after they are born. As to specifics of the family bed, they vary widely. Some proponents say that keeping a cradle next to the parents' mattress qualifies, while others say that a true family bed means that everyone sleeps together on the same surface until the children are well on their way through elementary school and even beyond.

Some people find the idea of the family bed unappealing; others say it's the only way to go. But even couples who enjoy sleep sharing acknowledge that it renders the bed off-limits to sex much of the time and requires them to come up with alternate lovemaking locations. This may or may not be a problem, depending on how much living space and creative energy the couple has. So when patients ask my opinion about sleeping in a family bed, I tell them that it works well for some families but that they will have to think about ways to ensure that their sex lives don't suffer.

SEXUAL INVENTORY

How Have Pregnancy and Motherhood Affected Your Sexuality?

1. Regarding pregnancy:

- In terms of how you felt—not how you looked—did (or do) the bodily changes of pregnancy make you feel more sexy or less sexy?
- When you looked at your third-trimester body, did you see Demi Moore or John Goodman?
- How did the baby's commandeering of your body make you feel about her or him before the birth? After the birth?
- How did the changes in your body affect your response to your partner's sexual advances? Did your bodily changes alter your feelings for your partner in other ways? Did you begin to see your partner in a different light?
- Did (or do) you have fears, regrets, and unwanted thoughts about pregnancy? If so, are you able to acknowledge them?

2. . . . and parenthood:

- How has becoming a mother affected your desire for sex? Your sexual self-image? Do you think others see you differently now that you are a mother?

- How do you apportion your physical and emotional resources between your mate and your child(ren)? Where are you on the list? Do you even have a list?

3. **How do you feel about your sex life now?** If you are dissatisfied, is your dissatisfaction related to not feeling like a sexual being? to depression? to an emotional change in your intimate relationship? to intrusions on your privacy and your time? to fatigue? to something else?

4. **Do you set aside time to focus on sex, or does it always come as an afterthought, taking a backseat to other desires and demands?** If so, can you think of ways to remedy the situation before it becomes a problem?

CHAPTER 6

After Puberty
Not with My Daughter!

There is nothing like early promiscuous sex for dispelling life's bright mysterious expectations.

—IRIS MURDOCH

I was having lunch with a colleague when he stopped eating and started talking about his daughter. She had just turned thirteen and would often spend weekend afternoons at the movies with her friends, one of whose parents would drive the girls to the multiplex, buy the tickets, and pick them up when the movie let out.

But he was starting to worry. He was hearing stories about an activity that had become all the rage among the middle school crowd. The activity involves groups of girls going to the movies and meeting up with groups of boys when they get inside—young kids, twelve and thirteen years old. They choose a row down at the front where no one sits and file in girl-boy-girl-boy-girl-boy. Once the lights go down, the girls ring their mouths with lipstick, each in a different color, and, when the movie starts, they slide to the floor and perform oral sex on the boys sitting next to them. The girls then sidle down the row and do it to the next boy and the next and so on until all the boys have been serviced by all the rainbow girls, so called because, by the time the lights come up, they have adorned each boy's penis with a spectrum of lipstick rings.

If you are shocked by this scenario, you are not alone: as I write this, a new young-adult novel about a rainbow party that never takes place can't get shelf space because booksellers are squeamish about stocking it (the fact that the party doesn't happen doesn't seem to matter; the subject it-self has sent the marketplace shuddering). And if you're not shocked by the image of girls just out of elementary school providing oral sex to boys whose faces are as smooth as theirs are—in public, no less—you must admit it's a far cry from spin the bottle.

My colleague had no reason to think his daughter had ever heard of such an activity, let alone participated in it. But if she had, how would he know? It wasn't the sort of tidbit she was likely to share at the dinner table. And her strong academic record provided little comfort: just because she made honor roll didn't mean she was smart enough to know that this sort of es-capade could lay waste to her self-esteem, her concept of who she was as a sexual being, and what she had a right to expect from an intimate encounter.

I don't blame my colleague for worrying; I worry about all the girls whose introduction to sex is kneeling on a grimy floor and performing an intimate act on a row of boys with whom they share no emotional connec-tion and from whom they get no pleasure in return. Not only am I worried, I'm angry.

I'm angry because these girls have no idea of what they are doing to themselves, and we, their parents, are driving them to do it. Literally: we pile them into our crash-tested SUVs and figure they're safe. After all, what could happen? They're in a group—no one would come on to a girl who's part of a group. And even if he did, the other girls would be there to protect her—unless, of course, they were pressuring her to get with the program and go down on their friends. I mean, no one's taking off any of her clothes or touching anything *down there,* so it's not really sex. And if everyone is doing it, how bad can it be?

Very bad, as a matter of fact.

It's bad because this age is when a person's identity starts to solidify, when we begin to own the notion that we will not always be predictable satellites of our parents, orbiting obediently within the gravitational range of Mom and Dad. This is when the boundary between parental edict and personal responsibility begins to blur, tossing the adolescent's evolving self into a welter of self-righteousness and self-pity.

This is also when a girl's sexual identity begins to form, when the yearn-ings swirling inside her coalesce into a sexual persona that she senses will one day find expression through her body. Her impression of this persona vacillates wildly; one moment she's a goddess; the next, a troll. Her self-concept is a fluid, evolving entity, suffused with pleasure when a popular boy smiles in her direction or wretched with humiliation when he walks past her toward someone else. She knows that one day she will be a woman and do what women do, but she knows this only in theory; in practice, she is a child whose sexual self is still evolving. If something interrupts the evolution of this self and makes her feel cheap or used or manipulated, or instills a belief that she is not supposed to derive any pleasure from sex, it can have a profound impact on the evolution of her sexuality, as well as other aspects of her personality. A 2003 study found that adolescents between the ages of twelve and sixteen who routinely engaged in sex with partners with whom they shared no romantic feelings or emotional connection were more likely than their celibate friends to become depressed and engage in delinquent behaviors such as smoking, drinking, taking drugs, getting involved in violent altercations, and attempting suicide.[1]

How could a child gain anything positive from being a rainbow girl? How could she emerge unscarred, with her dignity intact? The potential for hitting the self-respect jackpot is slim when you're part of a ritual in which one group of your peers receives toe-curling bodily pleasure through the intimate exertions of a separate-but-equal group that gets no bodily satisfaction in return. And who are the celebrants of this ritual? A generation of children whose parents have been obsessed with making sure their offspring feel good about themselves.

For a society that worships at the altar of self-esteem, we're strangely averse to shedding the blood, sweat, and tears required to build it. We overpraise the average and enshrine the mediocre, thinking we can make kids feel good about themselves by lauding their every act. We present every kid on the team with a trophy, even if the kid blew every play, even if the team lost every game, and the kids learn that all you have to do to be a champion is show up. The kids feel good and the parents feel good because everyone's a winner, but not really; there are no winners when no one is allowed to lose. In our frenzy to spin a cocoon of perfect happiness around our children, we deny them the freedom to struggle, fail, persevere, and succeed, and we curtail their opportunities to rebound from defeat and learn from loss. In so doing, we also rob them of any dignity they might have earned in the process. Without a lot of dignity at stake, it's easier for them to go along with the crowd on a clandestine adventure whose thrill is probably enhanced by its gross-out factor.

Once you get past your initial distaste for the whole enterprise, it's not impossible to imagine a boy agreeing, perhaps reluctantly, to be part of it; all he has to do is stay in his seat and keep quiet. The payoff for him is a sequence of intensely pleasurable encounters that are intimate, fleeting, and free of obligation. There is no pretense of devotion or even affection; the lack of privacy grants the participants neither the burden nor the hope of meaning anything to one another. It is an act of breathtaking cynicism, a crude enactment of the easy-come, easy-go ethos that pervades the culture.

Why would a girl do this, collaborate with her friends to stage a pleasurefest where she is doing all the giving? What is she getting out of it?

It's hard to know. Perhaps it's a status thing and she achieves the distinction of being bold enough to engage in an X-rated public parlor game. Or maybe she thrills to the subterfuge of having her parents unsuspectingly deliver her unto an adventure that would paralyze them with shock, awe, and revulsion were they to find out about it.

What about the pleasure she might feel at her newfound ability to render a boy helpless with ecstasy? While it may be comforting to think that a girl might derive a sense of power by driving these alternately goofy and swaggering boys to lose control, I doubt that's the case. I think it is far more likely that she is besieged by feelings of confusion and shame. She is on her knees in a subservient position; she may be gagging and fighting to keep her popcorn down; the boy may be holding her head in his crotch; and to top it off, all his friends are watching. No, I don't see a girl getting anything out of this except a distorted view of her sexual self, a bad reputation, and possibly a disease that could torment her for the rest of her life.

The rainbow phenomenon is not the only sex game that young people are playing, although color is a recurring theme. At a middle school I heard about, some seventh- and eighth-grade girls were coming to class wearing thin plastic bands of various hues around their wrists. When a boy saw a girl he fancied, he could walk up to her and pull off a band, obligating her to perform with him (at a later time and off school premises, I imagine) the sex act denoted by the color he chose: red for intercourse, blue for a hand job, green for oral sex, and so on. An attentive adult got wind of this and notified the principal, who banned the bands. Degrading and distasteful, perhaps; unprecedented, not quite: these bands seem to me to be descendants, however squalid, of the dance cards that women wore to fancy-dress balls during the nineteenth century. An orchestra would play a program of dances at these events, and women would wear on their wrists a device containing a small card listing the dances and a tiny pencil that each man would use to sign himself up as her partner for a particular number. If a man excelled at the waltz, he could sign his name next to the waltz and the woman would be obliged to dance it with him. Some dance cards—especially those crafted in Europe—were ornate, sculptural works of art bearing no resemblance to the plain wristlets worn by girls today. But the concept is eerily familiar: a guy comes up, decides what he wants, fiddles with your arm, and commits you (with your implied permission) to being his partner in one sort of dance or another.

When people are having sex without knowing what it means, it's not a good trend—especially when the people involved are very young and poised on the cusp of sexual self-knowledge. It is during this transitional time, just past childhood, that girls and boys start to become aware of who they are, what type of people they are becoming, and what gender they are attracted to. It usually starts gently, with faint stirrings of interest in the kid who sits next to them in math whom they never really looked at before but who becomes, by the end of the marking period, the most fascinating human on the planet.

As they enter puberty, their bodies dump more hormones into the bloodstream. The stirrings get stronger as hormones sharpen fascination to the point of sensual attraction, and the child responds by thinking, or feeling, or in some inchoate way knowing *I find this person erotic; this person makes me feel aroused.* It is between the ages of thirteen and nineteen that a person's sexual identity solidifies, that he or she begins to intuit *I'm straight* or *I'm a lesbian* or *I'm not sure what I am—maybe I'm bisexual.* The feeling can be rather amorphous for a while, which is why you see young people experimenting sexually with persons of their own sex. But most people seem to sort it out one way or another by the time they are out of their teens.

As perplexing as adolescence is (for adolescents as well as their parents), it is also a time of momentous change and growth. As a girl's body matures, she inhabits it with a growing sense of ownership and begins to grasp her female potential: she has the capacity, presumably, to have sex and enjoy it, and to conceive and bear a child. When a girl has the time and psychic space to establish her sexual self-concept free of the pressures conferred by sexual intimacy, she has a shot at emerging from adolescence healthy and whole, with her choices intact.

But when she slides into sexual liaisons too early, without a solid sense of self, her sexuality can become distorted, her self misshapen, and her health permanently compromised. If her earliest sexual experiences have her providing assembly-line fellatio in movie theaters, she may learn to equate sex with sacrifice and consign herself to the role of giving pleasure with no expectation of receiving it. If she is gratified when a boy plucks a promise of sex from her wrist, she may come to prefer the flutter of being chosen to the exhilaration of choosing and jettison a lifetime's worth of passion into the sea of self-sacrifice. Even if her early sexual experiences are consummated with someone she cares for, she may still come to grave psychological harm.

The health risks are no less profound, as they may corrode both body and soul. Sexual contact, oral and otherwise, is an effective way to transmit a host of diseases, including genital herpes and warts, chlamydia, genital ulcers, gonorrhea, and syphilis, not to mention the HIV virus and AIDS. And while the odds of contracting a catastrophic illness such as AIDS from a youthful sexual spree might seem low, they're much higher for catching a standard-issue venereal infection. If a girl contracts pelvic inflammatory disease because she is having unprotected sex with a lot of different guys, she may never be able to have a baby. The damage may be done decades before she wants to have a child; it is only later, when her mind and her bank account are ready for motherhood, that she learns her body won't cooperate. That's a bitter pill for a woman to swallow, made more bitter still when she realizes that, had she insisted the guy use a condom twenty years earlier, she might have preserved her fertility.

Which brings me to a brief but heartfelt appeal to girls and their parents alike: don't underestimate the usefulness of condoms—there's a lot they can prevent besides pregnancy. At the time I am writing this, many sex education programs are admonishing young people against using condoms, saying they aren't 100 percent effective in preventing pregnancy.

Which is true, of course; the only birth control method that is 100 percent effective is abstinence, the current curriculum's method of choice. But let's not kid ourselves: young people are going to have sex. They are going to do it because the sex drive is stronger than their self-control, and I believe there's no point in scaring them into distrusting condoms and using nothing instead. A good-quality condom, properly applied, can not only prevent pregnancy, it can also inhibit the transmission of disease and place a barrier between sperm and cervix, protecting a woman's reproductive organs from exposure to infection and disease and the compromised functioning they can cause. While I wish we lived in a perfect world where teenagers would abstain from casual sex and save themselves for the rewards of mature and meaningful monogamy, I am also the mother of two adolescents and am not living in a fool's paradise. So I urge all young people who are thinking about having sex to think about using condoms.

If it seems that kids are becoming sexually active younger and younger, it's because they are. The average age at which girls start to develop has dipped steadily lower, with some girls exploring their sexuality while they are still in elementary school. We are not sure why this is happening; one theory is that television and movies are bombarding children with so much implicit and explicit sexual content that the kids' systems are being overstimulated and becoming sexualized earlier. So seven- and eight-year-old girls are going to school with exposed midriffs and platform sandals and imitating the provocative moves of Britney Spears and Christina Aguilera (or whoever has supplanted them by the time you read this). Their innocence undercuts the threat of their incipient sexuality: that's a belly, all right, but there are no breasts yet, so it's okay to show it. Or it's okay for her to be shimmying her hips back and forth because she doesn't know what it means; she's just dancing, after all, and it's poignant and sweet to see her enjoying her body, so chaste and unaware.

Perhaps, but I usually witness these displays with a measure of discomfort, because the child's lack of awareness—the aspect that makes it look so cute—is the very essence of the danger. By the time these girls are ten and eleven, some of them will be menstruating; by twelve and thirteen, many will have breasts and hips and a theoretical if not working knowledge of the behaviors of seduction. They will have pierced ears, if not navels; they will wear lipstick and revealing clothing and look very much like the women they will someday become. But that's just it: they are not women, even if they look like women, even if they have the occasional cunning to act like women. No matter how voluptuous the body and convincing the costume, they are still girls. And because they are still girls, they are woefully ill equipped to stand up for themselves, set limits, and know what they are getting themselves into when they get into sex.

What, then, defines womanhood? When does a child become an adult, and when is it appropriate to treat her like one?

Once again, it's hard to know. When you have twelve-year-olds trading sexual favors, on the one hand, and twenty-eight-year-olds returning home to live with Mom and Dad, on the other, it's not clear where childhood ends and adulthood begins. In some societies, children are trained from birth to subscribe to clearly circumscribed sex roles. In cultures where the first menses heralds a female's readiness for marriage, girls learn early how to prepare a particular fruit or root so it is edible, how to weave grasses into baskets in which to transport food, and how to weave fibers into fabric that will clothe them, their husbands, and the children they may bear while they are yet children themselves.

But our society's emphasis on intellectual development serves to delay psychological maturity rather than hasten it. We educate girls and boys until they are at least eighteen, with many not completing advanced degrees until they are in their mid-twenties. It's hard to be grown up and go out and work and take care of yourself if all you've been doing is going to school; you haven't been forced to do that, and you haven't been taught to do that. And now there is the phenomenon of educated, able-bodied adults in their twenties and thirties—sometimes with a spouse and children in tow—moving back into their parents' houses because they cannot find work or lack the funds to establish a home of their own.

So when does a girl become an adult? When she begins to ovulate and menstruate and is capable of bearing a child? Physiologically, you could say that is true, but I don't think it is at all true from a psychological point of view. In our culture, eleven-, twelve-, and thirteen-year-old girls are still very much children and dependent on adults for food, shelter, and good judgment. Moreover, our society doesn't celebrate when twelve- and thirteen-year-olds give birth; we say that babies are having babies and mourn for mother and child, children both.

Is a child an adult when she can support herself? When she can take responsibility for her own well-being? Or when her mother and father nudge her out of the nest and tell her they aren't going to take care of her anymore?

There is no set answer, but one thing is clear: engaging in sex neither betokens maturity nor bestows it on girl or boy, woman or man. It intensifies a person's experience of the self by thrusting her or him into intimate contact with another being and either defining or obscuring the boundaries of where one person ends and the other begins. At its best, sex is an act of communion between two fully formed selves. But when a girl has sex too soon, her fluid self may take the shape of whatever source she sprang from or whomever she pours herself into, with potentially catastrophic results.

Felice: From Denial to Cataclysm

I knew more about Felice than I usually do about a new patient because I had read about her in the newspaper before she came in. Campus police at her university had found her unconscious the week before on a wooded path well past midnight. I was a psychiatry intern at the time and not much older than she was; I was about twenty-seven, she about nineteen. I was old enough to be stricken by the sadness of her case but too early in my career to know it would still be with me more than twenty years hence.

She looked remarkably normal, a fresh-faced teenager who had recently finished her freshman year of college. A little tired, perhaps, and distant, but someone whose grip on reality I would not have questioned. It was one of my earliest instances of having a patient whose appearance was vastly at odds with her inner reality.

"Do you have any memory of what happened?" I said.

"No, not really," she said. "I remember meeting up with Lisa and Jennifer and we had dinner at the deli and then we went to the movie at the campus center. I don't remember anything after that."

"How about before that evening? What do you remember?"

"Just regular things. I went to classes, studied for finals, you know, normal stuff."

"But you do know why you're here."

"I know what people have told me, and what the policeman said. But it's like it happened to another person. I don't remember any of it."

"Can you accept what the policeman said? Do you believe it's the truth?"

"I guess. But it doesn't feel real."

It had begun the previous August, when Felice had left for college. The second eldest of four children born to devout Catholic parents, Felice was the first girl in her family to attend a university. Her mother and father sent her off with a new wardrobe, great expectations, and the hope that she would try to attend Mass at least now and then.

Felice had not dated much in high school, and about two weeks into the term, a guy in her anthropology class asked her out. He was smart and funny and a sophomore, and Felice soon fell in love. The boy returned her affection, and they grew close, spending evenings together at her dorm and weekends at his apartment. They were still together at Thanksgiving, but by Christmas, things had started to cool. He had to study more and more on weekends, and the distance between them grew. Felice said she had tried to woo him back, to no avail: he thought she was a great girl, but his feelings had changed. They parted amicably, albeit with some regret on Felice's part.

Felice went home for winter break and returned for the second semester. Nothing major seemed amiss; when questioned, Felice's roommate said she had seemed to be putting on weight, but the roommate had attributed this to the breakup and didn't think much of it. "She was a little withdrawn and didn't want to go out as much," the roommate said, "but she was still going to classes and carrying fifteen, maybe sixteen credits." As it turned out, Felice was carrying more than a normal course load: she was pregnant.

But here's where the story goes haywire. It seems that no one knew— neither Felice's roommate nor her friends; nor her former boyfriend, the child's father; nor anyone in her family; nor, it would seem, Felice herself. Even when she stopped menstruating, even when her belly began to swell and none of her jeans would fit, Felice remained oblivious to the pregnancy, at least consciously.

How could this happen?

Denial is a primitive defense, one of the most basic techniques we use to bear the unbearable. Persons who suffer from serious psychological problems often use denial as a coping mechanism, as do rational people who must act in defiance of their instinct to survive: soldiers running onto a battlefield must to some degree deny the likelihood that they will perish there, or they will be paralyzed with fear, unable to fight. Denial manifests in many ways: the seventy-year-old wearing a short skirt and go-go boots is in denial about growing old, as is the eighty-five-year-old who continues to drive despite her failing eyesight. Denial can even be good for you, at least in small doses: heart patients who exhibit high levels of denial in the first days of hospitalization tend to suffer less anxiety, less depression, and fewer medical complications.[2] Denial serves to keep any number of howling truths at bay and, if used in moderation, isn't always a bad thing.

But Felice used denial to an extent that bordered on psychotic. And in so doing, she managed to induce a seeming state of group psychosis in the people who knew her, none of whom seemed to notice the change in her appearance or felt compelled to mention it. She even showed me a photo that her sister had taken when she was home on spring break. Felice was standing with her arms around her parents and wearing a large sweater that swelled on her abdomen as if over a basketball. Any sane person looking at her would see that she was in the latter stages of pregnancy.

"What did people say when they saw you?" I asked.

"Nothing. They just said hello, that was all," Felice said.

In fact, a few people outside the family did say something. Felice said a dietitian at a campus dining hall once approached her as she was loading her tray and asked her if she thought the food was nutritionally acceptable for a pregnant person.

"I don't know; I guess so," Felice said. "Why are you asking me?" Another time, a gray-haired man on a bus offered Felice his seat. Felice took the seat but never figured out why he had offered it to her, as he was much older than she.

Why would an intelligent, seemingly stable young woman be so unable to accept the reality of a pregnancy? How could she so thoroughly divorce her mind from her body?

She could do it because the bodily reality of the pregnancy was, to her mind, unbearable. When the mind encounters a reality it cannot bear or accept, it sometimes adjusts its perception of reality to ensure its survival.

Felice came from an observant Catholic family; she knew her parents disapproved of sex before marriage and could not picture them providing succor to a daughter pregnant out of wedlock. She remembered the pride on their faces when they had dropped her off at her dorm; to disappoint them in this way flooded her with shame and anguish. Nor was ending the pregnancy an option; as a Catholic, Felice believed abortion was a sin: she could no sooner contemplate aborting the fetus than she could imagine carrying it to term. Seeing no way out, Felice constructed an edifice of denial and retreated within it.

No one knows precisely what happened the night Felice collapsed in the woods, but some facts have emerged from interviews with her friends and eyewitnesses, and we have surmised the rest. We know that about ten minutes after the movie started, Felice whispered to her companions that she had cramps and left for the bathroom. Once there, she sat down on the toilet, went into full labor and, oblivious to what was happening, passed what she thought was a bowel movement. I believe that at this point she must have been in a fugue state, a condition in which a person has minimal if any awareness of his or her surroundings. She then left the bathroom, exited the building, and was wandering across the campus when she collapsed. No one knows how long she lay bleeding before some students happened by and called the police, who took her to the infirmary. In the meantime, a young woman entered the campus center bathroom stall that Felice had occupied and found the walls smeared with blood and a tiny baby in the toilet. She screamed for an ambulance, but it was no use; the child had already died of exposure. The police arrived, phoned the infirmary, and confirmed that the student who had been brought in had the symptoms of having recently gone through childbirth. The story made it into the newspaper because there was talk of placing Felice under arrest. I left for two years in Chicago as a Navy physician before the case was resolved, so I don't know if charges were filed, but I cannot imagine the state imposing on Felice a punishment more severe than the torment to which she had already condemned herself.

What are we to make of this case? How do we think about this contemporary young woman whose story resonates as deeply as Greek tragedy?

Part of what makes Felice's case so horrific is that the circumstances surrounding it are so ordinary: a bright young woman reared with what we call family values leaves home for college, falls in love, has sex for the first time, and gets pregnant. It is reasonable to assume that Felice knew she had options for dealing with the pregnancy; she might have sought support from the campus health center or Catholic campus minister or both. But she did neither, being utterly unable to cope with precisely the sort of circumstances her upbringing was meant to forestall. Felice's self was so closely bound to the beliefs of her family and her religion that she could not imagine deviating from them and surviving intact. She was not yet sufficiently differentiated from her upbringing and parents to hear her own thoughts or know her own values apart from theirs; she literally did not know her own mind.

But if Felice's case is extreme, it is also universal: while it might be hard to imagine ourselves doing what she did in that bathroom stall, it is not at all hard to conjure up the feelings of shame, guilt, and self-recrimination that drove her there. All of us have felt these things. And that is precisely the point: any one of us might have found ourselves in Felice's situation, and many girls and young women still do. We have read enough stories about newborns found in Dumpsters to know that it happens all too often.

The catastrophe of Felice's life was not that she had sex but that she had sex before her self was fully formed. Her identity was undefined, her wants, needs, and values indistinguishable from those handed down to her. She did not yet see herself as separate from her parents and could not forgive herself for her perceived transgressions any more than she imagined they would be able to.

This was not a case of superficial, anonymous sexual contact wreaking havoc on a young woman's ego; still, the fact that the sex took place within the context of an affectionate alliance did not mitigate its devastating outcome. This nineteen-year-old was not ready for a sexual relationship of any kind because she was psychologically unprepared to deal with its most logical outcome—a pregnancy—not only for what it meant to herself and her family but also for what it meant to how she saw herself and how she imagined her family would see her. Felice's tragedy may have been rooted in her body, but it was nourished and brought to dreadful fruition by her mind.

Felice's behaviors—leaving home, falling in love, and having sex with her boyfriend—were not destructive; nor are, strictly speaking, those of a bunch of seventh graders providing oral sex to their classmates. What *is* destructive is the outcome of these escapades: they reverberate, sometimes forever, in the minds and bodies of the women these girls become. When you're a kid, you don't realize that the mischief you are making might haunt you as an adult because you can't imagine that you'll ever be an adult. All you know is that you want to do this now and you're going to do it *now,* period.

That's the problem with puberty: you have all kinds of impulses but not a lot of control. While the hideous outcome of Felice's story is not typical, most of us have had some bad outcomes, especially when we were young. And an outcome need not be hideous to be catastrophic; anyone who's had a weekend fling and ended up with a lifetime supply of genital herpes knows that's a calamity in its own right. A teenager might get an infection that responds to antibiotics only after it has rendered her infertile for the rest of her life. Or a girl might get pregnant at sixteen, when she's in tenth grade and in no position to be a mother. What can she do? (Let us assume she is fortunate enough to have parents to whom she can turn for help.) If she chooses to have an abortion, it could impair her psychological capacity to enjoy sex: she may feel guilty and worry that it could affect future pregnancies or that she'll get pregnant again; if she is unable to conceive a child later in life, she may castigate herself for squandering her one shot at motherhood. If she bears the child and gives it up for adoption, she may spend the rest of her life wondering if she should look for the child or if she did the right thing by giving it up in the first place. If she decides to keep the child, she loses what little of her own childhood remains to her; even if she has a family who will support her and the child, she will never be the same. If going through pregnancy and childbirth (not to mention accepting the responsibilities of motherhood) permanently changes even stable, mature women who are ready for it, how can we measure the effect of its rigors on a tenth grader whose biggest responsibility up to now has been feeding the cat and emptying the litter box?

We cannot, of course, but we do know that having sex too soon can devastate a girl's future capacity to make love and enjoy it and to be an advocate for her own sexual pleasure. It can also pervert her fundamental view of what her role is in the world and undermine her motivation for remaining in it.

Maya:
When Bad Romances Happen to
Good Middle School Kids

I saw Maya only once, when the pediatric resident on duty called me down for a psychiatric consultation. He said he had a thirteen-year-old female who had broken her ankle after either falling or jumping from the roof of the family home and landing in a holly bush. She was scratched up all over, but her wrists bore several bloody cuts that looked as if they had been made with a knife. Her parents were emotionally overwrought; they said that she had threatened once before to do away with herself but they never thought she would actually try anything. The resident thought it might be wise to admit the girl for observation and wanted my opinion.

Maya's skin was pale, her hair pulled back in a braid. She wore a hospital-issue bathrobe; her arms, crisscrossed pink and red where they had encountered the holly bush, looked raw against the white sleeves. Her ankle was encased in a fresh plaster cast, and the toenails that peeked out were painted blue. Maya's face was devoid of expression; she did not look up at me for a long time and instead stared dully at a scuff mark on the linoleum floor.

Maya said she had been depressed ever since her boyfriend had broken up with her. She and Keith had been together forty-two days; she had tracked the progress of the romance in her diary. He hadn't given a reason for the breakup; in fact, he hadn't broken up with her at all: he had just stopped calling. When she had tried calling him, the answering machine would pick up; one day she had left more than twenty messages. Keith had picked up only once, Maya said; he'd told her he was sorry, but she should probably stop calling him because he'd met someone else and didn't think they should see each other anymore.

That was three weeks earlier. Timing is significant when you're dealing with depression: a patient must experience depressive symptoms for at least two weeks to be diagnosed with the disorder. The emotions of a thirteen-year-old can be volatile on even a good day, so the duration of

Maya's symptoms was of interest to me: if the romance had ended a day or two earlier and she'd tried to kill herself, I would have diagnosed her as having not depression but an adjustment disorder, which is how we describe a situation where a person takes prompt, drastic measures in response to an upsetting event. But Maya's depressive symptoms—apathy, lack of appetite, insomnia, loss of interest in schoolwork and extracurricular activities—had lasted for three weeks, which led me to believe she was clinically depressed.

"Tell me about Keith," I said. "Was he in your class?" Maya looked surprised.

"No," she said. "He doesn't go to my school. He's starting college in the fall."

"College?" I was taken aback. This girl was in seventh grade. "How old is he?" I asked.

"He's eighteen."

Eighteen? *Eighteen?* I tried to shift my face into neutral.

"So you were dating this eighteen-year-old guy," I said. "How did you explain this to your parents?"

"They were like, 'Okay, if you really want to.' They said I could go out with Keith as long as I kept my grades up."

"And did you keep your grades up?"

"For a while. But lately I can't concentrate and I've screwed up on a couple of tests. Then I went out with Brandon, just a few times. That didn't work out, either. By then I was, like, really depressed."

Brandon was sixteen and a friend of Keith's younger brother; Maya had met him at Keith's house. The pattern repeated itself: Brandon would pick up Maya at her house, take her out to a movie, and then they would park somewhere and have sex in his car. This time Maya didn't hold back; she had sex with Brandon on their first date. This is typical of girls who become sexually active very young: once they have crossed the line and had sex there's no going back, so they go forward. Maya had had two boyfriends in her life, and already she was becoming promiscuous.

After meeting with Maya, I talked with her parents. They were middle-class, well spoken, and clearly concerned about their daughter. Yes, they knew Keith, they said; he had come to the house quite a few times. The other boy, Brandon, had taken Maya out only once or twice. Keith was a nice boy, well dressed, polite; his parents were lawyers and had a very nice house. Maya seemed to like him and was eager to go out with him, so they told her she could as long as her schoolwork didn't suffer.

"But what about the age difference?" I said. "Did it concern you at all that your thirteen-year-old daughter was dating a high school senior?"

"Maya has always been very mature," her mother said. "She's a good student, she's on the student council, she plays flute in the school orchestra. She really wanted to do this, and we figured, okay—she's a smart girl and she's never given us any trouble. We didn't want to say no."

Why not? I wanted to ask. What were they afraid of—that their daughter would be angry with them and pitch a fit? That she'd cry and stomp upstairs and slam her door? That she would hate them? These well-meaning people were too insecure to carry out their most sacred duty as parents: to protect their child. Instead, they allowed their seventh-grade daughter—a child, let us remember—to take up with an eighteen-year-old boy. He takes her to the movies and, after a few dates, back to his house. They have sex; she thinks there's a relationship there, and she falls in love. Six weeks later, he loses interest—how much do a high school senior and a middle school student have in common, after all?—and ends the romance. The girl is devastated: she has given this boy everything—her innocence, her trust, and her heart. When he leaves, she feels used and abandoned, guilty and ashamed. She reproaches herself for sleeping with him; at the same time, she wonders if he'd still be around if she had been better at sex. She hates herself for going out with him in the first place; she despises herself for not being able to hold his interest. She hates him for leaving her; she loves him for having wanted her at all.

If these feelings ring a bell, it's because they resonate so strongly with many women when we're in the midst of a breakup. But for Maya, the breakup was far more loaded because she was only thirteen; this was her first crush, her first hint of the exhilaration of romantic love. And that part is all quite normal: girls fall in love with boys all the time, as they sometimes do with other girls (although I don't think they always act on those impulses). Being in love is fun because it feels good: when the object of your affection rounds the corner, your heart pounds, your skin prickles, and you feel indescribably, deliciously alive—and he doesn't even have to know about it. Even if he does, if he's the first guy you go out with, you probably won't "go all the way" with him: you might kiss him or he might kiss you, but probably nothing more than that, so it doesn't seem dangerous. But it is dangerous if you're thirteen and he's eighteen because he is at his sexual peak: hormones are cascading through his system, every cell of which is primed to want sex—and he's going to want it unless there's something wrong with him. And at thirteen, you can't hold him off: what thirteen-year-old can tell any eighteen-year-old no about anything, much less sex?

The most disconcerting aspect of this case for me was neither Maya's having had sex with older boys nor her suicide attempt; it is not unusual for teenage girls to take some pills or make halfhearted attempts to cut their wrists after they've had sex with a boy who then breaks up with them. What disturbed me was her parents' abdication of authority: *We didn't want to say no.*

Well, why not? Why can't we say no to our kids?

The reluctance of parents to exert control over their children's behavior is a fairly recent phenomenon. Somewhere between when I was a kid and now, we became convinced that it is hazardous to children's self-esteem to tell them what they may and may not do. There was no such notion when I was growing up: I remember my mother telling me the whole time I was in high school that I was not allowed to date anyone who was more than a year older or younger than I was. I'm not sure why it wasn't acceptable to go out with someone younger; perhaps it was so I wouldn't take advantage of a younger child. But I wasn't invited to question the policy, which I now understand was all about sex. Nor was I allowed to date anyone who drove a van, because my parents figured there was likely to be a mattress in the back (they weren't fools, either).

Make no mistake: these were not decisions I made because I was smart or savvy or wise. These were my parents' rules—which, I should add, seemed totally uncool to me at the time and against which I railed with a stridency usually reserved for those unfortunates who suggested I attend nursing rather than medical school because it would be easier for a girl. But rage though I might, my parents stood firm; they could not have cared less whether I liked them or not. What they cared about was my well-being, and they knew better than to entrust it to someone as malleable and naïve as I. In removing my right to choose whether or not I had sex, they took out of my hands a decision I was utterly unprepared to make. And it helped me, because when that sweetly seductive guy with the VW van asked me out and I wanted to say yes (and might have said yes to a lot more), I couldn't. I could only tell him that I'd love to go out with him but my parents wouldn't let me. I was able to say no to him because my parents had said no to me.

We're hypocrites, really; we exhort our kids to renounce drugs and sex and alcohol and Just Say No, when it's *we* who can't say no: we're so desperate for our children's affection that we yes them and yes them until they've forgotten what no sounds like, let alone what it feels like. It starts early, when they carry on in the market about wanting that nutrition-free, sugar-laced breakfast cereal and they're making such a racket that people are glancing your way and you can feel the blood rushing to your face and you say, "Don't cry, don't cry, sweetie, here's the cereal, just drop it in the cart." Miraculously, the wailing stops and peace reigns—that is, until you get to the checkout line, where candy bars lie in wait.

Kids aren't fools; they quickly learn that all they have to do to get their way is howl and bawl until you feel like one of the wicked stepmothers who populate their video classics. They know that if they whine and complain long enough, you'll cave in and acquiesce to even the most outrageous demand—anything to shut them up and preserve your self-image as a caring, open-minded parent. The irony is that we are most caring when we *don't* give in, when we are confident enough in our children's love for us and our own sound judgment to stand our ground, save them from themselves, and say, "No, you may not have that cereal"; "No, you may not speak that way to me"; "No, you may not date a boy five years older than you are or any other boy, for that matter, because you are too young to be dating in the first place." But we don't say no, or, if we do, we don't say it often enough. And then we're shocked to learn that our young daughters are having sex in movie theaters and in cars, apparently of their own free will.

The thing is, a thirteen-year-old cannot give consent: she doesn't know what she is consenting to (that's the rationale behind the felony charge of statutory rape, which is defined as nonforcible sexual intercourse with a person who is under the statutory age of consent).[3] When a thirteen-year-old becomes sexually involved with an eighteen-year-old, the younger of the two, girl or boy, is likely being coerced: the power dynamic between them is clearly not in the younger one's favor. And if the younger one is a girl, the psychological consequences of being coerced into sex can be especially devastating.

If you can remember what it was like to be a teenager—or if you are the parent of a teenager and wish you could, for a blissful interlude, forget what it's like to live with one—you know that it is a time of unprecedented physical, emotional, and psychological change. Nothing feels right, because the inner territory is new and unfamiliar: adolescents' feelings about themselves, their families, and everything else veer so wildly between funk and euphoria that the people closest to them don't know who they're going to be the next time they shuffle or sashay into the room. We don't know them because they don't know themselves, and spiking the brew with sexual intimacy provokes too big a change, early on, for them to handle.

Which is not to say the urges aren't there: they are, in gale force. But because of society's taboos against frank and open acknowledgment of our sexual nature—whether in the form of religious prohibitions or the subjugation of public education to political pressure—we continue to fail miserably in our mission to teach young people about this most primal life force. If you try to broach the subject of sex with a middle school student, you will likely be greeted with a groan of condescension, complete with eye rolling and a weary assurance that "they taught us all that in school."

They may be teaching it, but are the kids learning anything?

When my eldest stepson was about fifteen, he came home one day fuming with righteous indignation because he had just learned that the boy down the street had gotten a classmate pregnant. My stepson was furious with the girl, saying the debacle was all her fault because she didn't tell the boy she was having her period.

"What in the world are you talking about?" I said.

"Well, if she'd told him the truth about having her period, she wouldn't have gotten pregnant."

Remain calm, Anita, I told myself, *and choose your words carefully.*

"First of all, if she were having her period, I think he would have known it," I said. "And second, that's not when a girl gets pregnant; in fact, a girl is least likely to get pregnant when she is menstruating. So let's go over these facts again."

I went over the whole process with him and was very clear about when during a woman's cycle she is likely to ovulate and thus be able to conceive. He sat there looking at once embarrassed and blasé about the whole thing, obliged as he was to sit through this birds-and-bees yawnfest. Which is exactly the point: it's not as if my stepson hadn't had sex education in school. He had been through at least six years of hygiene, health, and family life classes, and what he and his friends had taken away from it all was the warped belief that a girl is most fertile when she is having her period. That misconception had a lot more staying power for these boys than all the facts their teachers had undoubtedly lobbed their way. It's no wonder that kids are making bad choices and that bad things are happening to them.

Sex is a force of nature, whether we like it or not. Religious beliefs will not quell its expression or restrict the mind's infinite capacity to reconcile faith with fact. Felice's religious beliefs kept her from using either birth control to prevent a pregnancy or abortion to end it, but they protected her neither from her body's natural receptivity to conceiving a child nor her mind's capacity to deny that it had happened. What might have saved Felice and her child? Maturity and education: had she been possessed of a fully formed self, she might have felt safe enough within its bounds to balance faith with reason; and had she been properly educated about the complexities of sexuality, she might have understood her own sexuality well enough to cope with the consequences of exploring it. She might have considered using some form of birth control, or she might have permitted herself to weigh the spiritual price of an abortion against the personal price of carrying and bearing a child that was unplanned at best and unwanted at worst. I believe that Felice's tragedy was the pitiable outcome of expecting the ethereal nature of faith to override the primordial force of nature. Had she seen herself as a rational yet fallible adult rather than a good girl compelled to please the adults around her, she might have been able to contemplate a flawed but fulfilled existence—the most that any of us can hope to achieve.

And what of Maya playing sexual roulette with her will to live? And the rows and rows of rainbow girls who are convinced that fellatio isn't really sex, so it isn't really dangerous? Were we educating our girls more aggressively about their sexuality, I am convinced they would not be so quick to offer up their bodies and souls for so meager a return when the risks are so great. I doubt that they would sentence themselves to life without the possibility of bearing a child if they understood how easily it could happen. I suspect they would be more serious about keeping their grades up if they were to spend an eight-hour workday flipping burgers at a fast-food joint or doing the kind of manual labor for which they might be minimally qualified if they drop out of school to have a baby. And I bet there wouldn't be as many thirteen- and fourteen-year-old girls conducting Internet romances with thirty-five-year-old men and sneaking off to meet them at motels if they knew that the excursion could haunt them for the next fifty years, assuming they live that long.

Nor would so many girls damage their sexuality if we, their parents, would disengage our heads from the sands of complacency and see these sensual, surly, psychologically perplexing creatures for what they are: children. Children with breasts, perhaps, as well as an expanding knowledge of the seductive arts, but children nonetheless. Children who will castigate your draconian child-rearing philosophy now but will one day thank you for putting their best interests ahead of your popularity and having the guts to say no. Saying yes is easier, of course, and it feels good: the kid is happy for a few minutes, and during that golden interlude you're the greatest mom or dad ever, which warms the cockles of your heart a lot more than when she screams that she hates your guts. But bringing up children isn't the same as running for office, so don't mistake your kids for your constituency. If you are a parent, you shouldn't worry about whether your kids like you or not. If you can't say no, then when you say yes, you're not really saying yes; you're just letting whatever happens happen.

SEXUAL INVENTORY

When Girls Are Sexually Active

1. If you are the parent or caregiver of an adolescent girl, here are some questions to ask yourself and discuss with

your daughter so both of you have a greater understanding of what is going on in her life:

■ How do you think your daughter views herself? Have you talked about this with her? If not, why not?

~ How does she see herself physically?

• Is she happy with her body, unhappy, or a little of both? What do you think the specific issues are—weight, skin, hair?

• Where does she get the images of womanhood that influence her most—from movies, television, magazines, friends, you?

• How does she think she compares to these images? Do you think she understands what these images actually project?

~ How does she perceive her intellect?

• Does she think she is very intelligent, of average intelligence, or below average?

• Where do intelligence and academic achievement lie on her scale of what is important in life? Does she distinguish between intelligence and academic achievement and/or perceive a correlation between the two?

• How is she doing in school? What do you think motivates her academic performance? Have you talked about it?

2. How high would you rate your daughter's self-esteem?

■ Do you believe she thinks well of herself? On what are you basing your opinion?

■ Do you believe she thinks ill of herself? Again, on what are you basing your opinion?

3. Does your daughter have friends?

■ If not, does she seem concerned about it? Are you concerned about it?

■ If she does have friends, how would you characterize the friendships?

~ Are her friendships mutually satisfying? That is,

• Does she initiate visits with friends?

- Does she wait until they call her?
- Does she do most or all of the calling?
- Is the power balance in her friendships distributed equally between her and the other person?

~ Does her circle of friends comprise

- Mostly girls?
- Mostly boys?
- Both girls and boys?

■ What do her friends tend to be like? Are they bright, athletic, intellectually curious, well liked by their friends? Do they seem responsible and motivated?

■ Is she romantically interested in boys? In girls?

4. What is your daughter's understanding of sex?

■ Does she think it's gross? Does she think it's supposed to be fun?

■ Does she understand little, some, or much of the mechanics of sex?

5. Is your daughter involved in a romantic relationship? If so:

■ Do you think the relationship is appropriate to your daughter's chronological, emotional, and intellectual age? Does she seem happy and stable within the relationship or unhappy and off balance?

■ How do you feel about the person with whom she is involved?

■ How do you think this person feels about you?

■ How does this person make you feel?

■ Is either your daughter or her romantic interest "in charge" of the relationship or more dominant than the other? Does the balance of power in the relationship shift? If so, why do you think it does?

⟨⸺⟩

CHAPTER 7

What Lies, Roils, and Festers Beneath

Resentments, Fears, and Worries

"I'm worried my husband is having an affair."

The woman was young, maybe twenty-six or twenty-seven, and petite, which is to say she stood no more than five-foot-one and had feet the size of granola bars. Her name was Stephanie, and she came in complaining of hypoactive sexual desire disorder; in other words, she had lost all interest in sex.

"Tell me more," I said.

"I just have this feeling, and it's scaring me because we've only been married a year and this isn't supposed to happen so soon. I don't know what to do—" She broke off and squeezed her eyes shut.

People often begin this way, awash in a sea of emotion. Sometimes, if they start to talk, the words buoy them up and form a sort of flotation device they can cling to until an insight arrives to hoist them toward self-awareness. I watched as the young woman's thumb worked her wedding band back and forth on her finger. Eventually she looked up and began to speak again.

"It's probably my own fault. I haven't been feeling very . . . I don't know what it is lately, but I just don't feel, you know, like I used to. I used to really get into sex. We once did it in the bathroom at my in-laws' house while they were waiting for us to come down to dinner."

A short laugh erupted before Stephanie bit her bottom lip and sighed.

"That was a really long time ago. I can't remember the last time I felt that way, and I don't know why. Everything's fine. I'm not depressed; at least I don't think I am. I go to work, I do my job; things are kind of intense, but I'm doing okay, and besides, that's not the point. The point is that I just don't feel like having sex anymore. And now Charlie doesn't want to, either. He doesn't touch me, he doesn't, you know, try to do anything. He works late a lot. He really likes his job, and he's already moving up. The company has offices everywhere, and there's lots of room for growth, but you've got to put in long hours at the beginning, so he's got to stay late a lot, or at least that's what he says. And I don't think he's lying. He calls me before he comes home and the caller ID always shows his work number, so I know he's there, although someone might be there with him. It's hard to imagine, it's just not like him. But the thing is, he doesn't want sex anymore. And he used to—we were even talking about having a baby in the next couple of years. That's what scares me. We haven't been married that long, and if it's like this already, what's the rest of our lives going to be like? Or maybe the marriage is over and I just don't know it. I'm really worried, and I can't sleep. I'm afraid I'll mess up at work—I forgot about a conference call the other day. I've never done that before in my life. This is not me. I'm not a flaky-type person, and I don't want to screw up this opportunity. I wish I could sleep. Maybe you could give me something to help me sleep."

There was a lot going on here. Stephanie had come in seeking help for low desire but spent relatively little time on that compared to other subjects. The first thing she said was that she was worried her husband was having an affair, yet she also acknowledged that this would be out of character for him. They had been married for barely a year, which is rather soon for a young couple to lose their erotic spark, especially when they had been attracted enough to each other to have sex in the ancestral bathroom.

The situation was rich in irony. Here was a young woman with little or no interest in sex, agitated because her husband wasn't pressuring her for sex. Her agitation was more intellectual than physical: she wasn't upset because her husband was withholding bodily intimacy that she craved; she was upset because her rational mind told her that happy young newlyweds don't go six months without having sex. Therefore she and Charlie must not be happy, he must be getting sex elsewhere, and she must be too naïve, distracted, or just plain thick to see it. I had no reason to think that Stephanie didn't love her husband, nor did she have reason to think he didn't love her, save for his alleged sexual reticence. She understood intellectually the duality implicit in her situation—that she loved her husband even while she felt little or no desire to have sex with him—yet did not see that the same duality might exist in him.

Stephanie's quandary intrigued me. From the way she had described Charlie, it was hard to imagine him engaged in late-night trysts at the office. I thought it more likely that he was putting in long hours at a new job in hopes of securing a promotion and a raise, perhaps to better support the family he and Stephanie had talked about starting. And their mutual loss of desire perplexed me; if either one or the other was avoiding sex, I might look for a medical explanation. But when a woman and man as young, healthy, and newly wed as Stephanie and Charlie both avoid sex for six months—half their married life—I tend to look to the relationship for clues.

I told Stephanie that I thought medication might help calm the anxiety and help her sleep. She was all for it, as long as it didn't cloud her mind and adversely affect her job performance. I decided to prescribe an antidepressant rather than an antianxiety drug, because antidepressants treat anxiety in addition to mood. Moreover, a few have been developed that produce the desired effects without diminishing sex drive, so I thought this would be a good choice for Stephanie.

Stephanie arranged to come in every two weeks on Thursday afternoons. I sometimes glimpsed her dashing from her car in the parking lot moments before her appointment, hair and shoulder bag flying. She would arrive at my door flushed and out of breath, gasping apologies for being late, even when she was right on time. She seemed to be in constant motion, juggling a travel mug of coffee, cell phone, and electronic organizer as she settled into a chair.

I began working with Stephanie on ways she might reclaim her desire. We discussed the importance of devoting time and energy to romance, and I suggested she talk with Charlie about setting aside time on Saturday nights for the two of them to be alone in a way that would encourage intimacy. This was not as obvious a prescription as it might sound; typically, they would spend their Saturday nights at home watching movies and playing video games until they dragged themselves into bed and fell asleep. They were together, but only in terms of vegging out on the same couch. I suggested they turn off the interactive media for an evening and spend time interacting instead.

In the early sessions, Stephanie focused on her courtship and marriage: how she and Charlie had met at business school when he showed up for a weekend study session splattered with paint and told her he had spent the morning working with Habitat for Humanity, and how that had made her pay attention to this otherwise ordinary-seeming guy and accept his invitation for coffee. I heard about their wedding in Pennsylvania and honeymoon in Mexico, and the job offer Charlie received that was too good to pass up, even if it meant moving farther away from their families. He would be working for a telecommunications conglomerate—his first choice—at a starting salary that would support them both. Stephanie agreed to accompany him and soon had an offer from a human resources consulting firm that specialized in creating corporate training programs. The salary wasn't as high as Stephanie had hoped for, but the company was young and growing, and the man who interviewed her was a real dynamo. Stephanie figured she could learn a lot from him, and she took the job.

As I got to know Stephanie, a picture coalesced of a high-achieving young woman, a straight-A's type who did well at whatever she set her mind to. As a girl, she had excelled academically, sung in both school and church choirs, and competed in scholastic chess tournaments. She was salutatorian of her high school class, attended a state university for her bachelor's degree, and went on to the Ivy League for her MBA. Stephanie said it had irked her when friends ribbed her about being so smart. "I did well, but I worked hard," she said. "They were all hanging out at the mall at night, but my parents only let me go when there was no school the next day."

Stephanie described herself as sexually open if not adventurous and cited the bathroom rendezvous as a departure for her—one that she would happily repeat if only she could feel that level of desire again. Stephanie said that she and Charlie would have sex almost every night when they were first married; then, after they relocated and Charlie began working, it slowed down to twice a week. But now, she said, months would go by without more than a perfunctory kiss.

I was doing some paperwork in my office one Thursday when

Stephanie called. Sounding flustered, she said she had a work emergency and had to cancel the session. Two weeks later, it happened again. When she finally came in, I asked if things had calmed down at the office.

"Not really," she said. "I've spent most of the last three weekends there. It's kind of a weird situation. The guy who hired me, he quit not long after I got there, and I've been doing his job, so it's pretty intense. He was in the middle of creating six employee development programs for three different clients—you know, leadership training, management skills, that kind of thing—so now I get to finish them. I did a similar project in grad school, so I know a bit about it, but it's a ton of work." She fidgeted in her seat.

"You haven't been there very long, have you?" I said.

"That's the thing—I've been there only nine months, and I've been doing this upper-level job for, like, more than half of it. It's a great opportunity. And if I like it and do okay, they'll give me a promotion and a raise." She nodded rapidly and clasped her hands in her lap.

"It sounds like a lot of work," I said.

"Yes, but I can handle it. I don't want to blow this. There's a real opportunity here, and I'd be crazy not to take advantage of it. I've got to do this. And I will. It's just a lot, that's all."

The story gradually unspooled: how the sudden departure of Stephanie's boss had left the company in a bind, and how she was the person who could save the day. She was working nights and weekends trying to get the work done, and a coworker was giving her trouble because he thought he should have gotten the job. To complicate matters, Stephanie's father-in-law had cancer and she had not been to Pennsylvania to visit him in months because she was working all the time. Charlie had made the trip four times in a row without her.

It was beginning to add up. This was a young woman who had always been able to manage everything that came her way; now, for the first time in her life, she was overwhelmed. She was working harder than she ever had before, and it wasn't enough. Stephanie had bought into the myth that she could do it all, and the stress was enormous. This happens to many women: they try to be all things to all people and end up lost to themselves. For Stephanie, to acknowledge that she was out of her depth would be tantamount to failure—a humiliation of epic proportions. To cope with the anxiety, she had battened down her emotional hatches and focused all her energy on her job, leaving precious little for her husband, their marriage, or anything else. Low desire wasn't making her anxious and keeping her awake at night; it was the other way around: stress from the job was tying her in knots and turning her obsessively inward, away from her husband and ultimately herself.

When a woman is wracked with stress, the feeling seeps through the seams of her psyche, pooling in the crannies and crevices of the self, including her sexuality. She can't simply stem the flow of stress, relax enough to make love, and resume worrying postcoitally. Men seem to be different. Generally speaking, guys tend to stash their interior goings-on in separate bins: work, play, home, love, sex, kids, relatives, friends; they're all in there, coexisting in separate-but-not-so-equal harmony. It's rather like an internal self-storage system, with separate lockers for each facet of the male self. This typically leaves them less immediately in touch with their feelings than women, which in turn enables them to get it up for sex more readily when they have other stuff going on.

I told Stephanie that I suspected job stress was the source of her desire problem and that if she addressed the work angle directly, the sex angle would improve. She looked at me blankly.

"I don't know," she said. "I'm holding it together; no one's told me I'm not doing a good job. I've been working for years now, and it's never affected me this way before. And what does my job have to do with Charlie not wanting sex?"

"It's not your job that's affecting Charlie; it's you," I said. "Think back to when your desire first started to go. What would you tell Charlie?"

"Tell him? I didn't tell him anything; what would I say?"

"If you didn't say anything to him, how did things play out between you sexually?"

"He'd, you know, try to get something going, and I guess I just turned over and went to sleep."

Stephanie recounted episodes when she had rejected Charlie's caresses, saying she was too exhausted to make love. He persisted, but she rebuffed him, gently but consistently. When his erotic overtures abated, Stephanie was relieved. She didn't stop to think about how her behavior was affecting Charlie, that he might be confused, frustrated, hurt, and too timid to confront her. She assumed, as many young people do, that marriage magically conferred intimacy and trust, that if Charlie still wanted to have sex with her he would be pursuing her. It did not occur to her that he might be aching to make love with her but fearful of being rejected again.

Armed with newfound insight, Stephanie vowed to reconsider how her actions might be affecting her husband. She started paying attention to how her job was affecting her state of mind and began coming in every week to talk about it. She stopped going into the office on Saturdays so she and Charlie could spend more time together and accompanied him to Pennsylvania to visit his father. They had sex that weekend, and two weeks later they had sex twice. They resumed talking about having children, and Stephanie began to entertain the thought that a less stressful job might enable her to have both kids and a career. When I last saw Stephanie, she told me that Charlie had won a transfer that would move them back to Philadelphia, which would not only provide a better job market for her but would also move them closer to their families. This would be helpful once they started their own family.

"The transfer was his idea," she said. "He wants me to find another job, and he knows there isn't much available here. And here I am, picturing him with somebody else. I feel like an idiot. You know, I'm a pretty perceptive person, but I couldn't see what was right in front of me."

Or rather, just below her line of vision. It seems so unmysterious: a young woman is in a new marriage, new city, new job; her boss leaves unexpectedly, and she takes on his job, for which she is neither qualified nor prepared; young woman becomes anxious, loses desire for sex, rejects husband's attempts to regain her favors; husband withdraws. Seems pretty obvious. But when the facts are yours and you're living them each day, they're not so obvious to you—to your mother, perhaps, or to your closest friend, but not to you. You just can't see the connection between what's going on in your life, how you feel about it, how your feelings are affecting what you're doing, and how what you're doing is creating a new set of circumstances that colors everything in your world, including sex. All you see is what is looming closest to your line of vision, which is usually what you happen to be obsessing about at the moment—in Stephanie's case, her husband's apathy toward sex. She was far too absorbed in her work to see that it was her own flight from intimacy that had prompted his.

Why didn't she just talk to him? Why didn't he talk to her? Why, for that matter, don't any of us talk to our mates when something is bothering us rather than retreating into strained silence, as we do most of the time?

Because it's easier, of course. Why confront your partner with a complaint and risk having him bristle through dinner when you can ignore the problem and hope it goes away? It goes away, all right, burrowing under your skin and into your psyche, pickling in a potent marinade of anxiety, guilt, resentment, fear, and whatever uncomfortable emotions you have come to repress.

Stephanie resolved her problem relatively quickly; within four months of starting therapy, she had resumed sexual relations with her husband, attenuated her stress by deciding to seek less stressful employment, and decided, with him, to move closer to their families in anticipation of having a child of their own. Contributing to her rapid recovery was the fact that she hadn't given her problem a chance to root very deeply before seeking help.

Renata:
Minimum Desire, Maximum Resentment

By the time Renata became my patient, she had been seeing doctors at the Women's Midlife Health Center for some time. Renata was fifty-eight, had been married for thirty-three years, and was the mother of two grown sons. Her gynecologist at the center had put her on hormone replacement therapy (HRT) several years earlier, when Renata had begun having hot flashes and night sweats. The treatment had served her well until she stopped, cold turkey, in the wake of reports citing its possible connections to breast cancer and cardiovascular disease. She had since resumed and quit HRT several times in response to media reports about its various benefits and risks, the most persuasive encomium coming from her twin sister, who had been taking hormones for years and told Renata, "I don't care if they take five years off my life—at least I'll enjoy myself while I'm here." Rebekah wasn't worried about getting breast cancer or cardiovascular disease; no one in their family had either illness, and neither she nor Renata had any other conditions, such as fibrocystic disease, that would have predisposed them to developing those illnesses. But Renata was not persuaded: hormones were out, no matter what Rebekah said, at least until they were proven safe.

Renata had also consulted an internist about recurring bouts of anxiety. About three years earlier, she had started having troublesome symptoms: racing heart, shortness of breath, and a creeping sense of doom, and the doctor had put her on an antianxiety formula that eased her worrying and enabled her to function more normally. But now Renata believed that the medication was destroying what little sexual desire menopause had left her. When she asked her internist to suggest a different drug, he suggested that she see a psychiatrist, as we are typically more familiar with the vast array of mood-altering medications and more experienced at prescribing them. Renata procrastinated another three months before calling me and did so only at the insistence of her husband, who was both concerned about her state of mind and frustrated at the sexual drought that was withering their marriage.

This isn't unusual: many of my patients, especially those who are middle-aged and older, resist acknowledging a sexual problem until it threatens the stability of their primary relationship. It's only when the husband or partner expresses unhappiness that the woman seeks help, and even then she may not be keen on the idea of seeing a psychiatrist. Many times she is convinced that the entire problem is due to Menopause, with a capital M, that catchall time of life that's to blame for everything from forgetting where you left your keys to blanking out on your children's names, as well as what it feels like to have an orgasm. And so it was that Renata appeared in my office, convinced that her apathy toward sex was a result of aging and taking an antianxiety medication.

My first session with a patient usually leaves a strong impression, and this one was no exception. Renata was beautifully dressed in an expensive tweed suit, and her silk blouse looked as if it had been dyed to match her shoes. Renata was both intense and opaque; her gaze was intelligent, and she looked me straight in the eye, but her eyes told me little about what was going on behind them. She spoke warmly of Harold, whom she had married when she was twenty-five and supporting herself as a piano teacher and he was twenty-nine and a junior executive at a bank. To hear her speak, you would think they lived in a state of connubial bliss: they had two lovely grown sons, lived in a lovely house on seven acres of land, and belonged to a lovely club where they ate dinner several nights a week now that the boys were gone. She no longer gave piano lessons; she had grown weary of teaching and, in a burst of empty-nest vigor, had several years earlier started her own business creating custom-designed photo albums. She worked with an upscale portrait photographer in town who referred more clients to her than she could handle and was doing very nicely putting in about twenty hours a week. It was a happy business, Renata said; she worked mostly with brides, who reminded her what it felt like to be young and just starting out, and it kept her mind off how empty the house seemed now that the boys were gone.

Toward the end of the session, I asked Renata about her relationship with her husband. She looked at me with those inscrutable eyes and said, "Oh, Harold is a devoted husband and father." The phrase struck me as odd. When I tried to probe a bit deeper, she assured me that she and Harold got along well; it was just their sex life that needed work. But something didn't seem right: her description of Harold sounded a bit too professional, as if it had come from a press secretary rather than someone who had been married to the man for over thirty years. It reminded me of obituaries that describe the deceased as a devoted husband and father or wife and mother; *devoted* is a word we use to publicly convey a world of private, turbulent emotion in a proper, controlled way.

I gradually grew acquainted with the facts of Renata's life. Her mother had ruled the household and been very strict with her twin daughters, dressing them in identical outfits and refusing to let them wear pants to school, even when the principal changed the rules to allow it. Talking back was forbidden, and Renata once got her mouth washed out with soap for calling her mother a witch. Rebekah was bolder, calling their mother far worse and, according to Renata, getting her mouth washed out so often she developed a taste for Zest. Renata talked about her mother with a degree of bitterness more typical of a teenager than a person in her fifties. The woman was living in an assisted living facility but had lost little of her grit; Renata said she had no trouble staying young at heart because whenever she visited, her mother made her feel like a three-year-old.

As time passed I focused less on the events of Renata's past and more on her behaviors, especially the ones I observed during our sessions. I watched her face as she spoke about her family. Her eyes grew soft and sometimes moist when she talked about the boys' early years, and a wistful smile would play about her mouth as she described the time this one had been a lamb in the Christmas pageant and that one had sent his gerbils for a spin on the ceiling fan. But when Harold's name came up, Renata seemed to stiffen, and her eyes would dart away before returning, neutral and veiled, to my face.

The plot thickened when Renata began to speak at more length about her sons. Thomas was thirty, had a master's degree in finance, and worked for an importing business. He was still single but had been seeing a lovely young woman for some months now whom Renata hoped he would marry. Her voice warmed when she spoke of Thomas's recent promotion to vice president in charge of sales and marketing, and the corners of her eyes crinkled with pleasure whenever his name came up, which was often. He called home on Wednesdays and Sundays and kept her and Harold up-to-date on his whereabouts, as he traveled frequently to Asia on buying trips. He had brought back some beautiful pieces from China—Harold was fond of small lacquered boxes—and had promised her a carved jade pendant when he found just the right one.

But when it came to the younger son, it was harder to get information. Renata mentioned him from time to time, but there were none of the tender, rambling narratives she lavished on Thomas. When she did talk about Dean, she would often refer to him as Thomas's younger brother rather than by name, and glance away and let her voice trail off with a sigh. I wondered what the story was.

Little by little, I found out. Dean was twenty-three and lived about fifty miles away in an apartment he shared with two other men. Renata described him as being between jobs, but it sounded as if he hadn't been employed for some time. He had never graduated from college, having left at the end of his sophomore year after Renata and Harold learned he was spending more time stoned in his dorm room than in class. Harold gave him an ultimatum: he could either pull up his average to a B, or the money would stop.

"And he kept his word," Renata said. "You couldn't talk to the man. Poor Dean. He tried his best, but it wasn't good enough. It never was."

"Never good enough?" I said.

"For his father. For Harold. He was always so hard on Dean. I don't know what it was, but he never warmed up to that child. No matter what the boy did, it never satisfied his father. Even in college. He went back to class, you know, and ended up with a C average. But no—Harold said he had to have a B, and if he didn't have a B, that was it. So that was the end of Dean's college career."

"What do you think should have happened?"

"I think we should have cut him some slack. I think a C was good enough, considering he was flunking out when this whole thing happened. Rome wasn't built in a day, you know."

"And what did Harold say?"

"Harold said he had to have a B."

"But you felt differently."

She paused for a moment. "Yes, I suppose I did." Her eyes grew opaque and distant.

I began to recognize a pattern: when I asked Renata about Harold directly, her responses were bland and vapid, but when his name came up in connection with Dean, something in her flared hot and red until her hostility seeped out like blood through a bandage.

Like the coalescing image on a Polaroid snapshot, the source of Renata's low-desire problem came into view. The picture was completed when she described an episode that had occurred just a week earlier when Dean had come to dinner. He had applied for a job at an organic foods market and thought he had a good shot at getting hired. Renata felt a surge of hope; Dean had always been attracted to holistic-type things—he had once taken a yoga class—and she thought this job might work out for him. When he got up to leave, Renata walked him to the door and was slipping a wad of fifties into his hand when Harold materialized and reminded her that Dean still owed him three hundred dollars that he really should repay before they gave him any more cash. Renata watched, stony and silent, as Dean wheeled around, snarled something vile about what his father might do to himself, hurled the money at the older man's chest, and strode out of the house. She then bent down, picked up and smoothed the bills, and thrust them into the pocket of Harold's cardigan before retreating to the kitchen to clean up from dinner.

"What were you feeling when all this happened?" I said.

"Harold had a point; Dean did owe him money, and it was only right that he pay back his father."

Renata inhaled sharply as if she were about to say something, then averted her eyes and remained silent.

"You just had a thought," I said. "What was it?"

"It's just that the money I was giving Dean was mine, not Harold's," she said. "I have a small account that I keep separate and that I use for special things, private things. This had nothing to do with Harold; it was supposed to be between Dean and me. That's why I waited until we were alone to give it to him. But Harold did have a point. Dean owed him money, and here I was, giving him more. So he stopped me."

"How did that make you feel?"

"Embarrassed, as if I'd done something shameful. Dean didn't even have a decent pair of shoes to wear to the interview. Is it a sin to give your child money if he needs it? Am I such a terrible person because I want to help my son?"

"What do you think?"

"What do I think?" She looked at me uncertainly.

"Yes. What do you think?" I said.

"I think—" She stopped and clasped her hands tightly in her lap. She then reached down for her purse, extracted a handkerchief, and pressed it against her eyes. "I don't know what I think anymore," she said.

"Here's what I think," I said. "It is true that growing older and the medication you're taking can affect sexual desire, and that's probably going on a little bit with you. But I don't think your problem is age-related as much as it is rage-related."

Renata looked up and sniffled.

"I don't know what you're talking about," she said. "Rage? That's not me. I'm not an angry-type person."

Renata insisted that she loved her husband and cited the longevity of their marriage as evidence of their compatibility. She could not see— at least not at first—that her problem wasn't menopause but rather her smoldering, decades-old resentment about her husband's tough-love parenting style, which she believed had ruined their younger son's childhood and was now depriving the lad, twenty-three and chronically unemployed, of the love (and cash) he needed. She kept insisting that she loved Harold and he loved his sons; everything he did, he did for the family's benefit. She acknowledged that she didn't always like the way Harold handled the boys, but he was their father, and that's the way fathers were with their sons. After all, she said, Thomas had turned out well; if Harold were such a terrible father, wouldn't Thomas have problems, too? And besides, Renata said, she and Harold hardly ever argued. How could they have gotten along so well all these years if she were as enraged as I said she was?

I said that I believed the reason they got along so well was because she had never confronted her husband with her true feelings. Instead, she had chosen to be a good girl, burying her rage deep within her, just as she had buried her resentment toward her controlling mother. Girls are taught to be good, to be pliant and agreeable, to acquiesce to the will of the adults—especially the men—around them. Like many girls of her generation, Renata learned early on that she would be praised for her winsome ways, her willingness to compromise, to behave and be nice. She conducted herself in marriage as she had in her parents' home, amiably, agreeably, and accepting of her husband's ways—at least on the surface. But that's as far as her serenity went. Renata had never consciously burrowed beneath the skin of her marriage to examine the muscle and bone that gave it shape. She had not looked there, so she could not see that her erotic feelings were inextricably bound to the hostile ones she was harboring toward her husband and hiding from herself.

I should mention here, as I have before, that the process of therapy does not resemble a string of pearly, incandescent revelations as much as it does a Jackson Pollock canvas, whose riotous energy and chaotic paint drips defy linear observation and interpretation. It took Renata nearly a year to exhume her anger, acknowledge its origins, and take responsibility for burying it—along with her passion—rather than face her husband with her displeasure. And when she finally could acknowledge her complicity in the death of her desire, bells did not peal nor trumpets blare to proclaim her redemption; nor did passion come flooding back in a tidal wave of joy and forgiveness. It took time for her to work up the courage to go home, talk to Harold, and reveal to him the feelings she had sequestered for so many years. And it took time for her to agree to try several new antianxiety medications until she found one that neither caused her to put on weight nor adversely affected her reemerging sex drive.

It also took time for her to entertain her gynecologist's suggestion that she try a low dosage of testosterone, which doctors are prescribing more and more often for women with low desire. We often think of testosterone as a man's hormone, but the fact is that women's bodies manufacture testosterone too, albeit in more modest quantities. Testosterone stimulates a woman's sex drive, as it does a man's, when she is in the prime of life, but her testosterone level drops dramatically once she enters menopause, which can cause her desire level to plummet as well. We know that moderate amounts of testosterone can boost desire in women who are in the menopausal transition as well as those who are beyond it, and doctors would prescribe it for them more often if the hormone were packaged in female-friendly dosages. But as it stands, testosterone is available almost exclusively in dosages calibrated for men, which, when taken by women over extended periods of time, can deepen their voices and cause them to sprout facial and chest hair (not what most gals have in mind). So when a physician wants to prescribe testosterone for a female patient, she or he must choose a form of the substance—pill, gel, or injection, to name a few—that delivers the hormone at a rate and in a quantity that can be adjusted, case by case, to be safe for and suited to the woman in question.

The rationale for the availability of guys-only dosages is shrouded in mystery and politics, but I believe it derives from the (overwhelmingly male) medical establishment's squeamishness about empowering women to boost their sexual appetites. It's a funny thing: just about any guy would love to come home to a lusty minx who would snake her tongue into his ear and drag him upstairs as he walked in the door—that is, as long as he could keep her locked in the house and all to himself. Some men are still prey to the medieval view of woman's sexuality as a voracious beast whose mesmeric stare will lure them to madness, ruin, and eternal damnation, and that the only thing protecting them from this wretched fate is the fiction that women aren't really that interested in sex. But if we give women hormones to increase their desire (so the superstition goes), the balance of power will tip in woman's favor, and off she'll go, laying waste to mankind in supermarkets and shoe departments everywhere and humping every guy who crosses her sex-crazed path. Which would be fine as long as the woman in question isn't *his* woman. And while I offer this scenario with tongue firmly in cheek, if not ear, I'm only half joking. If men were more comfortable with the idea of sexually assertive and independent women, we would be as inundated with ads for women's testosterone supplements as we are with commercials for erection-enhancing drugs.

When I first talked to Renata about trying testosterone supplements, she balked at the idea because the regimen would require her to also take doses of estrogen, and she was still anxious about the possible risks of hormone replacement therapy. In time, however, she became more receptive and agreed to try it. She has been taking the supplements for several months now, as well as a newly prescribed antianxiety medication. She reports that she has begun to feel the stirrings of desire again, along with the news that Dean got the organic market job, Thomas became engaged, and she *convinced* Harold to agree to join her for sessions with a marriage counselor.

While it is interesting to contemplate the prime motivators in Renata's recovery—going into therapy with Harold? increasing her testosterone level? euphoria at her sons' good news? all of the above?—an even more captivating issue is what caused her dysfunction in the first place. While I believe that both the hormonal shifts of menopause and the original antianxiety medication's side effects played a role in dampening Renata's desire for sex, I am convinced that the most potent force at work was her two decades' worth of fury at her husband. This was a woman who never acknowledged her anger—neither to her husband, nor to her mother, nor to herself, nor to anyone. Slowly and inexorably, rage and resentment had wormed their way deep into her psyche and eaten away at her erotic core, as they would in any woman who squelched her true feelings for as long as Renata did.

Repressing your feelings can damage not only your marriage but also your health. Looking at data from a ten-year follow-up to the Framingham Offspring Study, researchers found that women who chronically suppressed their feelings when disagreeing with their partners were four times more likely to die during the follow-up period than women who spoke their minds. According to Nieca Goldberg, a cardiologist in New York City, this may be because when a woman perpetually presents a smiling face to mask rage, stress hormones repeatedly pump into her system, elevating both her level of strain and her chances of developing heart disease, as well as depression and sexual problems.[1]

Most striking, as was the case with Renata, she may be oblivious to her tamped-down fury and what it is doing to her, so much so that she denies having felt anger in the first place. When you think of yourself as a good girl, expressing dissatisfaction, let alone rage, is unthinkable. Renata's self-respect resided in no small measure in her willingness to subjugate her wishes to those of her loved ones—her mother, her husband, and, to some extent, her children. She was the peacemaker in the family, the loving counterpart to Harold's rigid disciplinarian. To contradict him directly would be tantamount to emotional mutiny; she would not dare threaten the family's equanimity, and her role within it, by expressing her disaffection. It was easier to pretend, to hide, to put a brave face on her discontent and go along with her husband's pronouncements. It wasn't until she lost almost all feeling for him that she realized how strong her feelings actually were.

Andra and Quinn: Anger Mismanagement

"I'm here because of my partner," the woman said. "She thinks I need to see someone, and she's threatened to leave me if I don't get help."

"What seems to be the problem?" I said.

"Well, I just . . . I don't know. We don't . . . we haven't . . . okay, I'll just say it: we hardly ever have sex anymore. I just don't . . . feel the way I used to."

Interesting, I thought. Like many patients, this woman came in at the urging of her partner. Gay or straight, when one partner gets unhappy enough, he or she will often press the other to seek help.

"How have your feelings changed?"

"Well, for one thing, I used to want sex. A lot, too."

"And now?"

"Now it's not . . . how do I say this? It's not very good anymore, at least not for me."

"I'm hearing two different things," I said. "First you implied you didn't want sex anymore, but now you just said that you don't enjoy sex anymore. Those are two different things."

Andra stopped for a moment to consider this, which gave me time to consider her. She looked to be in her late thirties and wore a dark pantsuit with black leather pointy-toed boots, which were in style that season. Her hair was short and well cut, and she carried a roomy, expensive-looking tote bag of supple, gleaming leather.

"You know, that's true," she said. "It's not that I don't think about sex anymore. It's just that I don't feel like having sex, at least not with Quinn. She thinks it's lesbian bed death, at least on my part. But I don't think that's it. I'm not even sure there is such a thing."

I was inclined to agree with her. "Lesbian bed death" is a jarring, if descriptive, term that has recently crept into the language and signifies the phenomenon of diminishing sexual activity in long-term two-woman couples. While I have no doubt that established lesbian couples do suffer from a drop-off in sex after a while, I am not convinced that they fare much worse than their heterosexual brothers and sisters (or two-man couples, for that matter). The decline of sexual activity in long-term straight couples is an oft-lamented and documented syndrome, especially on TV sitcoms (and, not incidentally, in this book), and has a lot to do with loss of novelty, overexposure to your partner and vice versa (a hottie seldom retains his heat when you're sharing a bathroom with him), fatigue, and everything else that happens to be going on in your life at the moment— all of which are effective desire-dampening agents.

Research is still sketchy about the syndrome, but one theory is that two-woman couples are more emotionally intimate than woman-man couples because women are allegedly more in touch with their feelings. As a result, their need for sex is less urgent because the partners are already connecting on an emotional level and deriving intimacy that way, or so the theory goes. Another theory is founded on the assumption that a couple's sex drive thrives in direct proportion to the testosterone levels of the partners. This would account for anecdotal evidence that long-term male-male couples have more sex than female-male couples, who in turn have more sex than female-female couples. Implicit in this theory is the supposition that men tend to initiate sexual activity more than women, which is at best a generality and at worst a biased one. For better or for worse, however, couples who have been together a long time tend to have a lot less sex than those who have just embarked on sexual intimacy, gay and straight alike.

"How long have you and Quinn been together?" I said.

"Almost three years. We met at a concert, hit it off, and have been together ever since."

"And things have been good until now?"

"I guess. We have our moments, of course, but so do all the other couples we know."

"Do you have any insight as to what might be causing your loss of interest? Are there any recent conflicts the two of you have had, or changes in the relationship?"

"Yes, I guess you could say that," she said. "Quinn had to leave her job and she's been taking it kind of hard, so we moved out here so I could go to work. A friend of mine has a sister who was looking to hire a physical therapist, so I interviewed, got the job, and here we are."

"Wouldn't it have been easier for you both to find work in the city?" I said.

"Not really. I've been out of the workforce for almost three years, but this old friend of mine talked me up to her sister so I was able to get an interview. And as for Quinn, she had a couple of offers, but they were for a lot less than she was making before. She was at this old, established Richmond law firm, you know, where the partners all belong to country clubs and play golf every weekend, that kind of place. She worked her tail off for seven years, and then, right when she's supposed to make partner, they inspect her résumé and find a—what did they call it?—a discrepancy. Seven years of work, completely lost, over a discrepancy.

"It's not as if she was practicing law without a license. You don't have to go to law school to be a lawyer, at least not in Virginia. So this whole thing about lying on her résumé is way over the top. Okay, maybe she shouldn't have made it look as if she had a law degree; I think that's what they were so ticked off about, you know, that she put the letters JD in there, so they thought she graduated. She did take some courses on campus, so she actually did go to law school for a while. But it really doesn't matter: Quinn says that in this state, you can practice law as long as you pass the bar, and Quinn passed the bar."

Andra's information was accurate; a newspaper story had recently appeared about law readers, people who study law and, in states that permit it, become attorneys without graduating from law school, assuming they have passed the bar exam.[2] While the practice is perfectly legal, it is not typical, and it sounded to me as if the law readers profiled in the article had probably been more forthcoming about their unconventional educations than Quinn had been with her employer. If Quinn had indicated on her résumé that she had earned a juris doctor degree without having graduated from law school, she had indeed lied.

"Getting back to you," I said, glancing at the clock, "can you pinpoint when your desire started flagging?"

"Well, ever since we moved here, Quinn has been kind of hard to get along with. Not that she's ever really easy to get along with. She doesn't have much patience for—what's that expression?—she doesn't suffer fools gladly, and as far as she's concerned, most people are fools. It's like she always thinks she's the smartest person in the room, which would be totally obnoxious, except she usually is the smartest person in the room, so you have to cut her some slack there, I guess. I'm usually good at getting along with her. But lately, she's been a little out of control."

"How do you mean?"

"Well, it's like . . . she's always liked sex to be a little, you know, a little rough. Nothing dangerous or really scary, but she likes to say things, to sound tough, when we're in bed. I go along with it because it's a turn-on for her, and it doesn't really bother me. But lately, she's gotten mean. She used to say stuff like, you know, she'd call me a nasty little bitch, stuff like that. But now she's started calling me some vicious stuff, the kind of things you'd expect to hear from a guy, and not a nice guy. It's a real turn-off, and I've told her so. But that just ramps up the excitement, at least for her. She gets into it, I get turned off, and we end up fighting. So sex is not something I'm interested in lately. I just want to avoid the whole thing, and that makes her even angrier.

"Which is exactly what she doesn't need. This whole job thing has been a disaster for Quinn, and I promised to do whatever it took to see her through. But it seems like the more I try to help her, the nastier she gets. It's like I can't do anything right lately. When this whole job thing happened, I said fine, I'll go back to work. So now I'm supporting both of us on a physical therapist's salary, which is a far cry from three hundred grand, let me tell you. When Quinn was pulling in the big bucks, I was a model wife; the house was perfect, the Sub-Zero was stocked, and we never ran out of champagne. We did save a little money, so we're actually in okay shape. And we can get by on what I'm making.

"But it's not as if Quinn couldn't find a job afterward. In, like, two weeks, she had an offer for a corporate position for two-fifty-five . . . I think. But she turned it down; she doesn't want to work for less than she was making before. She says she shouldn't have lost her job in the first place, and to work for a lower salary would be internalizing her old firm's opinion of her. So she's holding out for something that pays at least as much as her old job."

Quinn sounded rather narcissistic. A narcissist is someone who perceives him- or herself as special and unique and who behaves in ways calculated to elicit admiration and attention from others. The name derives from the myth of Narcissus, the beautiful Greek youth and scorner of maidenly affection who stooped to drink from a pool of water and fell in love with his reflection. So smitten was he with his own face that he was unable to tear himself away from the water, and thus he languished, pining and miserable, until he died. Narcissists have an exaggerated sense of their effect on the people around them, imagining that others are as preoccupied with their actions and accomplishments as they are themselves. They typically exhibit a sense of entitlement, manifested, I felt, by Quinn's refusal to consider working for less than her former salary. Another common hallmark of the condition is a lack of empathy; narcissists are notoriously self-centered and unable to see things from a vantage point other than their own. For all their eccentricities, narcissists are often highly intelligent, articulate, and entertaining, and can be a lot of fun to be around— that is, unless you're in an intimate relationship with one. Then it can be hell, as I suspect Andra knew only too well.

I was curious about Quinn, and at the end of the session, I asked Andra how she would feel about bringing Quinn to the next one. She said she was fine with the idea and would try to persuade her to come in.

A week later, they both appeared in my office. Quinn was in her early forties, taller than Andra, and dressed in a man-tailored shirt and slacks. She slouched in her chair and gazed stoically in my direction. When the session ended fifty minutes later, she had barely moved.

Whereas Andra was forthcoming, Quinn was reserved. Several times during the session, I noticed her eyes meandering about the walls of my office, fixing on a drawing my daughter had done in preschool or on the screensaver that unfolded continuously on my computer monitor. She said little, with the exception of one tart exchange when she took issue with Andra's description of her professional travails. "I did not quit, Andra," she said, her voice slicing through the air. "I was forced out. They left me no choice."

"Can you tell me a bit about what happened?" I said. Quinn shifted her gaze in my direction.

"What happened is that I made the mistake of thinking that a bunch of rich, white country-club types would accept someone like me into their pantheon of legal deities," she said. "The fact that I spent seven years working sixty, seventy, sometimes eighty hours a week didn't seem to matter. When it came to making partner, I was never going to qualify, that was clear—that is, to everyone but me. There's only one woman partner there—one out of sixteen. And she was the worst of all of them, a real sweetheart." Quinn exhaled derisively and directed her gaze out the window while Andra studied her lap.

"What about this woman partner?" I said.

"She instigated the whole thing. If it weren't for her, I'd probably still be there. But you know, I'm not sure we should get into this now. It's a long story, and this session is supposed to be about Andra, isn't it?"

I seized the opening. "You're right," I said. "Maybe we should take this up at another time, when we can speak privately." Quinn's head swiveled toward me.

"You want to see me alone? I'm sorry, but aren't we here to deal with Andra's issues?"

Andra's issues. Another characteristic of narcissists is that when they are in conflict with someone, it's always the other person's doing, never their own. I chose my words with care.

"Yes, absolutely," I said. "But you're the person closest to Andra, and your perspective is both unique and invaluable. You aren't obligated, of course, but if you're willing to come in on your own, and if Andra doesn't object to it, I think you could help me get the bigger picture. Andra, you can go home and think about it—"

"No, it's fine," Andra said, looking up. "I think it's a great idea." I turned to Quinn.

"We're not talking about me going into long-term analysis, are we?" Quinn said.

"No, not at all," I said. "But Andra's feelings are causing you to have some partnership problems, and I can better help you both get to the core of the problem if you'll come in and give me your take on things." She appraised me coolly.

"You think it will help Andra?"

"Yes, I do."

"Then I'll come in," she said.

When Quinn arrived for her session two days later, she ambled into my office at a leisurely pace; she was in no hurry to get started, and she made no attempt to hide it. When she had settled herself in the chair, she interlaced her fingers like a zipper and looked up.

"So, what did you want to talk about?" Quinn said.

"I was hoping you would talk about your relationship with Andra," I said.

"Well, she's having some struggles, and I think she's transferring her frustration onto me."

"What do you think she is struggling with?"

"She's struggling with everything: moving out here, living in a smaller house, going back to work. She's having a hard time adjusting to the change in our circumstances, and she's holding it against me."

"Why do you think she's doing that?"

"I think she's doing that because she liked staying home while I went to work. Who wouldn't? But I'm in a tough spot right now and I need her to be supportive, which she isn't, at least not in the way I need her to be."

"Can you be more specific?"

"Andra is acting as if she's the injured party, when she's the one who won't have sex with me. I'm the one with the complaint, not her. She accuses me of being distant, but when I come on to her, she pushes me away—she's tired, she's premenstrual, she's postmenstrual, she's arguing with her sister—and instead suggests we curl up and cuddle. Well, I'm not somebody who is satisfied with cuddling. Sex is important to me, and it used to be a big part of the relationship. But instead of sleeping with me, she's reading these self-help books. She thinks I've got an anger problem—as if I didn't have a right to have an anger problem."

"So what is it you're angry about?" She looked at me as if I were speaking in tongues.

"You're kidding, right? I thought we went through all this."

"You're referring to the way you were treated by your employer—"

"I was treated like crap by my employer. Look, you don't know what happened."

"Why don't you tell me?"

She did: how she worked like a dog for seven years, that her partner review was generally favorable, although a couple of clients had found her abrasive ("If I were a man, they would never have said that; it's just because I'm a lesbian"); that the lone female partner took it upon herself to go back through Quinn's dossier and call the law school listed on her résumé; that they told her Quinn had taken some night school courses but had never matriculated, let alone graduated from there, whereupon this woman had called a special partners' meeting to announce that not only had Quinn not graduated from law school, she had lied on her résumé, willfully misrepresented herself, and embarrassed her colleagues (and the firm) by allowing them to labor under the misapprehension that she had a law degree. Not only should the firm not make her a partner, this woman said, but it should terminate her employment and consider taking legal action against her.

In fact, the partners did not take legal action against Quinn and voted instead to allow her to resign. Citing the high quality of her work, two colleagues even offered to recommend her for other jobs, with the understanding that they would advise the person doing the hiring that Quinn did not have a law degree.

"It sounds as if you had some supporters there after all," I said. She stiffened.

"You call that support? Offering to chat me up to their cronies as long as they could warn them about my moral failings? That's not supportive; that's condescending."

"I suppose you could see it that way," I said carefully. "But you might also interpret it as an expression of confidence in your ability, considering the circumstances."

"What do you mean, 'considering the circumstances'? What are you saying?"

"I am saying that your colleagues felt betrayed by your lack of honesty, yet some still were willing to recommend you to people they knew. That's quite a testament to your skill as a lawyer, as well as their fundamental faith in you." Quinn stared stonily ahead, refusing to meet my eyes. I saw that we had run ten minutes over and told her I hoped she could come in the following week.

"I thought this was a one-shot thing," she said. "Why do you want me to come back?"

"Because I think you do have an anger problem," I said. "I think you are living in a state of rage about being forced out of your job, and it's eating away at you, at your partner, at your sex life, and ultimately at your relationship and your health—"

"Absolutely not!" she snapped. "This has absolutely nothing to do with my job. This is not about me; it's about the woman I live with, who couldn't keep her hands off me before and who is now refusing to have sex with me. This is about my partner, who, incidentally, is the person who came in for psychoanalysis in the first place, and the person who should be sitting here instead of me. You know, you're not a very good doctor. You've got a real attitude."

I told her that my attitude was probably a reaction to the hostility she had been expressing throughout the session, which made her even angrier. She then said she didn't want to see me again, but, oddly, demanded a referral to another psychiatrist. And she had requirements: it had to be a woman who was at least forty years old with a lot of experience—she didn't want a kid who was just out of medical school or someone who was going to ask her about her relationship with her father and how old she was when she was toilet-trained; it had to be someone well versed in treating people with anger problems, and it had to be someone outside the university. That ruled out about 95 percent of the people I might have recommended. I told Quinn I didn't know anyone who specialized in anger management, but I did know a psychiatrist in her fifties who had trained at the university and had not only a good success rate with her patients but also a no-nonsense therapeutic approach that I thought Quinn might like. I told Quinn her name and wrote it down on a piece of paper along with her phone number.

Quinn became furious. It just so happened that this doctor was and is a lesbian, and Quinn knew her. She started shouting, accusing me of recommending the doctor because she was homosexual and declaring I was even more sexist than the men who ruled the patriarchal medical establishment. I remained calm and said no, I had recommended this doctor because she was well trained, she was a woman, she was roughly my age, and she had a private practice in town; everyone else I might recommend was younger, and Quinn had said she didn't want someone younger.

But Quinn was not to be appeased. She got angrier and said the difficulty between us was emanating from me, that I was patronizing her and treating her like a fool, which she certainly was not; fools don't make three hundred thousand dollars a year. This blindness to her complicity in the conflict confirmed my impression that she probably suffered from narcissistic personality disorder.

There are two kinds of narcissists: those who believe they are nearly perfect and superior to others, and those who believe they should be that way but know they aren't and are deeply shamed by their shortcomings. In an attempt to hide their shame, they will sometimes present a grandiose exterior and other times try to get people to admire and compliment them. But when such people are narcissistically injured—that is, when someone confronts them with their imperfections or, as in Quinn's case, says, "You lied, you committed fraud, this could be illegal"—it hurts them. They are humiliated and ashamed but don't want to acknowledge being hurt, so instead they get enraged. Narcissists who believe they *are* perfect project their fury onto whomever they think caused their problem; narcissists who believe they *should be* perfect turn their rage inward and become depressed.

Quinn had endured a critical narcissistic injury when she was forced to resign, especially if she was able to see that the fiasco was, underneath it all, her own fault. She was both furious with her colleagues for catching

her in a lie and humiliated at being found out. Deeply ashamed, she subli-
mated her wrath and projected it onto the people around her, pelting Andra
with hostility for some time and venting her spleen with me. When Andra
withdrew sexually, Quinn gave her an ultimatum: Either you get help for
your problem—not *the* problem or *our* problem but *your* problem—or I
will withdraw the beneficent light of my favor. So Andra had come in for
treatment, only to learn that the problem was not hers alone.

This was a situation where anger obstructed the flow of the entire relationship, including sexual intimacy. Sex doesn't necessarily suffer when
a couple isn't getting along; some lovers find hostility invigorating and cultivate it for its aphrodisiac properties. But this was not the case with Andra
and Quinn, whose anger had reduced them to little more than housemates, and not very cordial ones at that.

Andra had an advantage because she was able to connect her loss of
desire to Quinn's maltreatment of her. Quinn, however, was less lucid
about the state of their union. So fortified was she against accepting responsibility for her troubles, she was blinded to the toll they had taken on
her and, by extension, her relationship. To heal the rupture that separated
Quinn from her partner, she would first have to recognize her narcissism
and the lopsided view it offered of her place among others. She would
have to relinquish her self-aggrandizing fantasy of personal perfection in
favor of a more realistic and less exalted concept of herself.

I do not know what happened to this couple. The day that Quinn
stalked out of my office, livid with rage, was the last time I saw her. I do
not know if she ever called the psychiatrist I recommended, nor whether
she commenced treatment with someone else. Nor have I seen Andra
since her joint session with Quinn, although she left a message to say that
she had found our work helpful but had decided to hold off on further
treatment. The reality is that many people leave a psychiatrist's care with
unresolved problems. I like to think that, as furious as Quinn was with me,
she did not reject everything I said and that an insight may have pierced
the armor of her fortified self and penetrated to the tender parts within.
Then, perhaps, she might gather the courage to see herself in a healthier
perspective and regard her flaws as evidence of her humanity rather than
a repudiation of it.

Are Repressed Emotions Hampering Your Sex Life?

1. **Are you easily distracted during sex? During any kind of intimate exchange with your partner?**

2. **If so, what thoughts, worries, and anxieties derail the increasing momentum of excitement?** If these distractions seem trivial, do you think they signal a larger issue you may not be acknowledging?

3. **If you are in a steady relationship, does your sexual ardor correlate with how you are getting along with your partner?**

4. **If you feel less desire for your partner now than you did earlier in your relationship, do you know why? Does it bother you?**

   ■ Are there aspects of your partner that used to irritate or frustrate you that no longer seem to do so? If so, is it possible you are repressing these feelings and that they are affecting your sexual interest in your partner?

5. **When you were growing up, how was anger expressed in your family?**

   ■ Did you express anger as a child? If so, what form did it take? How did your parents respond to your childhood expressions of anger?

6. **How do you handle your anger now?** Do you blow up, let it simmer, or repress it so well that others have to remind you that it's there?

   ■ Do you think you may be repressing feelings of frustration and anger? If so, what do you think is the source of these feelings?

   ■ If your partner is not the source of your anger, who else or what else may be causing it?

~ Is there a family dynamic that displeases or upsets you? If so, have you discussed the problem with the people involved? If not, why not?

~ Is there a situation at work that is upsetting you? Again, if there is, have you discussed the problem with the people involved? If not, why not?

7. **Do you have anxiety symptoms that could be manifestations of underlying anger?**

8. **If so, are these symptoms aggravated by tension between you and your partner?**

CHAPTER 8

Under the Covers with the Lights Out
The Hidden Face of Shame

> We live in an atmosphere of shame. We are
> ashamed of everything that is real about us;
> ashamed of ourselves, of our relatives, of our in-
> comes, of our accents, of our opinions, of our expe-
> rience, just as we are ashamed of our naked skins.
> —GEORGE BERNARD SHAW, *Man and Superman*

Nowhere is shame more pervasive than in the realm of sex. No aspect of human endeavor is more freighted with cringing and
wretched self-denigration than the urge to connect intimately with another person. It makes slaves and fools of us all and, unlike the tax code,
offers loopholes for neither the rich, the famous, nor the clueless. We
cackle into our double lattes when we open the newspaper and read about
the married governor and father of two who resigns from office when he is
revealed to have appointed his boyfriend to a high-level government job or
the perky middle school teacher from the heartland who goes to prison for
taking a sixth grader as her lover and marries him after she has served her
sentence. We roll our eyes at the shocking lack of character displayed by
these weakened vessels of unbridled lust, while in the recesses of our consciousness, a sneering voice whispers that there, but for the will and grace
of a higher spiritual power, go we.

I am not saying that we are all closeted homosexuals and latent child
molesters. I am saying that sexual hunger is a feral force, and most of us
struggle at some point in our lives to cover its claw marks on our skin.
There's the person at work you have never gotten along with until one day
you are wedged together in the elevator and you pick up the musky scent
of his skin and you are inexplicably stricken with longing. Or you go to

pick up your kids at their friends' house and are ambushed by a twinge of desire when you see their daddy mowing the lawn without a shirt. The fact that his kids play with your kids and that you're good friends with his wife doesn't unman him in the least: for a fleeting, sun-kissed moment, he is not the playmates' papa but a virile, muscular, glistening hunk of manhood (especially if he's using a push mower).

Within a nanosecond, shame sets in. *What's up with that?* you wonder, shrinking back from yourself. *That's Steve, Connor's father. He's a friend; I see him all the time. I'm happily married. How can I be feeling this? What am I thinking?*

You are not thinking, of course; you are feeling, which is precisely what normal, robust people do. A healthy woman sees an attractive man: Why shouldn't she feel something? Why shouldn't her body respond? It does, naturally, with a gusto that has nothing to do with relatedness or commitment or love and everything to do with the lusty, primal urge of the species to perpetuate itself.

Why do we equate the quickening of desire with something illicit and shameful? Rather than celebrate the life force, why do we fret that there is something wrong with us when we are moved by intimations of grace? We admire a girlfriend's child without fear that we love our own any the less; why, then, can we not acknowledge her husband's beauty without anticipating the imminent arrival of a serpent bearing a Golden Delicious?

Because, according to our culture—and just about every culture on earth—a woman is not supposed to feel anything sexual for anyone except the man to whom she is married (if she is partnered with a woman, most cultures decree that she shouldn't be feeling anything for her in the first place). We are taught to deny the sex between our legs, deprecate its extravagant promise of pleasure, manage its effusions with tidy dispatch, and perfume it into floral-scented submission. And we are quick learners, spending billions of dollars every year on feminine hygiene products to protect us from the horrors of our femaleness. (As for masculine hygiene products, the only one I've ever run across is a bar of soap.) God forbid we should have an accident and bleed through our clothes; many a woman has a story of when this happened and she had to make a sudden escape, sidling out of the room with her back to the wall. Most of us know the thrill of frantically rinsing out the crotches of our underwear in the sink of a public restroom and returning, soggy-seated, to our companions, whom we hope are none the wiser.

With so much of woman's sexuality suffused with embarrassment, it is no wonder that we strive to keep it quiet; even those of us acquainted with our sexual selves are loath to reveal the brazen hussy lurking beneath our unisex T-shirts. So we ignore, if not stifle, the wench within and subdue her rowdy presence with a bashful smile.

But what of the woman who has suppressed her sexual self, for whom sex is so intertwined with shame that they are one and the same? Countless women live with men in marriages and partnerships that are, by their standards, happy and secure; who insist they enjoy making love with their husbands, yet whose core sexual identities are so encrusted with layers of self-loathing that their defining characters are profoundly obscured. It is only when a crisis cracks open the marriage's amiable façade that the underlying decay is exposed. These cases are notoriously hard to treat, as they confound logic and inhabit the shadowy territory between psychology and pathology.

Peg: Guilt-Edged Shame

In the mid-1990s, I treated a woman named Peg who came in for help with depression. She was fifty-three years old and an adjunct instructor in the education department of a small private university. Peg had been married for twenty-eight years to Philip, the managing editor of a midsize metropolitan daily newspaper. Their only child, Sheila, had graduated from college a few years earlier and relocated to New York City, where she worked as an editorial assistant at *Vogue*.

Peg said she often felt blue in autumn but was missing Sheila more acutely than usual this year. There were other factors in play as well: it was the twentieth anniversary of the death of her mother, a heavy smoker who had suffered a massive heart attack at a young age while visiting Peg, Philip, and five-year-old Sheila at their suburban Chicago home. Louise was only twenty when Peg was born and widowed several years later when Peg's father died fighting in World War II. Louise's natural intensity was magnified by her husband's death; straitlaced and demanding, she raised

Peg under the banner of imperial motherhood, brooking no opposition from her daughter. Peg chafed under Louise's rigidity but chose a path of reconciliation rather than rebellion, acceding to her mother's wishes whenever possible and choosing her battles judiciously. Now Peg was the same age as her mother had been when she died. Melancholy would descend over Peg every November as the anniversary approached, but this year her anguish was crippling.

Peg spoke of her mother's death in halting cadences. Several times she was overcome with sobbing and paused to collect herself. The extent of her grief was remarkable, considering the antagonism that had plagued the women's relationship. Louise was one of those mothers whose daughters squander much of their lives trying to please, with little success. Louise was unable to perceive the boundary between herself and her daughter and would vehemently oppose Peg's decisions when they did not mirror her own. To Louise, Peg never outgrew her status as a fatherless young girl in dire need of her mother's guidance.

Things between the women deteriorated when Peg, Philip, and Sheila left their apartment in Louise's downtown neighborhood and bought a house in the suburbs with an in-ground swimming pool. Louise was appalled—how could the mother of a toddler be so foolish as to buy a house with a built-in drowning hazard? Peg's reassurances that a fence would be installed did little to assuage her mother's fears; no sooner would Louise arrive for a visit than she would begin muttering, castigating her daughter's poor judgment and her son-in-law's refusal to make her see reason. Philip exercised considerable restraint during these episodes, remaining above the fray and allowing Peg to defuse the crisis. Peg was twisted in knots; any suggestion she might make, however tactful, that her mother was overstepping her authority would send the woman into a rage and storming out of the house. On one level, this would have provided Peg with a measure of relief, but she felt too loyal to her mother to risk wounding her and escalating the conflict.

On the night she died, Louise announced after dinner that she was going outside to smoke a Chesterfield and get some air. Peg became concerned when she finished cleaning up from dinner and realized her mother had still not returned. Grabbing her coat, she went outside and found Louise unconscious. Peg said she had blocked out the exact sequence of events but she knew that she had screamed and Philip had come running outside barefoot. By the time the ambulance arrived, her mother was dead.

Peg did not offer many details, but I knew that she and Philip sold the house shortly thereafter and left Illinois. Philip took a job at the paper he now managed, Peg began teaching at the college, and Sheila grew up with little memory of her grandmother or her death.

Meanwhile, Peg's periodic bouts of melancholy and annual depressions gradually worsened until she came for help. In treatment, Peg talked about the trauma of her mother dying at her house and how fresh the memory seemed even twenty years later. She also spoke of the personal liberation she felt now that her mother was gone but then would remark on how guilty it made her feel to say it. When I asked about her relationship with her husband, she said things were fine but would not elaborate.

Peg started taking an antidepressant that worked pretty well, although it sometimes upset her stomach. After five months, she felt well enough to stop therapy; a few months after that, she called for advice on how best to phase out the medication. I heard from her once more when she left a message saying she had successfully stopped the antidepressant and, outside of occasional blue moods, was doing fine.

I was surprised, then, when she called one January day to say she needed to see me on a matter of great urgency. It was seven years since we had last spoken, and my recollection of that conversation was pleasant and upbeat. Now she sounded distraught but would not say anything other than that she was in a crisis and needed to see me. I told her to come in.

Peg arrived and sat down without smiling. Her hair was grayer than I remembered it, but she would have been about sixty now, so that made sense. Her demeanor was what struck me; wan and pinched, she looked as if she had not slept in a long time. I asked her what was going on. She looked up at me, and I saw the eyes of a frightened animal, inarticulate and poised for flight.

"I don't know. It's not easy to talk about. I've never talked about this kind of thing before. But I have this problem, this condition. I don't know how I got it, and Philip swears I didn't get it from him, and I know I didn't, but . . . he hasn't touched me since we got back and I don't know what to do."

"Got back from where, Peg?"

"From the Caribbean; that's where it started. We went on a cruise to celebrate our thirty-fifth wedding anniversary. We took Sheila with us. We booked a room at the Plaza, flew up to New York, and left from there.

"We'd been out for only three days when I got this . . . these blisters . . . down there. They really hurt, and we couldn't have . . . relations."

She could barely get the words out. I knew from our work eleven years earlier that Peg didn't feel comfortable discussing sex—I had once asked about her sexual relationship with Philip, and she had stammered so awkwardly I had dropped the subject—so I didn't press her now other than to ask if she had been examined by a doctor. She stared down at the handkerchief, which her hands had twisted into a tight cotton cable. She nodded and wept again.

"The doctor says it's . . . it's . . ." She murmured something I couldn't quite hear. It took at least thirty seconds for her to look up again.

"Peg, what is it?" I said.

"It's . . . herpes."

Herpes? Peg had herpes? I could hardly have been more startled had she announced she had a prostate condition.

"Peg, what does Philip say? What does he think is going on?"

"Philip? I can't talk to him about things down there. I've never talked to anyone about it in my life, except just now, with you. It's bad enough I had to tell him I had herpes. He looked at me as if I'd told him I had cancer.

"I don't understand. I've been married for thirty-five years. I've never been with anyone but my husband. He . . . I . . . we haven't been . . . my marriage is falling apart. Philip hardly looks at me in the morning; half the time he leaves for work so early I don't even see him. I feel so dirty. I can't face him. I'm so ashamed, so, so ashamed."

My heart went out to my patient. How could a sixty-year-old woman who had gone through pregnancy and childbirth be too shy to talk with her husband about *this*? It was hard to envision living with a man that long and still being too bashful to speak about a skin eruption, even one *down there*. Her use of the expression was sad and quaint and reminded me of the way girls used to talk about their bodies when I was growing up. There was no such thing as vagina monologues, let alone dialogues. We spoke of a redheaded friend coming to visit each month, or how this girl had let that boy touch her "below the waist." Nowadays, with people publicly jabbering on their cell phones about hot dates and the government snooping into what books we read and who has had an abortion, we forget that for some people, the loss of privacy can be a matter of life and death.

More to the point, it simply did not make sense. How could a woman of such prudish sensibilities have contracted a venereal disease? I had not met Philip, and it was always possible that he was the source of the infection. But assuming Peg knew him well enough to vouch for his fidelity—and that was the assumption I had to work with—it was ludicrous to picture this couple committing adultery with herpes-ridden floozies and gigolos.

I went back and pored over Peg's medical records. Her gynecologist had diagnosed her with herpes even though three different cultures had been taken, tested, and turned up negative. That was odd; when test results come up negative three times in a row, that usually rules out the condition. Compounding the mystery was the fact that the blisters weren't responding to the medication Peg had received. Surely an eruption of herpes, a virus, would have subsided after three weeks of treatment.

I was confounded. Something was wrong with this picture. I stared at Peg's chart. If she were younger and more liberated sexually, I might have been more cynical about her avowals of fidelity. But this woman had never had sex with anyone except her husband and claimed never to have talked about sex with anyone outside my office. How could she contract herpes in her sixties?

I recalled something one of my medical school professors once said: Sometimes you hear hooves and you think it's a horse, but it turns out to be a zebra. Suddenly, it galloped into view: what Peg probably had was an outbreak of herpes zoster, better known as shingles. Shingles is caused by varicella zoster, the same herpesvirus that causes chicken pox. When you get chicken pox, the varicella zoster virus travels into your nerve cells and remains there, lying dormant in your nervous system, whence it may rouse itself at any time and manifest as shingles, a very painful epidermal eruption of fluid-filled blisters that look and feel just like genital herpes (an infection caused by herpes simplex, the other herpesvirus). We do not know definitively what causes latent herpes zoster virus to reactivate as shingles, but it tends to happen when a person is under stress, exhausted, fighting an infection, or in some cases, on a drug regimen that suppresses the body's natural immunity.

The more I thought about it, the more certain I was. This diagnosis made sense for this patient; it felt right. I phoned Peg and told her to call her gynecologist and go back for reevaluation. She was skeptical because she had never heard of shingles occurring in the genital area, but I assured her that it was possible. She went back to the doctor, and sure enough—it was shingles.

But Peg continued to flounder. She felt tainted and guilty, although of what she could not say. She described a sensation of feeling defiled, as if what had once been good and pure within her was irrevocably lost. She avoided all but the most superficial interactions with her husband, remaining in bed until he left for work and reading in her study until after he had turned in for the evening. On the rare occasions when Philip initiated lovemaking, she shrank away from him. Philip was staying later at the newsroom and becoming increasingly withdrawn at home. Peg was becoming increasingly distraught.

I coaxed out more details about their intimate life. Peg said she had always felt squeamish about sex, wearing flannel nightgowns to bed and insisting on total darkness when she and Philip made love. It had always been this way, even when they were younger. She said she had enjoyed their lovemaking but always felt guilty afterward, as if she'd done something dirty. She also said she preferred not to disrobe when having relations but would allow Philip to rearrange her nightgown as needed to proceed with the act.

Peg spoke of Philip with affection and confided that, years before, he had given her a sexy outfit for Valentine's Day—a corsetlike affair with red satin garters—but she had never worn it because just looking at it made her uncomfortable, and picturing herself in it made her redden with shame. She then recounted an episode from when she was thirteen years old. She had asked her mother if she could have a miniskirt for her birthday. Instead of the skirt, she had gotten a lecture about the two kinds of females in the world: good girls like Peg and sluttish ones who used their bodies to seduce men. Louise's lesson had stuck.

Louise—of course! Themes from our earlier work resurfaced—Louise's hypercritical personality, her death in Peg's house . . . I knew she had been gone for nearly thirty years, but I was convinced that something about her—the way she had treated Peg as a child and her dismissive attitude toward her as an adult—held clues to Peg's problems.

"Peg, if I recall correctly, you used to become depressed every year on the anniversary of your mother's death, is that right?" I said.

"Yes, every November," Peg said. "But it hasn't been that bad the last few years. I distract myself by preparing final exams and grading papers."

"And the cruise was in December?"

"Yes, right before Christmas."

"Peg, think back if you can to the time leading up to the cruise. How was your state of mind?"

"I didn't have much time to obsess about my mother, if that's what you mean. I thought about the anniversary as it grew closer, but I was busy with Thanksgiving, and then final exams, and then packing for the trip, so I didn't get as caught up in it as I have in the past."

"And did your good mood continue in New York and on the cruise until the shingles began?" She paused, and a disconcerted look passed over her face.

"You know, that's strange," she said.

"What's strange?"

"I'd forgotten until now. Something funny happened on the ship. After we unpacked we went exploring and ended up by this enormous swimming pool. It was December in New York and freezing cold, and the pool had a cover on it. I had a funny reaction; it reminded me . . . it made me feel . . ."

Peg stopped and looked up uncertainly. I watched as the color drained from her face.

"Peg, what is it?"

"The pool," she murmured.

"The pool?"

"Yes. That's where I found her."

"Found who, Peg?"

I saw the face of a ghost.

"My mother. I found her in the pool. That's where I found her. I never told you before; I couldn't bear to say it. But that's where I found her, floating in the pool."

Peg was sobbing now. Gradually, the story came out. There had been an argument that night at dinner, and Louise had jumped up from the table, snatched her coat, cigarettes, and lighter, and stormed outside. Philip took Sheila upstairs to give her a bath, and Peg started cleaning up.

Peg thought she should give her mother a chance to smoke a cigarette and cool off before trying to talk to her. When she finished the dishes, she realized that her mother hadn't returned, so she went outside to look for her. To her horror, Peg found Louise floating facedown in the swimming pool. The rest was pretty much as she had described it before: Peg screamed, Philip called an ambulance, and the paramedics pronounced Louise dead at the scene. An autopsy revealed she had suffered a major coronary and fallen into the pool, where she drowned. The pathologist said she almost certainly would have died even if she had collapsed at the dinner table, but the image of her mother floating in the frigid water seared Peg's soul. Compounding the anguish was the shattering irony of the episode: in Peg's view, her consistent repudiation of Louise's warnings about the pool had proven calamitously ill founded. Louise had been right all along—about the pool, the house, the move to the suburbs, everything. As the ambulance pulled away that night, Peg remained in the backyard, paralyzed with horror. When Philip tried to lead her back inside, she asked him to put Sheila in the car and drive them to a hotel. The next day Philip brought suitcases of clothes for his wife and daughter. Peg never slept in the house again.

The family left the Midwest, but Peg's shame moved with her. Peg spoke of her mother as a selfless single parent who had sacrificed her youth and personal gratification for her daughter's sake. She gilded her mother's memory with layers of guilt, rehabilitating her from a scold to a prescient saint. Her mother was right; she had always been right.

"She warned me it was dangerous, she told me something would happen. So I made sure my baby never, ever was out there alone. I kept my baby safe. And the more she nagged me, the more I told her, 'Look—Sheila is fine. You worry too much—would you just please trust me to protect my own child?' So that's what she got for her trouble: a terrible death. She was only fifty-three years old.

"What was she doing out there? Why couldn't she smoke on the patio? She hated that pool! It's like she did it on purpose, to spite me, to prove that she was right and I was wrong." She looked up, an expression of horror twisting her face.

"My God, how can I even *say* such a thing? She's dead because of me. You know, if she'd lived, she'd only be eighty now. She could still be alive. I killed my own mother. I am so . . . so . . . so ashamed, so horribly ashamed."

If ever there was a case that illustrated the convoluted interplay of woman's psychology and sexuality, this is it. There is no single thread that, if you followed it to its source, would reveal the origin of Peg's problem. Instead, there are numerous intertwined strands of feeling and memory, fact and myth, love and revulsion. Reading about Peg's therapy sessions and seeing her words on the page, you can pick out a fiber here, a filament there, that suggests a connection between an ancient scar and a freshly opened wound. There were undoubtedly numerous lectures and arguments, but one stands out in the patient's memory: her request as a young girl for a miniskirt and her mother's harsh rebuke. Peg learned long ago how to coexist with her mother; rather than rebel, she accepted what came her way and wove the string of invective into a shroud to cover herself.

Peg grew up, obedient yet sturdy, and made her way. The scope of her intelligence was limited only by the shame that shriveled her nascent sexual self. She graduated from college, fell in love with Philip, married him, and bore a child. She functioned within the multiple intimacies of marriage, yet would not allow her husband to see her naked. She lined the bedroom draperies so light could not penetrate when they were drawn and wore cotton nightgowns from Austria with tiny printed flowers and high, lace-trimmed necklines. Philip wished she were less self-conscious but learned to accommodate her eccentricity. She was a wonderful person, after all, a constant wife and loving mother, and they had sex frequently enough to satisfy him and covertly enough to mollify her. Before they were thirty years old, they had established a template for intimacy that would define their marriage for decades to come.

Now, years later, Peg's outbreak of shingles had sparked a psychological crisis. Why did the lesions erupt when they did, and what did they mean? The varicella zoster virus tends to resurface when the body's natural resistance is compromised, which in Peg's case may have resulted from psychological distress. She said she had not had time to dwell on ghosts from her mother's death that particular November, but I suspect they had haunted her nonetheless. At sixty, Peg was already seven years older than her mother was when she died, a footnote that would not have escaped her guilt-ridden attention. Fatigued and anxious, she was both eager to go on vacation with her husband and daughter and riddled with guilt and shame. Peg was living with more than enough stress to trigger an outbreak of shingles.

But shingles was not the crisis; rather, it was Peg's shame that had catalyzed the crisis. Had the blisters appeared on her abdomen or face, they would have had a far less traumatic effect on Peg's state of mind; also, they would probably have been diagnosed correctly. But the location of the blisters, compounded with a (mis)diagnosis of genital herpes, exacerbated her distress and inflamed her shame. So appalled was she at her allegedly sordid state that she could not bring herself to speak honestly with her husband of thirty-five years—a marriage that they were in the midst of celebrating—about her confusion and pain. Instead, she retreated within herself, fleeing the one person whose love might redeem her.

It took Peg nearly eight months of work and weekly therapy sessions to get to where she could grieve for her mother and renounce enough of her guilt and shame to allow Philip to touch her again. When she did, it was with a renewed sense of erotic possibility. They began making love in the light of a candle, and Peg allowed Philip to see her unclothed.

"It's intense, and it's still sometimes hard to do," she said. "There's much more feeling, much more tenderness. And I welcome it. But it makes me sad, too. I keep thinking of how much time we lost, especially when we were younger and I was a lot more lovely than I am now. Philip always wanted to look at me, and I wouldn't let him. Now that I'm able to let him, all he gets to see is an older version of the young girl he fell in love with. All those years that we might have loved each other better, that I might have let him love me, all lost, wasted, gone. It breaks my heart."

Rochelle: DES Daughter

Rochelle was referred to me by her gynecologist, who thought she needed help dealing with unresolved grief over her difficulty having children. She was forty-five, married to her second husband, and had had two miscarriages, one during her first marriage and another during her second. She attributed the miscarriages to pelvic abnormalities she had sustained as a result of being exposed to diethylstilbestrol (DES) while her mother was pregnant with her. Rochelle's parents were still alive, but she seldom saw them. She had one sibling, a sister named Sheryl, who lived in another state and with whom she stayed in touch.

Earlier, I talked about the introduction of DES and its wide use in the 1950s and 1960s. The drug was thought to prevent miscarriage and was prescribed widely for women who had experienced uterine bleeding early in pregnancy. By the end of the 1960s, doctors noticed that an unusually large number of young women were being diagnosed with clear-cell adenocarcinoma of the vagina and cervix, a rare form of cancer previously seen only in elderly women. Researchers began studying these young women to learn what, if anything, they had in common. It turned out that their mothers had all taken DES in the early stages of pregnancy.

The connection between this rare cancer and in utero exposure to DES sparked further investigation, which revealed the prevalence of uterine deformities and other reproductive problems in young women whose mothers had taken the drug. DES had long shown itself to be ineffectual against miscarriage, and in light of its apparent connection to catastrophic cervical and vaginal problems, the U.S. Food and Drug Administration outlawed its use in 1971. But the tragedy was far from over: from 1938 to 1971, between five million and ten million people were exposed to DES, including women who had taken the drug and the children they had borne while under its influence. Boys exposed in utero to DES seemed to have suffered no ill effects. But millions of girls exposed to the substance were born with uterine deformities or developed cancers that devastated their ability to have children of their own.

Rochelle had been married for ten years to Owen, whom she described as a gentle Paul Bunyan type of guy. He worked on an organic farm owned by his cousins and attended a Friends meeting several Sundays a month, to which Rochelle accompanied him with burgeoning interest. She told me this with a sardonic half smile, citing her Jewish background and her mother's fear that she would become a Quaker. "My mother fed me oatmeal for years," she said, "so now it's payback time."

Rochelle said a defining event in her life had been the miscarriage she had suffered when she was twenty-six and married to her first husband. Jerome was a nice enough fellow, earned a good living, and came from a wealthy family. He wooed Rochelle with five-course dinners in five-star restaurants and a single-mindedness that distracted her from the lack of common feeling between them. His attention made her feel important, and her mother lobbied energetically on his behalf. Despite some misgivings, Rochelle agreed to marry him.

Not long after the engagement, Rochelle went to her gynecologist for birth control pills. During the exam, he detected pelvic abnormalities consistent with in utero exposure to DES. Shaken and disbelieving, she went home and confronted her mother, who told her that yes, she had taken DES when she was pregnant with Rochelle.

"I was upset," Rochelle said. "I'd never heard my mother mention having a miscarriage before I was born, and I wanted to know why she took the stuff, I wanted to understand. So I asked her, 'Did you have problems having a baby? Did you have a miscarriage before you had me?' And she said no, she didn't have a miscarriage. But she did have a friend who was pregnant at the same time she was, and this friend started to bleed and her doctor told her about this new drug that would stop the bleeding. And so my mother, who is a world-class hypochondriac, goes to her doctor, lies and tells him she's bleeding, and talks him into giving her this wonderful new drug.

"She tells me this like it's no big deal, and I feel like I'm going to pass out. I got so dizzy, I had to sit down. So I kind of lost it, and I started to cry, and I guess I was yelling at her, and you know what she says? She says she's not about to commit suicide because of a decision she made twenty years ago for me—*for me!*—and if I think I'm going to make her feel guilty about it, I can just forget it." Rochelle's mother clinched the episode by telling Rochelle that if she had any hope of marrying this nice boy Jerome, she should keep her mouth shut; there would be plenty of time after the wedding to explain the situation to him.

Rochelle and Jerome had been married for more than two years before she summoned the courage to divulge the secret. She might not have told him then were it not for the fact that they had been trying to conceive for nearly a year with no success. Rochelle said she felt she had wronged

Jerome by not telling him sooner and regretted that she had caved in to her mother's decree of secrecy. She was also anxious about Jerome's reaction and feared he would experience buyer's remorse, as she put it. Rationally, Rochelle knew that being a DES daughter did not necessarily mean she could never have children, and she believed that a woman's essential worth transcended her fertility. Nevertheless, she said that she had felt like damaged goods ever since the doctor had discovered the deformities and had been loath to tell anyone about it, including—and perhaps especially—her husband.

Jerome was hurt that she had not told him sooner. But his resentment was short-lived: two weeks later, Rochelle learned she was pregnant.

Rochelle described the ensuing months as a uniquely happy time. The pregnancy dispelled her feelings of inadequacy, and she experienced a newfound sense of well-being and acceptance. Both her family and Jerome's bided their time quietly until the first trimester was over and then spoke of little other than the new baby. But the idyll ended abruptly in the seventeenth week, when Rochelle began hemorrhaging and was rushed to the hospital. Two days later, she lost the baby and plummeted into a depression that lasted for the better part of a year. Jerome, ill equipped to cope with the needs of his severely depressed young wife, flung himself into his work and away from Rochelle. The marriage could not withstand the stress, and several years later, Rochelle and Jerome divorced.

Rochelle went to work for a small company that sold high-end building supplies and was soon managing the office. On summer mornings she would attend a local farmer's market to stock up on produce, and it was there that she met Owen. Rochelle had been divorced for nearly five years and, at thirty-five, had had her fill of romantic flings. She said she was immediately drawn to Owen's friendliness and guileless smile. She began lingering at his booth and struck up conversations about how to cook the mysterious-looking squashes he sold. He offered to cook dinner for her, and she agreed. Before long, they were living together, and two years after they met, they married.

Rochelle described the early days with Owen as blissful. He was strong and much bigger than she, yet gentle and considerate. The seventh of eight children, he was accustomed to taking care of himself. Owen liked to cook, helped with the laundry, and enjoyed tinkering around the eighty-year-old farmhouse they lived in. He found Rochelle extremely attractive and in his typical self-effacing way was perennially astounded that she could be so drawn to him. Their sexual relationship was erotically and emotionally charged, and Rochelle reveled in her good fortune. It sounded corny, she said, but she felt she had found the man of her dreams.

The subject of children came up early in their courtship. Rochelle told Owen about the miscarriage and that she might not be able to have children. He accepted the news with equanimity and said that his siblings had produced plenty of kids and having his own was not necessary to his happiness. They wed content with the notion that their marriage would probably comprise just the two of them.

And so it was with shock and trepidation that Rochelle learned she was pregnant again. She was thirty-eight, Owen was forty, and they were quietly and cautiously ecstatic.

"I knew better than to get too excited, but I did anyway," Rochelle said. "I couldn't help myself. I'd already had a miscarriage, and I thought maybe I'd paid my dues and now I could have some happiness. His parents were so happy for us. They gave me all this attention they'd never given me before. I mean, it wasn't as if they'd been rejecting me, but all of a sudden I felt this warmth and acceptance. It felt as if I could finally be like the other women in the family.

"It didn't work out, of course. I miscarried in my eleventh week. It wasn't as bad as the first time; miscarrying in your third month isn't quite as horrific as when it happens in your fifth. But I was also older, and there was a finality to it that was hard to accept. Owen felt bad, too, but it wasn't the same for him as it was for me. He tried his best, though, I guess."

But now the marriage was foundering. Rochelle said she and Owen had not made love in a year. They still loved each other and enjoyed holding each other in bed, but there was no significant physical intimacy.

"It's mostly me," she said. "I haven't felt normal sexually for five or six years now."

"Since the miscarriage?" I said.

"I guess, or maybe a little after. It's as if something shifted inside me. I can't . . . I can't get into it. And it hurts. Owen's not exactly small."

"Has sex always been painful for you?"

"No, it used to be okay. But now it isn't, now it hurts. But a lot of things have changed between us."

"Can you identify anything specific?"

"Well, we fight more. We never used to argue, but now we do a lot."

"What do you argue about?"

"Nothing and everything. He's just, I don't know, he does things that never used to bother me before but now they drive me crazy. I think I'm still mad at him for what he said. We had this argument a long time ago. I think I'm past it, but it just comes up again. And when I think about it, I get angry all over again and feel this empty space inside."

The cataclysmic conversation had begun harmlessly. It was two weeks after the miscarriage, and Rochelle was talking about how much she had wanted this baby, how she knew Owen's parents wanted him to have kids and were disappointed that she wasn't able to have any, how she felt everyone was measuring her womanhood and finding it lacking.

"He looked up at me," Rochelle said, "and he said, 'Look, you're making too much of this'—that's what he said—'you're making too much of this. We don't need a baby to be happy. We've been fine until now, and we can still be fine.'

"Those were his exact words. It was six years ago, but I remember it as clear as day. I couldn't believe it. This was my husband, the person I thought knew me better than anyone. But he didn't know me at all.

"A shock went through me. I got this terrible feeling, as if I didn't know him, like he was a stranger I was living with. If he really knew me, he couldn't have said that."

That conversation marked a turning point in the marriage. Owen tried to explain his meaning, but Rochelle would not be moved. To her, his words symbolized a fatal breach in their connection. All she could hear was a dismissal of her feelings, a trivialization of her grief. She appeared to be incapable of imagining another interpretation of the words her husband had used, another way of seeing, thinking, feeling. That Owen had meant to comfort her was immaterial. For Rochelle, the words had an innate significance that transcended whatever Owen may have meant by them. Owen had betrayed the sacred oneness she imagined they shared, and she could not forgive him.

In subsequent sessions, Rochelle returned frequently to her anger, which she seemed to have focused with laserlike intensity on her husband. His crime—trying, however clumsily, to comfort her—did not seem to merit the severity of the sentence she had imposed upon him. She knew she was angry and occasionally brought it up to him in the context of other disagreements. And he would apologize and say that he had not meant what she had taken his words to mean, but none of that fixed it for her. It was as if the break could not be repaired and she wanted it that way.

Rochelle was stewing in a bitter brew of her own making, and it had seeped throughout the fabric of the marriage. She had made it clear to Owen that sex was no longer part of their relationship, and he had grown to accept the drought with grim resignation. It seemed to me that he had embraced her view of him and accepted the loss of sexual intimacy as the price he had to pay for his catastrophic utterance.

At this point, you might wonder why I did not include this story in the chapter about unresolved anger and worry. And I might have: Rochelle's seething resentment toward her husband certainly qualified her for inclusion in that group. But, as with many cases in this book, Rochelle's story spans several categories and defies simple definition. She was angry, that much was obvious. But the quality of her anger—the tenacity with which she held on to it despite her husband's pleas for forgiveness, and her indictment of him as the author of her anguish—made me want to look beyond the obvious source, beyond the argument, toward something deeper.

What would make a woman unable or unwilling to forgive a beloved husband? Rochelle had described Owen as the man of her dreams. Yet she was stonewalling him and, in so doing, had hastened the demise of their sexual relationship and the marriage beyond that. Rochelle's first marriage had collapsed after a miscarriage, so there was a precedent for what was happening now. Still, she had been much younger then, and the match itself had been far less satisfying than her current one. She had had more than a decade of history with Owen, during which he had been a faithful and engaged partner. Why could she not trust his love enough to forgive him?

I thought back to when Rochelle had spoken about the first miscarriage and her anguish at learning of her mother's ruse to get a prescription for DES. She had also spoken of her sister, Sheryl, who was three years younger, married, and the mother of two teenage sons. Rochelle struggled with the knowledge that her mother had not taken the drug when she was pregnant with Sheryl and alluded to harboring resentment toward her sister, who had produced two children, while Rochelle was unable to bear any.

"I know it isn't my sister's fault that she was born okay and I wasn't. And I know my mother didn't know what she was doing when she lied her way into that prescription. But I'm the one who has to live with it, not her. What did I do to deserve this? Why are my insides messed up? I feel like I'm being punished for something my mother did. But I also know it isn't right to blame her as if she knew what she was doing. She wanted to have a baby, just like I do, and she thought she was doing the right thing."

Just as Owen had thought he was doing the right thing when he said the words that rocked his world. Was that why Rochelle had lost desire for her husband? Was she punishing Owen for what her mother had done, transferring her fury from her to him?

It made sense in a convoluted sort of way. Rochelle's desire to have children was made more poignant by her fertility problems. Her internal abnormalities had come to symbolize, for her, a fundamental flaw in her womanhood. Owen's virility only exacerbated her diminished sense of womanliness: as she perceived it, he was man enough to get her pregnant, but she was not woman enough to nurture and protect the pregnancy. And this is where the shame came in, the feeling of being inadequate, of being not enough: not enough of a wife to bear children, not enough of a daughter and daughter-in-law to bear grandchildren. Rochelle had spoken of the warmth and acceptance she had felt from her in-laws when she was pregnant, the sense they gave her that she was fulfilling her destiny by making Owen a father and expanding the family. Feeling loved and accepted is a powerful elixir to a person who has gone without it much of her life, as is the leap in status she achieves when she becomes a mother-to-be. And then to have to announce that there would be no baby after all, for the second time: it does not take much imagination to conjure up the feelings of failure, despair, and shame that a woman might feel, especially if she was a DES daughter.

One day Rochelle came in eager to talk. She had heard from an old acquaintance, a fellow she had had a crush on in high school, who had located her using one of those reunion Web sites. His name was Vincent, and he was bombarding Rochelle with messages at work, telling her how he had always liked her in high school but knew she was out of his league. Vinny's messages were flowery and romantic, replete with descriptions of how Rochelle had used to look when she was a teenager and fantasies of how he had hoped to seduce her. Rochelle was giddy with pleasure when she spoke about him. This was a guy her mother would never have let her date, a bad-boy type who smoked Lucky Strikes and drove a muscle car to school. They had been in the same class once and exchanged a few words, which Rochelle remembered with surprising clarity. She told Vinny she was married, but he was not discouraged. Instead, he reminded her that he had known her long before her husband did and had staked a prior claim to her affections.

I wondered at the power this man wielded over Rochelle. It was as if she were sixteen again and in the thrall of a boy whose sole allure was his connection with the forbidden. No doubt he reminded her of her youthful, innocent self and awakened something in her that resonated with pleasure. But it also seemed distressingly naïve: how could a forty-five-year-old woman be seduced by flirty, flowery e-mail messages? I could understand that she might be flattered by Vinny's ardor and tickled that her infatuation with him had not gone unrequited. But a red flag went up nonetheless when Rochelle said she had made plans to meet him after work one night. All she would say was that she was curious about Vinny and thought it would be fun to get together after all these years. She had neither invited Owen to come along nor told him where she was going, and a whiff of sexual adventurism wafted through the air.

Thus began a series of secret dinners and meetings. Rochelle reported that Vinny looked decidedly middle-aged and had a paunch, and his adolescent good looks had not worn well over time. But he made her feel special, buying her a rose from a girl selling them table to table, presenting her with handwritten notes, and showering her with compliments. He was openly emotional and spoke freely of his feelings, whereas Owen was more reticent and reserved. Rochelle had collected a sheaf of several hundred of Vinny's e-mails and would sit up late at night, reading them over and over again. She said that although she was not all that attracted to Vinny, his messages filled her with a longing that overcame her sexual ambivalence.

When Rochelle began talking about having an affair, a second red flag went up. In more than twenty years as a psychiatrist, I have never seen a couple mend their differences by sleeping with other people, and I told her so. (This is not a moral judgment but a statement of fact: adultery does not make a marriage better. Having an affair when your marriage is in trouble is like treating the measles by rolling around in a patch of poison ivy: you may distract yourself from the original itch, but ultimately, you're only compounding your problems.) I told her that I thought she might be in love with the idea of Vinny more than with Vinny himself, that she might be falling for his words rather than for the man. I said repeatedly: Be careful. Are you sure this is what you want? What are the possible outcomes if you take this step? Do you think cheating on Owen is in keeping with the honesty with which he has conducted himself in the marriage? I told her: Before you do anything, stop and think things through, for his sake as well as your own.

You sit there, and you see it coming. You know your patient is considering taking a drastic step, and however open-minded you try to be, you know it is not likely to turn out well. You want the best for her, and you try to help her take into account possible outcomes she may not have considered. But despite your best efforts to the contrary, patients still sometimes make decisions that don't make sense—at least not to you. At those times, all you can do is urge them to consider, to weigh, to think, and to take your phone number with them when they go.

Rochelle decided against conducting an affair with Vinny while Owen and she were living as husband and wife. Instead, she sat down with Owen, told him that she could no longer continue in the marriage, and offered to move out of the house so he would not have to. She got a lawyer, began divorce proceedings, and made plans to move with Vinny to Las Vegas, where he knew some people and had a lead on a job.

I did not hear from Rochelle for several years, but then one day an e-mail arrived. Things had not worked out for her and Vinny. He turned out to be different than she had thought: underneath his romantic veneer lurked a rock-solid traditionalist who expected Rochelle to pick up after him, do the housework, and prepare all the meals. Their sexual relationship was likewise lopsided, consisting of predictable bouts of missionary-position intercourse, after which Vinny usually fell asleep. He had become demanding and possessive, and she had soon felt imprisoned by the very intensity that had once made her feel secure.

Rochelle came back east. She had no hope of reconnecting with Owen, who, she heard from his sister, had recently become involved with someone else. The sister said that Owen had gone through a difficult spell but was more like his old self now. "You know," she told Rochelle, "you broke my brother's heart. All he ever wanted was to make you happy, and you treated him like garbage. It was very hard on him, and on the family, too." Rochelle hung up the phone, stung.

When I last heard from Rochelle, she was living on her own and earning a good living. She said she now understood that she had had to disconnect from Owen to get beyond the self-recrimination that had defined her life up to and including their marriage. She said she was able to love herself for the first time in many years, and that at last she felt there was room in her heart to truly love someone else. She sounded stable and sensible yet resigned and lonely. Those partial to silver linings might point out that Rochelle finally came to love herself, and I agree that that is all to the good. But it is still sad that she could not learn to love herself without rejecting the love of a good man.

There is no one right way to look at this case (or any other, for that matter). You might see Rochelle as a woman with intimacy problems or one whose inability to express anger had poisoned the well of her sexuality, and you would not be wrong.

But I believe that Rochelle's retreat from sex was due in large part to the psychological wounds she sustained from her exposure to DES. I believe her mother's defensiveness about having taken the drug and her lack of empathy for her daughter's pain hobbled Rochelle's ability to redefine her concept of womanhood and situate herself within it. Rather than owning the fury she felt toward her mother for taking DES, the doctor who prescribed it, the FDA for approving it, or the universe for aiding and abetting the calamity, Rochelle had thrust the feelings aside, where they festered and ate away at her sense of wholeness.

Isolated in her resentment, she lashed out at her husband, the person to whom she had entrusted her true self, for failing, in her view, to comprehend the vastness of her loss. She could neither quash nor condone this destructive progression because she was not aware of it. As her sexual feeling for Owen abated, she told herself it was because of the gulf of understanding separating them. The tragedy is that the gulf existed not between them but within her own being, and it was she, not her husband, who had put it there.

It may have been Rochelle's heightened sensitivity to words that smoothed the way for Vinny's entrance. Rochelle was vulnerable to verbal cues the same way another person might have a weakness for blue-eyed blonds. Just as Owen's well-intentioned but ill-considered words had numbed her to his pleas for understanding, so did Vinny's overwrought prose blind her to his less admirable traits. Remember, too, that Rochelle met Vinny when she was in high school. I suspect that part of his latter-day appeal lay in his ability to evoke in her the feeling of wholeness she had had as a young girl, before she learned of her disfigurement. The naïveté with which she invited him into her life and her vulnerability to his flattery were consistent with a teenager's myopia.

So, too, was Rochelle's insistence that her husband's words betrayed a profound and fatal lack of empathy. After all, Owen had also lost a child. But like a girl in the throes of adolescent angst, Rochelle was too absorbed in her own pain to be aware of his. She began to withdraw from Owen during her postmiscarriage depression, much as she had withdrawn from her first husband. Increasingly detached from her husband and persuaded that he shared little of her grief over the miscarriage, Rochelle fell prey to doubts about the fundamental rightness of the marriage. Rather than call upon Owen to dispel her doubts, she marshaled her doubts to build a case against him. When Owen tried to comfort her and draw her closer, she used his words to fortify the breach.

I believe that Rochelle was looking for a way out of a relationship whose intimacy had emphasized her feelings of inadequacy. I do not believe she did this consciously; indeed, when I asked her why she was leaving her husband, a man of proven character and loyalty, she was unable to cite any concrete evidence of their incompatibility beyond her conviction that he did not understand her. Something was urging her away from him, something inchoate and irrational, and it was this that had deadened her sexual feeling for him.

Of course, a woman need not have been exposed to DES to harbor feelings of inadequacy and shame about her womanhood. The nature of

shame makes us turn away when it catches our inner eye; in that split second of wincing recognition, we blot it from our vision and turn our gaze to
the more acceptable aspects of ourselves. Peg's shame was the legacy of
her upbringing, and it prompted her to renounce her sexual self. She was
able to have sex, but only under carefully controlled conditions. Rochelle's
shame was less clearly outlined. Her concept of herself as a sexual being
was intact until the DES bombshell splintered its framework. Thus weakened, Rochelle's sexual self-concept could not withstand the battering
assault of two miscarriages, and she withdrew from intimacy.

Shame is not fashionable these days, so we speak instead of low self-
esteem and being unhappy with ourselves and not liking this or that about
our bodies. Call it what you will, but I believe it is shame that prompts
women to pay doctors thousands of dollars to cram baggies of gel into their
breasts to enlarge them and peel layers of skin from their faces to make
them appear younger. I believe it is shame that prevents many women
from leaving the house unless they have coated their faces with cosmetics
and lacquered their hair into helmets.

I also believe that shame, amorphous in shape and hard to track, bur-
rows deep within the heart of sex. It plagues men and women alike and affects both sexes' capacity to engage intimately with others and give and
receive pleasure. A teenager's remorse at having had an abortion may crip-
ple her capacity for pleasure years later, when she makes love with her
husband, for how can one who valued her own life over her unborn child's
deserve happiness? Another girl finds herself pregnant at fifteen, bears the
child, and gives it up for adoption, only to be besieged with guilt and sexual numbness when, years later, she marries and starts thinking about having a baby.

Shame need not have its origins in sex to affect sexuality. People may
lose sexual desire or have trouble becoming aroused or achieving orgasm
because of doubts about their worthiness as daughters and sons, wives
and husbands, or mothers and fathers, and never connect their loss of libido to a dearth of self-respect. For example, a woman with unresolved regrets about her relationship with her father may be sexually drawn to only
those men with whom she unconsciously thinks she can revise her unhappy history.

A person's attitude about right and wrong and where she locates herself between the two can also affect her sexuality. A girl brought up in a religious household who finds herself attracted to women may be so repelled by her urges that she vows to squelch all sexual feeling for the rest of her life. Or a woman may give birth to a severely handicapped child, take it as a sign of her inherent unworthiness, and grow numb to her erotic self in an unconscious repudiation of the flawed woman she deems herself to be.

Shame has many faces, most of them hidden, and any one of them can insinuate itself into your sexuality: an ill-considered decision you made long ago; religious beliefs that denounce sexual feelings as sinful; something you did that you regret or did not do that you wish you had; a voluptuous body you think is fat or a plump body you believe is obese.

Or it may be something as mundane as desiring a variety of sexual play that you have been taught is kinky, weird, or sick. You may secretly yearn to be restrained during lovemaking but be afraid your husband will think you're perverted, so you never say anything (and never find out that he's been dying to try it, too). Or perhaps your partner would like you to dress up in a black satin corset but you refuse because, even though the idea turns you on, you are embarrassed at the prospect of flaunting your sexuality. The fact is, sex brings out the saucy wench in most of us, and we do ourselves a disservice if we are too ashamed to let her run wild from time to time.

SEXUAL INVENTORY

What Are You Ashamed Of?

1. Think about the family and cultural values and beliefs that shaped your inner world when you were a child.

- How have these values and beliefs shaped your sexuality?
- Are the views of family members overshadowing your own?
- Are you embarrassed by your sexuality or comfortable fulfilling it?

2. How do you view yourself physically?

3. **What parts of your body do you find especially attractive or appealing?**

4. **What parts of your body do you dislike, find unappealing, or obsess about?** Is your obsession valid, or is it possible you are holding yourself to an unrealistic standard?

5. **How do these feelings shape your concept of yourself as a sexual being?**

6. **Have you ever participated in a sexual behavior that you did not feel comfortable with or approve of?** If the answer is yes, why did you participate? Did the experience turn out to be pleasurable or unpleasurable?

7. **What have you never admitted to anyone about your sexual desires or self-image?** Why have you kept these thoughts to yourself? Do they make you feel ashamed? disgusted? frightened?

8. **If you do feel ashamed about an aspect of your sexuality or past behavior, what do you need to do to let go of the shame and forgive yourself?**

CHAPTER 9

"I Want It to Be Like It Used to Be"
The Menopausal Transition and
Getting Your Groove Back

In her book *The Wisdom of Menopause,* Christiane Northrup writes:

> There is much, much more to this midlife transformation than
> "raging hormones." . . . [I]n addition to the hormonal shift that
> means an end to childbearing, our bodies—and, specifically, our
> nervous systems—are being, quite literally, rewired. It's as simple
> as this: Our brains are changing. A woman's thoughts, her ability to
> focus, and the amount of fuel going to the intuitive centers in the
> temporal lobes of her brain all are plugged into, and affected by,
> the circuits being rewired. . . . [M]enopause is an exciting develop-
> mental stage—one that, when participated in consciously, holds
> enormous promise for transforming and healing our bodies, minds,
> and spirits at the deepest levels.[1]

Menopause isn't what it used to be.

It wasn't long ago that the end of menstruation signaled the death of a
woman's vitality and desirability, consigning her to crone status and forever relieving her of both the exigencies and ecstasies of sex. Her mothering done, she could now devote herself to doddering about, indulging her
grandchildren, and caring for her spry and aging mate, who could be forgiven if he sought out, from time to time, some extraconnubial bliss with
an obliging nymphet.

But women at midlife are crones no longer. Today menopause—the
time in a woman's life that commences one year after her last menstrual

period—is hailed as the dawning of her latter-day liberation. Her mothering done, she can rededicate her energies to all the things she has postponed for the preceding twenty or thirty years, including reconnecting with her mate and making love in every room of the house with the doors wide open. Freed of the constraints imposed by monthly bleeding, menstrual discomfort, and the possibility of becoming pregnant, she can abandon herself to the pursuit of those projects and passions that shaped her unique identity before she became a wife and a mother. She can, in short, return to herself.

But will she? Many women do. In a Gallup survey of 752 postmenopausal women sponsored by the North American Menopause Society, more than half said they felt happier and more fulfilled between the ages of fifty and sixty-five than they did in their twenties, thirties, or forties and reported that their sexual relationships had made it through the transition unchanged (of course, this goes both ways: if the sex was good before menopause, it remained good afterward, but if the sex was not so hot before menopause, it didn't get any better, either). More than three quarters of the women said that going through menopause had motivated them to make changes in their way of life; of these, roughly half improved their diet, a third either started an exercise program or increased the amount of exercise they were already doing, and a quarter reduced their stress levels by taking more time for themselves.[2]

These are encouraging, if not exactly recent, statistics; the survey was done in 1998. And while I love the idea of rehabilitating midlife and menopause from an era of decline to one of rejuvenation and personal fulfillment, I also know that not every woman experiences it that way. Some women are relieved to be done with childbearing, while others mourn the loss of their fertility. Some women send their kids off to college and rejoice in having more time for their husbands, while others are bereft at having no one but their husbands to tend and talk to.

As a woman moves through midlife, a multitude of physical, psychological, cultural, and familial factors commence pushing and pulling, stretching and compressing her into forms she may neither recognize nor admire. Her various identities—wife, lover, mother, daughter, sister, friend—periodically take on the distorted aspect of fun-house mirror reflections: one moment she is commander of all she observes, the next, a feckless imposter at the mercy of her body's thermodynamics. And while some women sail through the transition without encountering more than an occasional squall, the majority endure their share of tempests, of both titanic and teapot proportions.

First and foremost are the symptoms, both familiar and exotic, running the gamut from hot flashes (or flushes, as they are sometimes called) to memory loss to anxiety to depression. During the course of her transition, a woman may experience one or two of these symptoms, all of them, or none. The fact that she develops some symptoms and not others will depend in part on the genes she inherited from her mother and father, but not consistently so; a woman whose mother began menstruating at age ten and was in full menopause at forty-five, for example, may be disposed to follow a similar pattern but is in no way abnormal if she doesn't. Likewise, a girl's genetic legacy may derive more prominently from her father's side of the family, and she may find herself replicating the reproductive development of his mother rather than her own.

Moreover, a woman's symptoms may differ from the ones her friends or even her sisters are experiencing. Hot flashes—sudden, powerful sensations of intense body heat, generated from within—have entered the common vocabulary and become a trademark of the menopausal transition, but they are far from the only symptom we have to look forward to. That said, they do get your attention, even when you are asleep: I know of a fifty-one-year-old woman who has been sleeping on a bath towel for a year and a half because every night, without fail, she breaks out in a profuse sweat and doesn't want to wake her husband to change the sheets (she says he isn't complaining, however, because for the first time since they had kids, she is sleeping in the nude). I know forty-year-old women who have been having hot flashes for years and fifty-five-year-olds who have never had one. While the majority of women who have come through menopause can regale you with entertaining tales from the hot-flash corral, there are also those who say they are not sure whether they have had one or not. (To my mind, this means they haven't. A hot flash is like an orgasm: if you had one, you would know it.)

In addition to hot flashes and night sweats, a woman may have headaches, problems falling asleep and staying asleep, and increasingly irregular menstrual periods that vary in duration and volume of flow: one month her period may require a total of four tampons; the next month she may bleed through her clothes within the hour. Her moods may fluctuate; she may become short-tempered and feel anxious or depressed; also, she may have trouble concentrating and become forgetful, misplacing everything from her cellular phone to her neighbor's name, which in turn makes her think she has a degenerative brain disease and exacerbates her anxiety and depression.

There are sexual symptoms, too. As estrogen levels drop, the walls of the vagina grow thinner, reducing a woman's ability to lubricate and leading to discomfort and sometimes pain during intercourse. And while the problem can be eased by using a lubricant (ones formulated specially for sex work far better than, say, petroleum jelly), not everyone slides easily into the routine. Some women interpret their lack of lubrication as meaning they are no longer aroused by their partners and see problems in the relationship that are not there. They may equate vaginal dryness with a supposed withering of their sexuality and feel they are too old to be having relations because their bodies don't respond as they used to, or they may believe their aging bodies are sending them a message their sex-crazed libidos are too wanton to hear. Others cringe at the thought of interrupting lovemaking to reach over, locate a container of ointment, and slather it on their private parts. What may seem like a logical step to one woman— supplementing her natural lubrication with some from a tube—may pose an intimidating obstacle to another who reads portentous meaning into a shift in body chemistry.

Not only does estrogen wane, but, as mentioned in Chapter 7, testosterone levels drop as well, causing many women to experience a sapping of strength, stamina, and zest for life, not to mention a distinct and lamented loss of libido. Testosterone belongs to a class of substances known as androgens, hormones that are typically associated with maleness but are actually associated with the development of secondary sexual characteristics in girls as well as in boys. While testosterone is popularly referred to as a "male hormone," it is in fact produced naturally in women's bodies, by both the adrenal glands and the ovaries (some of the ovaries' testosterone output is converted to estrogen), and it plays a key role in triggering female sexual desire. Yet ask a heterosexual woman about the role that testosterone plays in her sex life, and she's likely to say something about her man rather than herself.

They say that knowledge is power, and sisterhood would be a lot more powerful if women knew more about testosterone, estrogen, and the roles that hormones play in their lives. In 1993 the North American Menopause Society sponsored a Gallup poll to get a sense of what women knew about menopause and hormone replacement therapy and find out where they got their information. Interviewers spoke to 833 women between the ages of forty-five and sixty and found that while 83 percent of them knew that a woman's body produces estrogen, only 167 of them—20 percent—knew that their bodies produced androgens. Of the 167 who knew their bodies produced androgens, only 42 women—5 percent of all women surveyed—believed that androgen production dwindled after menopause.[3] If most women, menopausal and otherwise, are unaware that their bodies produce testosterone and that it powers their sex drive, how could they know that a dilapidated sex drive could be due in part to a natural and manageable deficit of testosterone?

I am reminded of the woman who came in for the Viagra-for-women study and flung up her dress to show me the alleged wreckage of her body. Yes, she was overweight and out of shape. But her body probably did not look all that different than it had five years before; she had not suffered an extreme and precipitous weight gain or loss that would load her frame with cumbersome rolls of fat or excess skin. What had changed more than her body was her perception of its decline and decay. It had become suddenly horrifying to her because she still wanted to have sex but could not become aroused. Her response was in some ways similar to what a man's might be—"I don't care if I'm fat, I still want to have sex!" (though a woman's response is more typically along the lines of "Ugh! I'm too fat to have sex!"). This woman's despair transcended her perception of what her body looked like; she was grieving the loss of the *feeling* her body used to have: the throb of desire, the melting sensation between her legs, the responsive wetness that had made her feel alive and engaged with her partner and in the moment. While there was no simple, straightforward formula for relieving this woman's distress, I believe she would have suffered less had she known that her feelings of inner flatness might have been due at least in part to a declining testosterone level rather than the death of her sexuality.

However discomfiting this woman's dress-flipping gesture may have been, the feelings that motivated it were shared by just about every other woman who applied to participate in the study. When women started calling, we first asked them a few questions to determine if they were suitable candidates. We then invited them in for a more detailed interview, during which time we tried to make sure that they did indeed have arousal problems, the condition the study was designed to examine. (Just because someone thinks she has a certain disorder does not mean she has it, nor does it mean she has a disorder at all. You may recall Holly, the college student who volunteered for a study on orgasmic disorder and disqualified herself by revealing that she was easily able to climax with a vibrator.) There are always a few applicants who do not qualify for a given study, but we usually attract enough volunteers who exhibit precisely the symptoms we wish to look at and, we hope, alleviate.

I conducted a fair number of the intake interviews myself. There was nothing exotic about the women I spoke with; most of them were between forty-five and sixty-five, had been married for many years to the same man, and had a couple of grown children who were living on their own. They were neither flamboyant nor eccentric; if you saw any of these women at the greengrocer's, none of them would be swooning over the asparagus or caressing the melons. But every single one of them expressed the same sentiment: she had lost her ability to become sexually aroused, and she wanted it back.

Each of these women had the same complaint: they loved their husbands, had had what they considered a really good sex life, and then had lost it. Menopause had done it to them. They reported that their nipples and clitorises were not as sensitive as they used to be, the sense of building psychic excitement was no longer there, and they no longer lubricated sufficiently to facilitate intercourse, if they lubricated at all. The possibility that these symptoms were the result of marital strife was quickly dispelled; when I asked about the emotional climate at home, they said their husbands were considerate and supportive and described their marriages as solid.

These were women who liked sex, who had had orgasms, who were adventurous enough to try new things (although it is probably safe to say they were not heavily into the bondage-discipline lifestyle). They enjoyed good communication with their husbands and had enjoyed sex consistently over years of change, compromise, child rearing, and the occasional crisis. Their husbands still desired them and they desired their husbands, but now they could not manage to become aroused. And they were unhappy enough to be willing to take an experimental drug and keep a diary about their sexual activities in the hope that things would get better.

If you are surprised that so many women in thirty-year marriages would still be attracted to their husbands and want to make love with them, you are probably reading too many celebrity magazines. In real life, many people manage to stay in love with and faithful to the men and women they married. They don't have affairs with every delectable hunk or babe who undulates their way; in fact, most of them don't have affairs at all. They may not be sleeping with whomever the media have proclaimed as the sexiest man or woman alive, but who cares? They are sleeping with the man or woman they love, they like it that way, and they don't want it to end. To the women I interviewed, it did not matter that for many of them, their husbands were the only sexual partners they had ever had, nor that the boundaries of their sexual experience did not slither over the edge and into the realm of kink. What mattered was that they had been happy with their sex lives and were despondent about losing them.

It bears mentioning here that you do not have to be in midlife to be in menopause. A thirty-year-old who undergoes chemotherapy to treat her breast cancer may find herself in abrupt and premature menopause because the drugs have decimated her ovaries and rendered them unable to produce enough estrogen to maintain menstruation. Instead of midlife issues, this young woman will be grappling with the psychological and emotional pressures of illness. In addition, she will probably suffer from some degree of sexual dysfunction generated much more by deficits of estrogen than by assaults to her self-image caused by surgery. In my experience, young breast cancer patients (and their partners) find it easier to adjust to bodily disfigurement than to cope with the vagaries of estrogen deprivation.

Symptoms of low estrogen—including hot flashes, thinning hair, vaginal dryness, and spotty memory—can be ameliorated by taking supplemental estrogen, and many chemo patients respond well to the therapy.

This is especially true of patients whose cancers are not located in the breast and whose disease is not stimulated by exposure to hormones. But breast tissue is sensitive to hormones to begin with, and many breast cancer patients have tumors that are estrogen receptor positive, meaning that they rely on estrogen to grow and may enlarge if exposed to supplemental doses of the hormone. Women with this kind of tumor are typically treated with tamoxifen, a drug highly effective at reducing both the recurrence of breast cancer and the number of women who die from it. Tamoxifen, an estrogen antagonist, blocks the body's absorption of estrogen by some body tissues but does nothing to impede its absorption by others. It is particularly effective in treating breast cancer because it blocks estrogen from entering breast tissue, but, for instance, allows it free passage into bones, where it defends against osteoporosis. In curbing estrogen absorption, however, it may diminish the hormone's salutary effects on a woman's sexual functioning and intensify menopausal symptoms, sometimes causing distressing hot flashes in premenopausal women and hastening premature menopause.

These patients are stuck, for lack of a better word, between the discomforts of estrogen deficiency and the unique hazards that estrogen replacement poses to them. To help them be more comfortable and reclaim their sexuality, we might prescribe an antidepressant, as some are useful in treating hot flashes and night sweats in addition to the anxiety and depression that often accompany the menopausal transition. We also suggest that they try lubricants and urge them to become creative at generating sexual excitement in ways they may not have tried before. The abrupt descent of menopause upon a young chemotherapy patient provokes an array of psychological challenges that is vastly different from the gradual transition to menopause of a healthy, middle-aged woman. To treat such patients effectively, physicians are wise to use a holistic approach to treat the whole woman and not merely her symptoms.

Likewise, a premenopausal woman who has a hysterectomy will find herself in abrupt menopause if her ovaries are also removed during the surgery. The procedure, known as oophorectomy, is less common than it used to be but is still performed as a preventive measure by some surgeons who want to quash a patient's chances of developing ovarian cancer. While removing a woman's healthy ovaries will indeed protect her from that form of disease, it will also deprive her of the hormones her ovaries would have produced, along with their considerable benefits. Our research into the importance of ovarian hormones to women's sexual health, along with growing respect for the desire of many women for a vital sex life well past middle age, has made surgeons think more carefully about recommending that a woman sacrifice her healthy ovaries to a preventive measure that is as extreme as it is effective.

Helga: Early Hysterectomy

For many women, a hysterectomy early in life means going through menopausal symptoms twice, once right after the surgery, and again later in midlife. That was the case with Helga, who was referred to me by a gynecologist at the Women's Midlife Health Center.

Helga was about forty-five when I met her. She had had a hysterectomy with oophorectomy a decade earlier in response to years of abnormal uterine bleeding. (Were the hysterectomy done today rather than in the early 1980s, her ovaries would most likely have been left intact.) Since then she had been treated with hormones at very low doses, which had eased her passage through her surgically induced menopause. When the uterus and ovaries are removed together, menopausal symptoms often begin immediately and with stunning intensity. A woman can awake after hysterectomy surgery in the midst of a hot flash, making it hard for both her and her physician to distinguish the symptoms from those that might, for example, accompany a high fever associated with an infection. For this reason, women undergoing a hysterectomy with oophorectomy may be given hormonal supplements before they leave the operating table, as had Helga, who had been on a low dosage for the past ten years.

Helga complained of general malaise, a continuing feeling of nonspecific, all-encompassing flatness of mood. Nothing had the power to rouse her from her ennui, not sex, not vacations, nothing. This wasn't entirely novel; after the surgery ten years earlier, Helga had gone through a time when she lost interest in sex and devolved into a state of bored detachment. She said this was partially due to the realization that she would never be able to have children, but she came to not only accept but embrace this fact and turned her energies toward her work as a museum curator. Eventually her mood stabilized, and she enjoyed seven or eight years that she described as emotionally steady, if not ecstatic. But Helga's melancholy had returned, and she had been struggling for the past five months. She said she knew things had gotten serious when she canceled an appointment with a client at the last minute and had to grovel to keep from losing his business.

"I'm an art appraiser now, and I work for myself," she said. "This man was liquidating his parents' estate, and he wanted me to come out to the house and look at eleven rooms of antiques. It was a big opportunity and I knew it, but I felt so low that morning, I could not manage to leave the house. I sat in the kitchen with my coat on until ten minutes before we were supposed to meet, and then I called him on his cell phone and made up a lame excuse about being sick. He was not amused—he had driven twenty miles to his parents' house and was waiting for me there—and I was sure he would never speak to me again. I felt like a worm. So I sent him a hundred-dollar floral arrangement with a note begging him to give me another chance. He did, but that's when I knew I needed to see someone."

Helga had been married for eighteen years to Clyde, a tax attorney. I asked how things were at home and was surprised when she said she had not seen him in a while because they were living apart at the moment. I asked her about the separation, and Helga said that it wasn't anything like that, the marriage was quite satisfactory, but she periodically went to live with other people. It might be a friend in a neighboring town or one clear across the country. She could not articulate why she did this. Helga said that Clyde had used to object to her absences but had grown accustomed to living without her for weeks and even months at a time. She said they got along okay; she was just the kind of person who needed space.

I wondered if Helga's serial flights and reunions might be manifestations of psychological problems either brought on or exacerbated by her early menopause. First, though, it was important to stabilize Helga's mood, so I suggested that she start taking an antidepressant, an idea she warmed up to when I told her we could choose one that would not further depress her sex drive. In addition, I boosted the amount of estrogen she was taking, as I believed the low dosage was insufficient to maintain her sexual functioning.

Within a month of her starting the antidepressant, Helga's mood had markedly improved. She was no longer awakening with an empty feeling inside and said that she and her husband were planning a week's vacation away—together—and that she was actually looking forward to it. The professional gaffe had not been repeated, and she reported a renewed sense of purpose in her work and that she planned to travel to France to take a workshop for art professionals on how to spot fakes in oil painting.

After several months of weekly visits, Helga tapered off to monthly sessions. She said that she had begun to feel twinges of desire again, and while becoming aroused was more of a project than it had been when she was in her twenties (as it is for most of us), she and Clyde were up to the challenge. She said they had found a lubricant they liked and had found a way to incorporate it into their lovemaking. Their relationship had improved markedly, Helga said, and they were spending more time together than they had in the last several years.

And their living arrangements? Had Helga changed her pattern of abandoning Clyde every few months?

Not a chance. Helga still packed a bag several times a year and went off to live somewhere else, and still could not explain why she did it. But the time she did spend with her husband was better than it had been in a long time, and that pleased her.

Helga has been in my care for about thirteen years now, and she comes in every three or four months for a catch-up session and medication check. She tells me that Clyde is making plans to retire to the West Coast, and she is mulling over whether or not to accompany him. At fifty-nine, she is not ready to stop working; nor is Clyde willing to postpone his retirement. If she decides to relocate with him, they will sell their East Coast house; if she decides to stay behind, she will continue to live in it and fly out to see him from time to time. Helga talked about this as if sending one's husband off to retire three thousand miles away were the most ordinary thing in the world. I suppose that for her, it is.

Helga and Clyde's marriage is not typical. But it is the one they have chosen and cultivated for more than thirty years. It seems to be a marriage that suits them and requires no tweaking from outside experts. My patient is content to confine our tweakings to her dosages of hormones and antidepressant medication, and I content myself with that.

•　　•　　•

On the opposite shore from the early-onset menopause group are women who do not experience symptoms until much later in life. In some cases, this is due to having a genetic disposition toward late-onset menopause, which can occur when a woman is in her late fifties or even her sixties. When a patient tells me she is fifty-five, still menstruating, and free of night sweats and hot flashes, I tell her to celebrate her good fortune, because the longer her ovaries continue to produce estrogen, the longer her sexual health is likely to prevail.

The late onset of distressing menopausal symptoms is far more common in women who have been on hormone replacement therapy for some time and then decide to go off it. A tidal wave of women quit taking hormones several years ago in the wake of findings by the Women's Health Initiative (a fifteen-year, multimillion-dollar study sponsored by the National Institutes of Health to address the health concerns of postmenopausal women) that taking HRT may increase a woman's chances of developing heart disease or breast cancer. Even though only a small percentage of women on HRT developed these diseases, many women became alarmed and were advised by their physicians to go off the supplements. Consequently, these women were besieged with a host of acutely distressing symptoms. On the other hand, there are also women who have taken HRT and found that it caused side effects more onerous than the ones it was supposed to relieve. HRT works well for some women and not so well for others, and how well it might work for you is something you can discuss with your physician. The bottom line for me is that, while HRT may not be the universal panacea it was once thought to be, it is a viable alternative for many women who want relief from menopausal symptoms that are causing them distress. And if you've been taking supplemental hormones for a while and then stop, the onslaught of symptoms can be distressing indeed.

Estelle is a good example. She was fifty-eight and had been on HRT for seven or eight years when the warnings first came out. She said that while she wasn't blasé about the possible hazards of continuing the hormones, her sex life with her husband, Pete, was still active enough to warrant staying on them a while longer.

Now in her early sixties, Estelle had decided she was ready to go off HRT. Her sister had just been diagnosed with high blood pressure, and Estelle had begun to worry that she might be predisposed toward cardiovascular problems as well. Her sex life had simmered down, as she put it, and she did not think a change in her sexual functioning would affect the marriage very much, if at all. She had spoken with her gynecologist and, under his guidance, phased out her hormonal supplements.

It wasn't long before Estelle starting feeling not quite right, as she put it. "I've always been even-tempered," she said, "but I began to feel . . . not exactly frightened, but nervous. I started worrying about things that I never even thought about before, like getting lost. There's this furniture showroom I sometimes go to; I've been there at least half a dozen times and I know exactly where it is. But when I went last week, I had all this anxiety because I was afraid I'd miss the exit. Then when I got off at the right place, I worried about finding the store and whether or not there would be a parking spot. It's like I've suddenly lost confidence in my ability to do things, to handle anything that doesn't go exactly according to plan. I feel like I've become an overnight incompetent, not because of anything I've actually done, but because of the way things seem. And that makes me feel even worse. It's like those movies where the sun comes up and they show a flower coming out of the ground and its petals open and then it gets dark and it folds up and wilts, all in ten seconds? That's how I feel, like time is flying by and it's getting dark and I'm wilting. And I'm only sixty-two years old."

Anxiety is a common symptom of the menopausal transition, as is depression. And while growing older doesn't fill most people past the age of three with unmitigated joy, Estelle's sense of living in a time-lapse video revealed a pervasive pessimism that could harm her over time. Part of the problem was exhaustion; Estelle was awakening several nights a week between two and three A.M., her nightgown sodden with perspiration. She would slink out of bed and shower in the guest bathroom so as not to wake Pete, then be unable to fall back asleep. She would sit on the living room couch fretting until five or six in the morning, when she would finally curl up under an afghan and doze off for a few hours.

I told Estelle I thought the right antidepressant would do a lot to alleviate most of her symptoms. Because she was not concerned about sexual side effects, we had a wide range of formulas to choose from and selected a medication that would help diminish the intensity of night sweats and hot flashes, in addition to treating depression and anxiety. Within three weeks of starting the drug, she appeared more relaxed and cheerful. Her night sweats had decreased in both frequency and intensity, and her mood had lifted to the point where she was making lunch dates with friends again and routinely going places without fear of getting lost. About six weeks after starting the antidepressant, she phoned to say she did not think she needed to come in because she was doing so well. I agreed to cancel her weekly appointments with the proviso that she come in several times a year for a medication checkup and call me right away if her mood began to darken or her night sweats worsened. That was two months ago.

That Estelle has not called in a while does not mean she is not having symptoms, but it does suggest that she is coping well with the symptoms she has. Which is precisely the point: every woman reacts differently to the vicissitudes of hormonal fluctuation and must decide for herself what she can and cannot live with.

Speaking of what you can and cannot live with, that's another thing you can thank your parents for. Along with their genes, mothers and fathers also pass on to their children messages about how to respond to bodily processes in general and sexual ones in particular. A girl whose mother greeted her first period with fretful counsel to take it easy while she was unwell might mature into a woman who anticipates the discomforts of menopause with trepidation and despair. Every family has its own culture of bodily endurance, and the intensity with which a woman experiences her menopausal symptoms will derive in large part from how she was taught to relate to her body, both sexually and otherwise. Chances are good that if she was brought up to stick a bandage on her bloody knee and get back on the monkey bars, her monthly bleeding and attendant discomforts will not cause her to succumb to fits of the vapors. By the time she enters the transition, she is likely to tell herself, "Look, this is no big deal. A hot flash won't kill me." But if she was reared in a culture of female complaint and inculcated with gloomy pronouncements about the woeful indignities visited upon women by their bodies, she is likely to suffer

mightily at twinges and flushes another woman might shrug off. If you expect to be accosted by a host of vile symptoms, you will tend to interpret
mild ones as intense and intense ones as catastrophic. You will believe
yourself to be suffering more than other people in the same situation,
and you may feel compelled to take action to correct symptoms that you
consider to be extremely distressing but that are, in fact, eminently manageable.

Complicating matters further are the shifting relationships, responsibilities, and obligations that characterize midlife. It takes forty years to figure
out who you are and what your role is in the world. Then, just when you
think you know what you're doing, the script changes and you are suddenly starring in a new drama you know little about. Not only can it make
you feel crazy, it can also make you act that way. One moment you are a
competent, rational being; the next, a hideous gorgon, hissing and spitting
and desperately seeking a competent exorcist. It happens to most of us
who are fortunate enough to survive past forty, and it ain't fun, let alone
pretty.

But it is common, and it is rooted in the internal commotion created
when your relationships with others are changing at the same time as your
body chemistry is changing your relationship with yourself. You may find
yourself locked in a kind of chemical warfare with your teenage kids as
their hormones scream in and yours skulk out: it's a kind of hormonal con-
vergence, if you will, and there's nothing harmonious about it. Maybe your
kids move out of the house but your aged father takes ill and has to move
in. Or your spouse becomes sick and, instead of devoting yourself to reju-
venating your marriage, you are thrust into the unromantic role of care-
taker. Or your prickly marriage of twenty-one years finally disintegrates
and you find yourself suddenly single in your fifties. Or you decide to
adopt a child and bring home a baby just as most of your friends are sending theirs off to college. Your heart may be surrendering to motherhood
just as your body is easing out of its reproductive phase, and the combina-
tion could be invigorating or overwhelming or most likely both, depending
on what day it is.

In addition, your partner, who is probably your age or older, may also be experiencing problems with sexual functioning. Age fifty is when we start to see erectile dysfunction in men, and that can be both a sexual and a relationship issue for women whose partners are affected. (If you and your partner are women, you may not share the same symptoms, but you will at least have an intuitive grasp of what the other is going through.) Sometimes the man will stop initiating sex for fear he will not be able to achieve or sustain an erection, and the woman must choose whether to back off and let him call the shots or lead her man back toward intimacy. For some women, this is a welcome opportunity to assert their sexuality, initiate sex, and reassure their partners that they have not lost their erotic appeal.

But sometimes it goes another way, and a man's erectile dysfunction intimidates rather than invigorates his partner's assertiveness. She may be feeling amorous but would rather forgo lovemaking than try to get something going and end up with her man feeling hurt and humiliated. So she may say she isn't interested in sex when she actually is, subverting her own pleasure along with her authenticity. The relationship can languish for years, perhaps forever, in the sexual doldrums, where neither woman nor man is confident enough to initiate an intimate encounter that could, in their minds, result in embarrassment and emotional turmoil.

Or it could go yet another way (when it comes to sex, there's always another way it could go). It could be that a man starts to have occasional erectile difficulties at the same time as his menopausal partner starts losing interest in sex. This is a natural progression for both of them: neither one has a medical problem that requires treatment—that is, as long as each person's alteration in sexual prowess or interest is closely matched by that of his or her partner, and not mistaken as evidence of declining affection and loyalty. I have worked with many patients who adjust to changes in sexual dynamics by attending to their partners' moods and needs and allowing themselves to go with the natural ebb and flow of midlife erotic energies.

But something happened starting back in 1998, when Viagra came to market and erectile dysfunction became a household (couple of) words: millions of men in their fifties, sixties, seventies, and even eighties went to their doctors without telling their wives, got prescriptions, and, later that night, ta-dah!—presented their spouses with an erection, expecting the womenfolk to swoon with gratitude and delight.

Not all the womenfolk were amused.

Many were shocked and angry because their husbands had gotten the medication and used it on the sly. Many of these were men whose wives had been begging them for decades to go to the doctor for a routine physical, a cholesterol check, or a colonoscopy, with no success. But here the men suddenly got the gumption to call and make an appointment, tell the doctor about their sex lives, pick up a prescription, and take a pill—all for the sake of buttressing their manhood. Some of these couples had not had sex for months; many of them had settled into a routine of making love sporadically, when they both felt amorous and were inclined toward intimacy. And now, all of a sudden, he turns to her in bed and presents her with the gift of his erection, expecting she will want to have intercourse just because he is able to. It drove the women wild, only not in the right way.

What we learn from this is that intimacy is not a commodity that can be bestowed upon a woman by a man, however beloved he may be. For a woman, intimacy is a state of feeling between her and her partner, a mutually tended patch of fertile emotional ground in which the fruits of their relationship bud and thrive. The organic growth of intimacy, the process by which it breaks the ground and blossoms, is what ushers erotic potential into the relationship. Sexual intimacy is not something a man can give to a woman or spring on her when she least expects it; he must create it *with* her.

Which is not to say that erection-enhancing drugs are an impediment to sex. When a couple wants to have intercourse and the man needs help sustaining his erection, these drugs are an excellent solution. But, contrary to the fantasies of older and younger men alike, such medications are not the be-all and end-all panacea for every man's sexual problems; nor do they create intimacy where none exists. In fact, the current demand for these drugs is lower than predicted, and industry-watchers are less sanguine about the future of erection-enhancing formulas than they used to be. In October 2005, doctors wrote 10 percent fewer first-time prescriptions for Viagra, Levitra, and Cialis than they did in October 2004. Some urologists attribute the decline to reports suggesting that the drugs may cause a rare form of blindness. But others say the reason is that there are lots of impotent men who are choosing not to use the drugs, despite the 70 percent success rate and limited side effects. This view seems borne out by Pfizer's estimate that while about half of all men over forty have at least an occasional bout of impotence, only fifteen percent of them get a prescription for an erection-enhancing drug in any given year.[4]

Another intriguing angle is that many men who fill prescriptions for these drugs never ask for refills. We know this because pharmacy computers track first-time prescriptions as well as refills, and there are many men who buy an initial supply of Viagra, Levitra, or Cialis who never come back for more. Some of them may be buying generic formulations illegally off the Internet, which might account for a small percentage of new prescriptions that do not get refilled. But a more likely explanation is that men are realizing that while these medications can help them achieve and sustain an erection, they cannot spark and stoke romance, which many women require if they are to be sexually satisfied.

The use of these medications by men who are not impotent also seems to have peaked. Some young men without erectile problems manage to secure prescriptions because they believe, mistakenly, that the drugs will intensify their arousal level and magnify their erections. Not so, according to urologists, who say the drugs do not increase arousal. These medications do not help healthy young men achieve larger or longer-lasting erections. As one physician put it, "If you have a full tank of gas or half a tank of gas, your car runs equally well."[5]

Not all men experience erectile difficulties, however, and some remain as ravenous for sex late in life as they did when they were young. A man once came to me to participate in an anxiety study I was running. Al was in his late sixties and in an acrimonious marriage to a woman many years younger than he. After the study was completed he remained my patient, and I worked with him over several years as he extricated himself from both the marriage and the depression in which its bitterness had mired him.

As unhappy as he was, Al declined my repeated suggestions to try an antidepressant. He had read up on the subject, knew that sexual dysfunction was a possible side effect of such medications, and was not about to do anything to ruin his sex life, such as it was. "We don't get along very well, but we do have relations," he said. "Once a week is better than nothing, and I'm not inclined to accept nothing." I told him that while erectile dysfunction was possible, some men took the medication without experiencing any sexual difficulties. He was polite but firm: when it came to sex, he was not willing to gamble. Even after he separated from his wife, he would not be persuaded. "What if I meet someone?" he said. "If I can't function as a man, it will be a lot more depressing than what I'm going through now."*

After the divorce, Al regained his emotional footing and began circulating as a bachelor. At a dinner party, he met a widowed nurse and, after a courtship of six months, announced that they were engaged to be married. She was sixty-two, he was seventy-three.

The union was an amiable one. Al was retired and often had dinner waiting for Angela when she got home from work. They socialized regularly with her friends and his and began talking about where they might retire when Angela stopped working. As for their intimate life, Al offered few details. But he did say that he found his bride lovely and they enjoyed regular marital relations.

About two years after the wedding, Al was diagnosed with bladder cancer. He said they had caught it early and were pretty sure it had not spread, and I said something encouraging about how fortunate that was and asked when he planned to have surgery. Al said he had decided against surgery; rather than have his bladder removed, he would combat the disease with anticancer drugs. I was taken aback, because the cancer would be far less likely to recur and metastasize with surgery than it would without it. But if Al's bladder were removed, he would have to wear a bag outside the body to collect urine, and that was something he would not consider. "I couldn't function with something like that on me," he said. "I know it sounds shallow, but I wouldn't want to have relations with someone who had something like that. And I wouldn't do that to my wife. She wouldn't say anything, but how could she not be disgusted by it? No— surgery's out."

---

* I know, I know: here's a guy in his seventies, expecting he's going to meet someone. Ever hear of a woman in her seventies—with the possible exception of Joan Collins—expecting she's going to meet someone?

"But you could die without it," I said.

"I'm going to die anyway," he said. "I'd rather live out my life in one piece and die a little sooner than live a few years longer with my insides on the outside. No, thanks."

At moments like this, I feel the scientist in me duking it out with her emotional alter ego. The feeling side of me understood how a man would recoil at the prospect of having his bodily waste collect in a bag on his abdomen, with the bag becoming a familiar presence at every sexual encounter. However, the scientist in me wanted to encourage my patient with stories of other men who had undergone the procedure and were not mere shells of their former selves but alive and well and enjoying sex with their partners. I was amazed at my patient's vehemence. This man would rather die than compromise his sexuality. It wasn't as if Al would have to give up sex; he was unwilling to give up sex *as he knew it.*

What was most poignant about Al's decision was how it affected Angela. When she met Al, Angela had recently emerged from a protracted period of mourning for her husband, who had died a few years earlier. They had been together for nearly thirty years, and she had nursed him through an episode of colon cancer made all the more intense by the fact that he had stubbornly refused, throughout the preceding decade, to go for a routine colonoscopy. By the time his cancer was diagnosed, it was too late to help him. So when Al's disease was discovered, Angela sprang into action, phoning a urologist she knew from work and promptly scheduling Al for a surgical consultation. She was immensely relieved to learn that the illness was in its early stages and so was devastated when Al rejected the option of surgery. She begged him to reconsider, assuring him that the appliance would, in time, recede into the background of their relationship, sexual and otherwise, and expressing her dread at the prospect of losing yet another husband to cancer. Al would come in and describe tempestuous scenes at home, with Angela weeping through the night and, at one juncture, threatening to divorce him. But Al stood his ground, and Angela ultimately stood by him.

Al endured several years of treatments that involved instilling medication directly into the bladder. As predicted, the treatments slowed rather than halted the disease. The cancer metastasized, and Al's existence gradually became limited by ever expanding onslaughts of pain. The sexual wholeness he had fought to preserve lasted less than a year beyond the diagnosis; thereafter, he began to suffer erectile dysfunction along with enough bodily discomfort to dull his sex drive. His final years were marred by not only his own suffering but also that of his wife. He died at the age of eighty, leaving Angela twice widowed and both grief-stricken at losing him and angry with him for ensuring she would lose him. Still, it was his life, and inscrutable though his priorities may seem, they were his to live with and die for. For him, and undoubtedly for other men as well, compromised sexuality would literally have been a fate worse than death.

Vera: Abused Child, Abandoned Adult

Al's decision to hasten his own demise rather than endure diminished sexuality would strike many women as self-destructive. Yet some of those women would be shocked by their own self-destructive behaviors, if only they could see them. This is especially true when they are in transit between the glow of youth and the patina of age, picking their way gingerly among the land mines that explode as they—*we*—realize that we are no longer young.

The moment I first saw Vera, I suspected she was wandering in a midlife wasteland. She followed me into my office and stood, uncertain and unsmiling, as I closed the door. I invited her to sit, and she wavered, unable to decide which of two guest chairs to take. I gestured to the one closest to mine.

"No, I think I'd rather have this one," she said, settling into it. "But I'll probably switch. No matter what I decide lately, it always feels wrong." I said nothing, hoping she would continue, but she sat in silence, staring out the window.

"How do you think I may be able to help you?" I said.

"I've never done this before, so I don't really know. Should I talk? Or do you talk?"

"Either way," I said. "Why don't you start, so I get to know something about you."

"I don't know what to say."

"How have you been feeling?"

"You mean since the hysterectomy? Or in general?"

"Either. Both."

"Physically, I feel okay. The fibroids are finally gone. That's a relief."

"Is there anything else you're feeling?"

She pursed her lips and shifted her weight in the chair. "Actually, I've been feeling lots of things. Disgusting. Horrible. Fat. Old."

I looked at Vera and saw a woman of fifty-five or fifty-six, with dark hair pulled back in a chignon. Her clothes were of good quality, and a designer logo decorated the bows on her patent-leather pumps. She wore little makeup aside from deep red lipstick. Her eyes looked weary behind the lenses of her glasses.

"You aren't old, you know," I said, "and you certainly don't look fat."

"You didn't know me before," Vera said. "I used to be a size eight. Now . . . let's just say I can't believe this is my body. It's hideous, what's happening to me."

"What do you think is happening to you?"

"I'm losing my life. My body. My family. And my husband. He's gone. Or at least he is most of the time, except when he comes home to pick up something he needs, some cuff links, a pair of shoes, you know, the little things one needs to conduct the well-dressed affair. That's one thing you can say about him; he always liked to look good." Her eyes darted around the room before resuming their vigil at the window.

"He didn't waste any time. That's another thing you can say about him. He's efficient." She swung toward me, her eyes hard and dark.

"Less than a week after the operation he tells me we need to talk. So he sits down on the couch and he tells me he's been doing a lot of thinking while I've been in the hospital, and he realizes how precious life is. And I'm such an idiot, I think he's going to tell me how much he misses the girls now that they're gone, and he's going to start coming home earlier so we can get reacquainted.

"And so I reach over to take his hand. And he just sits there, not moving. Like a dead fish. And I'm leaning over, and my stitches are hurting, so I lean back and he gets this look on his face. And he says, 'Life is too short to spend it unhappy, so I've decided it would be best if I moved out.'

"Just like that. 'I'm moving out.' And he pats my hand and gets up and goes into the bedroom and comes out with his suitcase, all packed. He must have done it while I was in the hospital. 'I think it best to make a clean break. You haven't been happy in a long time,' he says. 'You'll be fine.' And he tells me I should call his cell phone if I need him." She struggled to maintain her composure.

Vera was convinced that her husband, Hasan, was having an affair, although she could not say definitively with whom. She suspected an old Turkish friend who had emigrated a decade earlier and with whom Hasan had been spending more and more time. She believed Hasan's concern with the details of his appearance bespoke homosexual tendencies that his native culture would deem abhorrent and that he had therefore squelched throughout their marriage. She also suspected him of contriving a dalliance with his dentist, a woman in her early forties who was married and the mother of a teenager. Vera acknowledged that both Hasan's family and her own would dismiss the notion of his bisexuality as absurd, yet she held fast to her suspicions. He had become secretive and withholding, she said; she knew him well and was convinced that his affections had fled the household long before he did.

Vera's story was convoluted and emerged in fits and starts. She came in each week, assured me she had nothing to say, and would then relate a seemingly bland anecdote that would open a vein of memory, often painful, about her past. Vera described her parents' relationship as distant; they had seldom touched each other and would sometimes go for days without exchanging more than monosyllables of acknowledgment. Her mother was obese and a source of embarrassment to Vera and her older sister, who rarely invited friends to the house for fear they would see her. Vera said her childhood had been unremarkable until she turned thirteen, which was when she awakened one night to find her father in her bed, whispering urgently that she was a good girl, and wouldn't she please make her daddy happy by holding his "thing"—that was the word she used—and rubbing it. She was repulsed by the episode and persuaded herself it had been a nightmare until he revisited her in bed several months later. These encounters happened four times over two years; when she tried to tell her mother, she accused Vera of lying and threatened to send her away if she told anyone else. When Vera was fifteen, her father suffered a heart attack and underwent bypass surgery; he never approached her sexually again.

Vera spoke of these encounters with reluctance. She understood that her father was to blame, not she; yet she neither cursed nor castigated him for what he had done, although she admitted she was angry that he had destroyed her innocence and any chance she might have had of a normal adolescence. Vera did not date in high school except for a dinner out with a young man whose mother was an acquaintance of Vera's mother and thought the two should get acquainted. He was nice enough but of no interest to her, and she declined his invitation for a second date.

Vera left for college when she was eighteen. Several weeks into the fall term, a young man approached her in the library on the pretense of borrowing a pen, a transaction that culminated in an invitation to try a real Turkish coffee in his dorm room later that evening. Hasan was dark and handsome, Vera said, and, at five-foot-nine, more than tall enough for her. He had emigrated from Turkey with his family when he was ten, spoke four languages, and held her eyes intently when he spoke. That evening in his room, he was respectful and proper, offering Vera coffee and sweet cakes and never once touching her other than to shake her hand after he walked her home. Hasan's manners were impeccable, his English more polished than that of her American-born friends. He phoned her the next afternoon with an invitation for a movie on Saturday night and presented her with a long-stemmed rose when he arrived to pick her up.

"He was very romantic back then," she said. "He would bring me chocolates, a book of poems, a hand-embroidered handkerchief from Turkey. He found me beautiful." Vera's eyes pivoted upward, and she blinked several times.

"I never liked my body. Growing up, I wanted to be like that skinny model, Twiggy. She was tall and blond, like a stick; the clothes just hung on her as if she were a hanger. All of us wanted to look like that. I would try to hide my chest, make it look as if I didn't have anything up there. But I couldn't, of course. People call you voluptuous when you look like me, when what they really mean is that you're fat.

"But Hasan, he loved it. Loved it. He couldn't get enough of me, my body, my hair, everything. But he never pressed himself upon me, he never forced me into anything. I felt so—so wanted, so desired, and yet so respected. For the first time in my life, I felt beautiful."

Vera and Hasan married a week after graduation. She worked as a buyer for a department store while he completed a master's in business administration. His first job was with a computer company, and within several years he was earning a six-figure salary—a big deal in the late 1970s. Vera stopped working to start a family and gave birth to two girls in the next four years. A stately Dutch colonial, matching Mercedes, and private school tuition followed in rapid succession. Everyone was working hard, Hasan at his business, Vera with the girls. Hasan sometimes didn't get home until after ten, at which point he would pour himself a drink and retreat into the room that served as his office. Vera would go to bed, and he would follow later, often waiting until she was asleep.

Over the last decade, their sex life had diminished significantly. Vera said they had sex perhaps once every six weeks, and then it was often perfunctory, with Hasan satisfying himself by rubbing against her, sometimes after she had already fallen asleep, or pretended to do so. It wasn't as bad as it sounded, Vera said; she did not desire sex very much anymore, and even when she did, it was hard to get excited the way she used to. Hasan usually climaxed quickly enough that she was able to fall back asleep with little difficulty.

But now he had moved out, casting Vera into a state of inner chaos. The timing of his departure probably had at least as much to do with his midlife tremors as with hers, but Vera situated herself at the epicenter of the quake: she had lost both her youth and her man. To Vera, the hysterectomy had been tantamount to the excision of her femaleness and sexual allure. That she was in full menopause at the time of the surgery mitigated the hormonal impact of the procedure, if not its psychological effects: for Vera, the hysterectomy added injury to the insult of aging. The ten or so extra pounds she carried on her hips weighed more heavily elsewhere: Vera saw herself as hideous and feared she would soon be as obese as her mother had been. She was furious both with Hasan for abandoning her and with herself for inspiring his defection. "He shouldn't have cheated on me—that's wrong, and I'll never forgive him," she said. "But then I look at myself—I'm fat, I'm ugly, I'm used goods. And now I'm alone. What am I going to do with myself? What will I live on? Who's going to want me now?"

While Vera did not feel sanguine about her future, she had not succumbed to depression, either. Her biggest problem was controlling the bouts of rage that would seize and wrack her body, leaving her weeping and trembling. We agreed to work on stabilizing her mood so she could get through the divorce. Vera did not want to take medication for fear of gaining weight but agreed to come in twice a week for therapy for the first few months and once a week thereafter. Over the following months, we talked about what kinds of work she might be qualified to do, and she applied for and got an administrative job at the university. The divorce agreement awarded her three years of alimony, which calmed her fears of imminent poverty and bought time for her to get back into the workforce and establish her own lines of credit.

Vera got through the divorce, sold the house and was awarded half the proceeds, and moved into a new condominium with a manageable mortgage and enough space to accommodate her daughters when they came to visit. She received a merit raise at work and was getting along well with her coworkers. She had bought some yoga tapes, was working with them three times a week before she went to bed, and said she was sleeping better. But she was lonely and came in one day saying she wanted to start dating and didn't know where to begin.

"I can't do these singles activities because I'm no good in group settings," she said. "I dated one man in my life, and I married him. That's the extent of my dating experience. I can't make small talk, and I'm not young anymore. I just want to meet someone I can go out to dinner with once in a while. A woman at work told me she's seeing a guy she met over the Internet, and she's not much younger than I am. So I think I might try that."

Before long, Vera was conversing with a variety of men online and had established a routine for getting to know them. After exchanging some chatty e-mails, they would arrange a rendezvous at the bar of a restaurant, identify each other, and have a few drinks. If the chemistry was right, they might have dinner. At some point, the man would look at his watch, or stretch and say it was getting late, or, in one case, feign an incoming call on his cell phone, at which point Vera would know he was about to leave, and a chilly sense of dread would snake through her body.

"It's not as if I even like these men," she said, "but I can't bear the thought of them leaving and me standing there, in a bar, by myself—it's pathetic. Something comes over me and I hear myself inviting them back to my place, and then it's too late to get out of it."

Of the dozen men Vera had met up with, only two had declined the postrestaurant invitation; the others had all returned to her house. Once there, after a drink or two and some chitchat, they expected sex, and she felt obliged to provide it. On one occasion, a visitor began pawing at her clothes before she managed to unlock the front door; when Vera told him to keep his hands to himself, he pushed her inside, knocked her to the floor, and slapped her face for good measure before taking off. Physically, she was not badly hurt, but her ego was another story.

I asked Vera if it had been her intention to sleep with all these men, and she said no; she had been attracted to only one of them, and his appeal had diminished substantially by the time she got him home. All she knew was that she could not bear the thought of these men walking away from her in public. She felt that everyone would know she had been abandoned yet again, and the humiliation was more than she could bear.

Like a lonely, insecure adolescent, Vera was sleeping with men she barely knew because it made her feel attractive, wanted, desired. Yes, she was old enough to know better, but no matter: at fifty-seven, Vera was as desperate for love as she had been at thirteen and as ill equipped to secure it within appropriate boundaries as she was then. If menopause marks a woman's return to her essential self, the quality of the return will reflect the essence of not only who she is but also who she *was*. Vera's transition into menopause was fraught with upheaval not just because her husband divorced her but because of everything else that had happened in her life, most notably the twin traumas of incest with her father and her mother's refusal to protect her.

Vera worked hard to reclaim her identity. She became more assertive in her online correspondence and more selective about whom she chose to meet. None of her Internet prospects proved suitable, but she did meet a widower through a colleague who invited her to share his season's opera tickets, an offer that Vera accepted with pleasure. She eventually decided she wanted to live closer to her sister, sold her condo, and moved to a distant part of the state. When last I heard from her, she was working on a state university campus, taking continuing education courses there, and studying to get her real estate license. Her social calendar was not clogged with invitations, but she was introduced to available gentlemen from time to time and no longer felt panicked as the evening drew to a close. "I'd like to find somebody, but it can't be just anyone," she wrote. "He can't be the only one doing the choosing. I have to choose him, too."

Maxine: Menopausal Turnaround

Many women make it through menopause with relative ease, managing their symptoms with patience, humor, and panache. Millions adjust to midlife changes in sexual dynamics without ending up in couples therapy, and many, many do it without the help of a psychiatrist. Of course, the ones I meet in my practice do want help from a psychiatrist, and some are wrestling with problems of daunting proportions. Yet even the most beleaguered patient can emerge from crisis strengthened if not unscathed by her ordeal.

Maxine was such a patient. When we met, she was forty-eight years old, the mother of twin teenagers, a girl and a boy, and working as a travel agent. She had been married for seven years to her second husband, a man named Drake who was a few years younger than she and ran the golfing program at a posh local resort. She was distraught because Drake had recently informed her that he just wasn't up to being a stepfather to teenagers and wanted out of the marriage. Maxine had pleaded with him to reconsider, offering to go for counseling and suggesting a trial separation before dragging lawyers into the mix. But Drake was adamant: living with teenagers was harder than he'd thought, and, more to the point, his feelings for Maxine had changed. He wasn't attracted to her anymore and didn't want them to spend the rest of their lives tied to each other when there was still time for them each to find someone else.

Maxine's first marriage, to the father of the twins, had ended when the kids were still in diapers and he took up with the mother of one of their playmates. Maxine, blindsided by his betrayal, waited several years before dating again. When she met Drake, she thought him a good bet. He was outgoing and confident, earned a good living, and got along well enough with Mitchell and Michelle, who were four when Maxine and Drake met and seven when they were married. Drake met interesting people through his work at the resort, and he and Maxine were occasionally invited to glamorous events, which she found exciting. The fact that he was younger than Maxine bothered her a little, as did the knowledge that he had left his first wife when their daughter, Zoe, was an infant. But he had gone into that marriage way too young and was never late with child support payments, and Zoe was like a sweet younger sister to the twins.

But now everything was spinning out of control. Drake was moving out, the twins were fourteen and a handful, and Maxine's job was in jeopardy because no one was using travel agents anymore. Any one of these stressors would be sufficient to frazzle an otherwise self-contained person; together, they had pressed Maxine into a state of near-paralysis.

"I don't know what to do," she said. "It's like I'm stuck in a hole and I can't climb out. I've got no fight left in me. The other night Michelle said she wanted to download more songs to her cell phone, but I said no because she'd already run up the bill enough this month. So she starts haranguing me like a lawyer. Ten, fifteen minutes, she's still going strong. And I've been up since six, I've worked all day, run to the market and been to the dentist, and it's nine-thirty and I'm tired. So I cave in and tell her she can do it, just so I can have some peace. So she disappears into her room and I sit up worrying that I'm going to get a three-hundred-dollar cell phone bill that I won't be able to pay. And now this! I can't believe he left me. I knew this would happen. I knew it!"

"What did you know?" I said.

"I knew I was too old! I'm almost fifty, but he's only forty-five, he's a guy, he's fine, he'll be young for another twenty years. But me, I'm not the same. I've put on all this weight. My whole shape has changed. And it's odd, because I'm still attracted to Drake but I'm not that interested in sex anymore. And when I am interested, it's just not the same as it used to be. I'm different now; I'm not the same person I was when he married me.

"But you're supposed to stay with your husband or wife, aren't you? You're not supposed to leave them just because their stomach sticks out. That's what he said—'You know, you'd look a lot better if you got rid of that tummy of yours.' He even offered to pay for liposuction. But I watched them do it on TV and it looked disgusting. And scary. You know, you can die from that stuff. And I told him that. But he wasn't worried. 'Lots of people do it,' he said. 'You'd look a lot better. Think about it.' And he's got a point—I would look a lot better. Maybe I should have done it. I don't know. But it doesn't seem right. It shouldn't have mattered that much to him, if he really loved me."

She was right that it shouldn't have mattered that much. She was also right in the middle of menopausal transition, which was making everything seem bleaker and more daunting than it would have seemed even a few years earlier. Her diminishing interest in sex was probably due at least in part to age-related arousal difficulties; had she been treated with supplemental hormones, Maxine would likely have felt more like her former sexual self. Perhaps the greatest blow was that Maxine's husband was pulling out of the marriage when she felt least like herself and most needed his constancy and support. It was as if her state of flux provided him with a pretext to drastically alter his own state of affairs, much as Vera's husband had done.

While you might be tempted to characterize these men as shallow cads whose love for their wives was no more than skin-deep (and you might be right), there is often more at work in the marriage than a husband's malice and deceit. Sometimes, as in Vera's case, there are ancient psychological scars that limit one person's ability to perceive and marshal her strengths in times of emotional crisis. And sometimes, as in Maxine's case, a person is guilty of ignoring information she would have done well to acknowledge. Maxine married a man whom she knew had walked out on his first wife and child. Some women would have seen this as evidence of an inability or unwillingness to adjust to the rigors of commitment and deemed him substandard marriage material. But Maxine was sufficiently smitten with Drake's good looks, personality, and glamorous profession to overlook the deeper implications of his actions. When he proved unwilling to adjust to the rigors of middle age and parenting two teenagers, he walked away from his second wife, just as he had from the first. Maxine should not have been shocked at his defection, and indeed she wasn't; in her deepest heart, she knew he had it in him to leave. That Drake left when he did was evidence less of cruelty than of cowardice: he was unhappy with his roles of stepfather to two kids who were no longer cute and husband to a woman who was no longer young. To stay the course required courage he did not have, so he left.

●　　●　　●

The menopausal transition allows us—in fact, motivates us—to revisit our lives. Many people who study aging agree that there is a point in our fifties or sixties when we do a life review, look back, and ask, "Have I accomplished what I wanted to accomplish? Am I who I wanted to be, or who I thought I would be, when I was twenty?"

If the answer is yes, a woman can stride into menopause as she would across a finish line, knowing she has run the course of youthful ambition and arrived at the threshold of a new phase of life. But if the answer is no—if she has not accomplished what she hoped to or if the particulars of her life are not congruent with the vision she held dear in her youth—she may feel confined in a quagmire of remorse, regret, and self-recrimination.

That is how Maxine felt when she began therapy. She came in once a week for about a year, during which time we worked on developing parenting techniques she could employ as a single mother (no small project with twin teenagers in the house), figuring out how she might use her travel agency expertise to craft a new career (she eventually found work as an online corporate travel consultant for a major hotelier), and renovating her self-image from an aging, matronly failure to a polished, seasoned professional. She began walking on her lunch hour twice a week, and, while she did not lose much weight, she was able to content herself with firming up what she had. She had her hair restyled, added copper highlights, and gave herself permission to pay for touch-ups every five weeks. Little by little, she commandeered her will to make changes to herself and her life, instead of passively waiting for time to wreak its changes on her.

And then she met Nathaniel. At fifty-nine, he was eight years her senior, divorced, and the father of a grown son who lived overseas. Maxine described Nathaniel as a real gentleman from North Carolina who treated her like the southern belle she would never be. He worked for a large insurance company, was popular with the people he supervised, and was well thought of by those who worked over him. He made a good living, was generous with Maxine, and insisted on always paying for their dates. He was also generous of spirit, reassuring Maxine that she was doing a fine job rearing the twins and reminding her frequently of what a remarkable person she was.

Nathaniel was persistent and forthright about his intentions: he had fallen in love with Maxine and wanted her in his life. Maxine was gratified to learn she was able to love Nathaniel back. For perhaps the first time in her adult life, she felt admired, respected, and adored. What she did not feel was a need to marry again. Her paramount goal was to shepherd the twins out of high school and into college. After that, she said, she would weigh her options.

Maxine and Nathaniel bought a house together, splitting the mortgage and the household chores. They live there with Michelle and Mitchell, who are seniors in high school. Maxine's career is flourishing and really took off when she was approached about becoming concierge of one of the area's most venerable historical resorts. She took the job and has become so committed to the hotel's clientele that I have counseled her to turn off her cell phone after nine in the evening so she can have uninterrupted time with the family.

Perhaps the best part of the story is that Maxine has reclaimed her sexuality. "It's new territory for me," she said not long ago. "He's sixty-one, I'm fifty-three, and we've got a sex life. And I ask him sometimes, 'How can you like my body?' I'm still carrying around fifteen pounds more than I'd like to, and it still bothers me. But it doesn't seem to bother him. He's never told me I should lose my tummy. You know what he says? He says, 'That's where your children came from. Don't apologize for it.' Can you believe it?"

As a matter of fact, I can. There are many men like that out there, more than you'd think. And they're not that hard to find once you decide you deserve one.

SEXUAL INVENTORY

The Menopausal Transition

If you are in or nearing menopause:

1. **What changes have you noticed in the shape of your body?** Have you noticed any changes in the texture of your hair, skin, and fingernails?

2. **What changes have you noticed in the way your body re-**

sponds to stimulation, sensitivity of erotic areas, and your interest in and thoughts about sex?

3. **What changes have you noticed in your partner's body and the way he or she responds to stimulation?** The sensitivity of his or her erotic areas? His or her interest in sex?

4. **What changes have occurred in your living situation, such as children leaving home, aging parents requiring care, having responsibility for grandchildren, or retirement, impending or otherwise?**

   ▪ How do you feel about these changes? Do you feel these changes liberate you or diminish you?

5. **What health issues affect you?** Consider both medical and psychiatric conditions.

6. **Are you using medication?** If so, how is the medication affecting your health generally and your sexuality specifically? Are you experiencing side effects? Have you noticed a decrease in physical functioning, mental functioning, or both?

7. **How has your upbringing affected your response to menopausal symptoms and your views about sex after menopause?**

8. **Have you considered hormone replacement therapy? If not, why not?**

   ▪ What potential benefits do you think HRT might have for you? What possible risks?

   ▪ Have you discussed HRT alternatives with your doctor?

9. **Have you talked with your doctor about how menopause might affect your sexuality down the line?** If not, would you be willing to? If not, why not?

CHAPTER 10

When It Really Is Your Body

"I haven't been doing too good lately. It just comes over me, and it's like I'm baking in an oven."

This was Toni's second session. We had spent the first doing little more than going over her medical history, which comprised a litany of problems including morbid obesity, borderline diabetes, borderline high blood pressure, depression, migraine headaches, hot flashes, chronic back and knee pain that had spawned a growing dependency on narcotics, and a recent hospitalization for a pulmonary embolism that had almost killed her. She had undergone a gastric bypass operation twenty years earlier when she was in her mid-thirties, but the effects of the surgery had not stuck; she had gradually gained back all the weight she had lost and put on even more. She had trouble walking, and any physical activity winded her. She appeared to be supporting more than three hundred pounds on what looked like a five-foot, four-inch frame, although I can't be sure of her height; I seldom saw her standing, because not long after starting therapy, she began using a motorized scooter.

"I was doing a little better until they took away my hormones," she said. "Now I wake up in the middle of the night, like I'm on fire. It's the most horrible thing. I'm fifty-six and still going through the change. I begged them to let me keep my hormones, but no, they couldn't do that."

"Do you understand why it was important for you to go off estrogen?" I asked.

"Not really."

"The blood clot in your lung most likely began in your leg," I said. "Some studies are showing that even low doses of estrogen, like you were getting in hormone replacement therapy, can increase your chances of getting a leg clot. And if the clot travels to the brain or the lungs, as it did with you, it can be fatal. So you're actually pretty lucky."

"Sure, if you think it's lucky to have arthritis in both knees. I had to stop assisting in the middle of a root canal last week because I couldn't stand up anymore. I've been with Dr. Hendricks for over six years now, but he says he's going to get someone else if this keeps up. The pain is terrible, really bad. But if I take enough drugs to get through it, I can't think straight. So I can't take anything when I'm working, but if I don't take anything, I can't work. I just can't win with this thing."

I had a feeling about where this was heading. I had had other patients like Toni, people for whom the question isn't whether the glass is half empty or half full but whether there's a glass in the first place. So far, Toni's way of describing her situation was emblematic of someone who perceived herself as a victim, a woman deprived of her hormones, beleaguered by relentless pain and an unsympathetic employer, and bereft of the means and wherewithal to improve her lot in life. People like Toni do see themselves not as autonomous entities acting upon the world around them but as hapless beings acted upon by other people and the vagaries of fate. I felt that Toni wasn't taking responsibility for the circumstances in which she found herself, but I also felt sorry for her. In an attempt to nudge Toni toward taking a more active role in her life, I deployed my standard opening salvo and asked her to tell me how I might be able to help her.

"It wasn't my idea to see a psychiatrist, so I don't really know," she said. "My doctor thought I should see one, so I came."

"Why do you think she sent you here?"

"Well, I'm depressed, and I could use some help with that."

"Is this a recent development?"

"No, I've been this way for a long time. I had that postpartum depression thing after Chuck Jr. was born; that's when all this started. It wasn't so bad with Teresa; I put on forty, maybe fifty pounds with her. But they say the second baby can really get you, and Chuck got me, all right. I put on another fifty pounds with him, on top of what I still had from Teresa.

Never managed to take it off. I lost a hundred pounds after the bypass, but it all came back."

"Do your children live at home?"

"No, they've been gone for years. Teresa's in Tennessee, Chuck's in Alabama. They come up for Christmas sometimes, but they can't always make it. We don't see much of them anymore." She set her mouth in a hard, straight line.

"Is there anyone else in your life you're close to?"

"Well, there's my mother."

"Tell me about her."

Toni stiffened. "Let's just say she's not my biggest fan."

"What do you mean?"

"I mean she's eighty-seven years old and she's still trying to fix me."

"How does she try to fix you?"

"She tries to make me into the person she wants me to be."

"What is that person like?"

"I don't know, easier on the eyes, with a richer husband and a bigger house. She can be a real pain, but she's the only mother I've got. She's old, and she's not doing so good lately, and sometimes I think about what it'll be like when she's not around anymore, and it's like being an orphan, only grown up. And my kids . . . like I said, I don't see much of my kids.

"So I've been kind of depressed and I thought the doctor would be able to give me something, an antidepressant maybe, but then I end up in the hospital with a clot in my lung and they take away my hormones. The only thing I have left is the painkillers. You going to take those away, too?"

"I hadn't planned on it, although I do think we should examine your dosage." At her first session, Toni had told me that the original dosage of painkiller was no longer effective and that she had gradually started taking more, breaking pills in half and taking twice as many as she should have, until now she was taking enough to nearly knock herself out. I told Toni she could keep taking the narcotic but that I would recommend placing a limit on the number of refills she could obtain.

"But I need the pills," she said. "My husband's retired, and I have to be able to work. I get migraines, and I have a bad back and two bad knees, and I have to have something to get me through. I'm not going to overdose, I know what I'm doing."

"Then you also know that narcotics are not designed to be taken for chronic discomfort," I said. I reminded Toni that narcotics don't work over the long term, and if you try to use them that way you can develop a tolerance for them and have to take more and more to get the desired effects. Even if you don't become addicted, these drugs still take a toll on you. They can make you constipated and give you digestive problems, and they also cause sexual dysfunction in a lot of people.

"Oh," Toni said, "that's another thing I wanted to talk to you about."

Toni and her husband used to have sex regularly but now would go for weeks without physical intimacy because she was unable to become aroused enough to have intercourse. I asked Toni if she was still interested in sex and she said yes, she was interested, all right, but she wasn't responding to Chuck's foreplay technique the way she used to. Toni still enjoyed the sensation of Chuck's touch on her body, but while it heightened her desire, the feelings stopped there and no longer caused her to lubricate. She would sometimes encourage him to go ahead with intercourse anyway, which resulted in painful coitus for her and postcoital guilt for him. Toni said Chuck was the one person in the world who cared for her, and she didn't think it was fair to deprive him of sex just because she was depressed.

I have learned to pay close attention when patients talk about sex, because you can learn as much, if not more, from what they don't say as you can from what they do say. Many women have sat in my office and told me how distressed they are that they no longer feel desire as intensely as they used to, or become aroused as much as they used to, or are able to have orgasms the way they used to, and they beg me to give them something, anything, that will restore the vital sexuality they miss so much. And many of these women will, after specific questions and gentle prodding from me, admit that it is not they but their husbands or partners who are distressed, and that they themselves would be perfectly happy having sex once a month, tops.

This did not seem to be the case with Toni, though; she looked right at me when speaking of her arousal problems and provided no evidence, verbal or otherwise, that her husband's unhappiness was motivating her complaint. Toni seemed genuinely distressed about the change in her sexuality. Also, I thought it was likely that she and Chuck were encountering logistical challenges faced by exceptionally large people in their intimate lives. Sexual intercourse is fundamentally an athletic act and requires, at the very least, a modicum of mobility and flexibility. When one of the partners is morbidly obese, it can be difficult for the bodies to mesh in a way that affords penetration sufficient to provide one partner, let alone both, with adequate stimulation.

But Toni did not mention difficulties related to physical exertion, awkwardness, or immobility when she talked about sex. Instead, she was convinced that depression was causing her arousal problems, which exemplified a can't-see-the-forest-for-the-trees phenomenon that I had seen in many patients. You did not have to be a physician to look at Toni and imagine the obstacles she must face in order to make love; she was too heavy to walk without becoming breathless and said that any movement involving bending or twisting would wrack her back with pain.

Toni illustrated perfectly women's tendency to diagnose sexual problems as psychological in nature even when there is massive evidence to the contrary. I believe women do this because physical illness frightens us more than psychological infirmity; we feel we can do more to cure mental malaise than bodily disease. The upshot is that we shift into self-help mode, focus on our attitudes and outside influences, and ignore the potent chemistry within us that profoundly influences our sexuality.

I was convinced that it was Toni's daunting health issues, not her depression, that posed the greatest threat to her sexuality, along with the hormonal fluctuations of menopause (there's nothing like a lowered estrogen level to stymie lubrication). Typically, we prescribe supplemental estrogen for menopausal women with hot flashes and lubrication problems, but Toni could not take supplemental estrogen because of her propensity for clots. We needed a different solution for her, and although I did not think depression was her main problem, she was convinced it was, so it warranted a closer look.

Why was Toni depressed? You might well ask yourself, how could she weigh three hundred pounds and not be depressed? But not so fast: it is presumptuous, in fact, to infer that an obese person is as put off by herself as you might be, or at all, for that matter. Our society makes no secret of its disdain for overweight people, and many of us harbor prejudice, whether we acknowledge it or not, toward those whom we deem too fat for their own good. All too often we assume that the person in question disapproves of herself (or himself) as much as we do, forgetting that we look different to ourselves than we do to the people around us.

Toni had not, in fact, complained much about her appearance. But she had had a gastric bypass when the procedure was far less common than it is now, which indicated that her weight had been bothering her for at least twenty years. She was anxious about her many medical problems and spoke often about how much the embolism had frightened her. She also spoke about her attempts to lose weight over the years, placing special emphasis on the bypass. She disparaged the surgery's effectiveness, saying she had initially lost one hundred pounds but gained back a hundred and fifty more. You can imagine my surprise, then, when she came in one day and said she was planning to undergo a second gastric bypass.

A blade of fear sliced through me. This was a woman who could very easily die on the operating table. I composed my face and asked why she was considering such a difficult surgery when she had so many other medical problems to deal with.

"Because I want to get rid of some of this"—she clasped her thighs with her hands—"this fat, and the operation will do it for me."

I had my doubts. First of all, a gastric bypass doesn't "do it" for anyone unless she is willing to overhaul her eating patterns. The procedure involves drastically reducing the size of the patient's stomach and rerouting the digestive system past much of the small intestine, and it severely limits the patient's ability to absorb the nutrients of what little food she or he is able to ingest. For Toni to have become obese after her first bypass meant she had worked hard to sabotage the surgery, most likely by consuming lots of calorie-laden fluids such as fruit juices, ice cream, and soda pop (the nondiet kind) and nibbling on sugary, fattening foods.

I was also astonished that she had found someone willing to do the operation. While a gastric bypass is not as risky as a heart bypass, it can lead to serious complications, such as a potentially fatal gastric leak, hemorrhage, or obstruction. Moreover, the risk of suffering one of these complications increases exponentially for a patient who is morbidly obese.

I told Toni that if she committed to eating smaller amounts of healthier foods and embarked on a modest program of physical exercise—walking only fifty yards twice a day would work—she could forgo the surgery and, over time, lose vast amounts of her excess weight. But Toni demurred, saying that she could not exercise because of her knees. When I suggested swimming, which offers a no-impact workout, she said she needed something she could do year-round, not just during the summer; when I mentioned the indoor pool at the community center, she said they kept the water there too chilly for her. As for the idea of changing her eating habits, Toni said she already ate like a bird, so cutting down would just make her sick.

You see the pattern: this woman was unwilling to do anything to help herself. She wanted to get rid of her excess weight but didn't want to do anything to make it happen except get operated on. Likewise, she wanted her knees to stop hurting but didn't want to do anything to make that happen except get operated on and take narcotics. She came in with anxiety, depression, and arousal problems but was not inclined to work through them. She preferred to take pills—hormones, painkillers, antidepressants—and have them ease her discomfort.

As it happened, I prescribed an antidepressant for Toni early in the course of her therapy, which helped her mood. It also reduced the intensity of her hot flashes and her migraines, as several of the newer antidepressants have been found to do. She responded well to the medication and, as far as I could tell, took it exactly as prescribed for the duration of therapy—a good thing, to be sure.

Now that her painkiller refills were limited, Toni was forced to deescalate her narcotics intake, which in turn somewhat reduced her lubrication problem. The antidepressant stabilized her mood, which was particularly helpful when Toni's mother died toward the end of therapy. Toni took it hard, considering that her mother was in her late eighties and had been ailing for some time. Although she did not dwell on it, it was clear that there was a lot of unfinished business between her and her mother, and to make matters worse, she and her brother became embroiled in an acrimonious battle over the estate. This was the time in our relationship when I felt the work had a significant impact, because the issues Toni was dealing with—grief, mourning, and feeling alone in the world—are well addressed by a psychiatrist.

But Toni's medical problems remained. She survived the second by-pass and lost fifty pounds but had gained most of it back by the time she left therapy. Her borderline diabetes improved right after the surgery, as did her ability to become aroused, but both problems returned when the weight did.

Which illustrates the point: Toni's sexual problem was medical, not psychological. Her arousal difficulties were a direct result of a constellation of medical problems caused by her obesity and the medications she was taking to control them.

Take Toni's borderline diabetes, for instance. Diabetes is a major cause of sexual problems. In fact, the most common causes of sexual dysfunction in men are diabetes and cardiovascular disease, so when men come in complaining of erectile dysfunction, doctors are wise to look for those two conditions. The same is true for women: when a woman comes in complaining of arousal problems, a doctor would do well to check immediately for diabetes and heart illness, both of which Toni had.

Diabetes affects circulation, which is a prime component of sexual arousal for both men and women. When a healthy person becomes aroused, blood surges into the genitalia, resulting in vasocongestion, a heightened concentration of blood in body tissues. In males, vasocongestion results in an erection; in females, it causes fluid to ooze out of the genital cells, resulting in lubrication.

But diabetes limits a person's circulation, resulting in vasocongestion levels too low to produce lubrication in a woman or erection in a man. Toni's compromised circulation was undoubtedly inhibiting her ability to lubricate, a situation compounded by her lowered estrogen level. Since she could not take estrogen supplements, her best bet would have been to improve her circulation by losing weight, which she did, however briefly, after the second bypass. The fact that her lubrication improved, albeit modestly, after the surgery indicated that her weight-related diabetes was indeed part of the problem. But obesity in women is associated with both depression and sexual dysfunction, so Toni's body remained unable to respond to her husband's touch sufficiently to facilitate intercourse.

Toni was a patient with multiple medical conditions—most if not all of which were self-induced—which, combined with the medications she was taking to alleviate their symptoms, greatly exacerbated her menopause-related arousal problem. I am not saying that Toni had no psychological problems; she did suffer from depressed mood and anxiety, not to mention a paralysis-inducing can't-do attitude. What I am saying is that her dilapidated health, not her psychological problems, was the cause of her sexual dysfunction.

Medical Disorders That Can Cause Sexual Dysfunction

There are many medical conditions that, along with the drugs used to treat them, can cause sexual dysfunction.

Diabetes is one **endocrine system disorder** that can devastate a person's sex life; thyroid dysfunction is another. The thyroid is a small butterfly-shaped gland located in the neck between the larynx and the collarbone that secretes a hormone that regulates metabolism as well as other body functions. If the thyroid does not secrete enough hormone—a condition known as hypothyroidism—cells throughout the body become inefficient at using energy, resulting in cells that are too sluggish to produce symptoms of sexual desire, arousal, and orgasm. At the other extreme is hyperthyroidism, a condition that occurs when too much thyroid hormone is produced, resulting in accelerated metabolism as well as nervousness, fatigue, insomnia, heart palpitations, and depression. In addition to thyroid imbalances, there are other endocrine system disorders that can affect sexual functioning, including polycystic ovarian syndrome (PCOS) and diseases of the pituitary and adrenal glands.

Numerous **neurological conditions** can also affect sexuality. A good example is multiple sclerosis, or MS, a progressive disease of the central nervous system. MS causes the gradual destruction of the myelin sheath that surrounds and protects neurons, nerve cells in the brain. The fatty myelin coating aids and abets neurons' ability to carry electrical signals, so its destruction disables the brain from making vital nervous system connections throughout the body, including the genitals. It is common for people with MS to take longer to become aroused and have diminished desire and altered patterns of orgasm. Other nonsexual MS symptoms that may affect sexuality include fatigue, muscle spasms, diminished sensation in the hands and face, changes in bladder and bowel habits, and depression.

Other neurological conditions that can affect sexuality include Parkinson's disease and various seizure disorders, commonly known as epilepsy. Sexual dysfunction can also result from nerve damage, which can occur in a variety of ways, including surgery, trauma, or pressure from an undetected growth such as a tumor.

Cardiovascular disease can also affect sexuality, although not in the way you might expect. Having a heart attack does not mean you cannot have sex again; it just means you have to pace yourself when you resume having sex and resist experimenting with strenuous, challenging positions until you have fully recovered. But heart illness will affect your sex life when cholesterol starts clogging your blood vessels, which will then be unable to deliver enough blood to facilitate vasocongestion. The genitals need abundant blood flow to produce lubrication, and if your arteries are clogged, not enough blood will make it down there, where it counts.

Autoimmune diseases such as systemic lupus and rheumatoid arthritis occur when your immune system gets confused and mistakes part of your body for an alien invader and attacks it accordingly. These diseases cause inflammation, which in turn affects sexual functioning.

Infections are among the more widely recognized sources of sexual dysfunction, with sexually transmitted infections, or STIs, some of the nastiest of the lot. You can get a lot more from STIs than sexual dysfunction—infertility, for instance—making them particularly unforgiving. One of the most common is pelvic inflammatory disease (PID), which occurs when a woman is suffering from infection and inflammation of the upper genital tract. A pelvic infection can travel up into the uterus and out through the fallopian tubes, where it can cause inflammation and scarring that may lead to infertility, abscesses, chronic pelvic pain, and ectopic pregnancy, among other things. According to the National Institutes of Health, PID is the most common preventable cause of infertility in the United States. Other infections associated with sexual dysfunction include gonorrhea, syphilis, chlamydia, genital warts, trichomoniasis, human papillomavirus, herpes, and human immunodeficiency virus (HIV).

Medications and Other Pharmaceuticals That Can Cause Sexual Dysfunction

More than one hundred medications have been documented as causing sexual dysfunction, but there are probably well over three times that number. Psychiatric drugs alone account for a good many of them.

As the gods of irony would have it, it turns out that **low-dose oral contraceptives** can dull sexual desire. When a woman takes estrogen orally, it increases bloodstream levels of sex hormone–binding globulin (SHBG). Testosterone is one of the hormones that bind to SHBG, so as more estrogen enters the bloodstream, more testosterone binds to the SHBG, causing sexual desire to flag (the body can utilize only free, unbound testosterone). The same thing can happen with **hormone replacement therapy,** but if you get supplemental estrogen through a patch-type delivery system, you're safer; the testosterone-depleting effect results primarily when the estrogen is taken orally, not when it enters the body transdermally (through the skin).

Selective serotonin reuptake inhibitors (SSRIs) are prescribed most frequently for people suffering from depression, but also for those suffering from anxiety, and are famous for wreaking mischief, if not havoc, with the sex lives of all the above. Depression is associated with low levels or poor functioning of the neurotransmitter serotonin in the brain, and SSRIs work by causing serotonin to linger a split second longer in synapses— spaces between neurons—enabling the body to use it more efficiently. SSRIs can affect both women and men by dulling desire, inhibiting arousal, and making it difficult, if not impossible, to achieve orgasm.[1] Many of the most widely prescribed antidepressants are SSRIs, and include fluoxetine (marketed as Prozac), citalopram (Celexa), escitalopram oxalate (Lexapro), fluvoxamine maleate (Luvox), paroxetine (Paxil and Paxil CR), and sertraline (Zoloft). Bupropion, marketed as Wellbutrin, Wellbutrin SR, and Wellbutrin XL, is effective at combating depression without inhibiting sexual functioning, and, in some cases, has been shown to enhance it.

Antianxiety medications can also cause sexual dysfunction. Benzodiazepines, a popular class of antianxiety drug, can either enhance or inhibit sexuality, depending on the size of the dosage. For instance, small doses of benzodiazepines can help men whose anxiety makes it difficult for them to achieve or sustain an erection; small doses can also help both men and women whose anxiety about sex inhibits their ability to feel desire. But larger doses can lead to unwanted sexual side effects, including decreased desire and ability to reach orgasm, painful intercourse (dyspareunia) in women, and ejaculation problems in men. Some popular benzodiazepines include diazepam (marketed as Valium), alprazolam (Xanax), chlordiazepoxide (Librium), clonazepam (Klonopin), and lorazepam (Ativan).

Many other medications can cause sexual dysfunction, including antihypertensives (used to treat high blood pressure), steroids (used to treat everything from poison ivy and other skin inflammations to autoimmune disorders and inflammatory conditions), H[istamine]-2 blockers (used to treat acid reflux and indigestion), and, of course, narcotics. As of this writing, cholesterol-lowering drugs do not seem to have a negative effect on sexual functioning (see, it's not all bad news).

Lidia: The Most Obvious Diagnosis May Not Be the Right One

I met Lidia when she interviewed to participate in a study we were doing on the antidepressant bupropion and its effects on sexual functioning (see p. 253). She was thirty-three years old, a college graduate, and a stay-at-home mother of three children aged seven, five, and three. An American citizen born in Colombia, she had come to the United States at eighteen to attend college. It was there that she met Hugo, a computer science major, to whom she had been married for nine years.

What I noticed first about Lidia were her dark, steady eyes. Sometimes an entire session will go by without a patient looking directly at me. Not so with Lidia; she sat calmly in her chair, ankles crossed and hands folded, and gazed right into my eyes.

"I'm hoping you can help me," she said. "My husband saw your ad and told me about the study. He's a very good man—he didn't force me to come here, not at all—but he just doesn't know what to do for me anymore, and I don't know, either."

"What seems to be the trouble?" I said.

"I've changed," she said. "Nothing sudden; it's been going on for a while. But I'm different than I used to be, and I think it's because I'm depressed."

"How are you different?"

"It's my sex drive. I . . . I just don't feel like doing it anymore. Not for a long time now."

"When did you notice the difference?"

"It was after David was born. He's three, which tells you how long this has been going on. After the birth, we were supposed to wait a while before making love again. And Hugo couldn't wait, saying, 'Just three more weeks, just six more days,' that kind of thing. And he turns to me in bed one night and says, 'Okay, Lidia, it's okay now,' and he starts, you know, doing what he does, and I'm lying there and I realize I haven't thought about sex in a very, very long time—years, not even months. Because I had just stopped nursing James when I got pregnant with David, so I wasn't thinking about sex then either, although Hugo was." She stopped and smiled sadly.

"And that's the way it's been ever since. My husband hasn't changed; the more sex he can have, the happier he is. He's a very good man, and we get along fine. So I don't think the marriage is the problem. The kids are a lot of work, I guess, but that's normal, isn't it? Arianna and James are both in school now, so they're not even home all day. And they're good kids, they don't give me a lot of trouble at all.

"At first I thought it was the baby. Having three kids is a lot more work than two; people told me that, and they were right. I had three kids under the age of four once David was born, and I was really tired, so I thought that was it. But it didn't go away. And the whole thing with my aunt made things really tough."

"What about your aunt?"

"It's not a very nice story."

"I'd like to hear it."

"My Aunt Blanca, my mother's sister, was a judge in the city where I grew up. This is not easy, for a woman to be a judge, where I come from. But my Aunt Blanca wasn't like other women. She and my Uncle Ernesto, they were both different. He was quiet but very educated, very smart. And she was quiet, too, but tough, really tough. She used to take me to the *bib-*

lioteca, the big library, on the weekends, and she got me a library card, and she helped me pick out books so I would learn to think for myself. It's because of her that I came here for college. It's because of her that I am who I am. They had no children, so I was more like a daughter than a niece. She was very, very good to me, and I loved her very much.

"A few weeks before David was born, I got a call from my cousin in Cali. He told me my Aunt Blanca had disappeared. Her car was in the parking lot, so they must have gotten her as she was leaving work that night. Just like that, she was gone. No one ever heard from her again."

The family was distraught. Lidia's parents and her cousins would call from Colombia at all hours, and every time the phone rang, Lidia's heart leapt into her throat. David's birth brought happiness to the family, but Lidia's joy was muted, and soon she was back in the grind of being at home with a two-year-old, a four-year-old, and a newborn.

For two months the family clung to shreds of hope. Then one afternoon the phone rang, and Lidia learned that her aunt's body had been found. She cried straight through the night, stopping only when the baby woke up at four in the morning for his feeding. It was the worst pain she had ever known.

"I haven't been the same since my aunt died. I read up on depression, and that seems to fit: I feel sad a lot, and sometimes I dream about her and wake up thinking she's still here, but then I remember she's gone and I get this sick feeling inside. So when I heard you were doing this study, I thought maybe I would qualify."

I looked hard at Lidia and saw an attractive, well-groomed young woman. Her clothes were clean, and her voice, which rose and fell expressively, bore no resemblance to the flat, monotonous tone that often betokens a depressed state of mind. She was sad, to be sure, but was it grief or depression that ailed her? Grief is typically more time-bound, and triggered by an identifiable event or loss. The murder of Lidia's aunt several years earlier certainly qualified as a grief trigger, so one could argue that Lidia was enduring a protracted grieving period. That said, the existence of a grief trigger did not rule out depression; moreover, low sex drive is a symptom of depression in women, and that had been Lidia's primary complaint.

It seemed to me that Lidia met the criteria for depression, so I decided

to put her in the study, which would last for three months. Each participant would take a pill each day that would be either a dose of bupropion
or a placebo (a pill that looks like the drug being tested but has no more
medicinal content than a Tic Tac); meet periodically with a research
nurse, who would check her vital signs and ask how she was feeling; and,
in some cases, keep a diary in which she would note any reactions she
might have to the medication, including changes in mood, anxiety level,
and sexual functioning. This was a double-blind study, which meant that
neither the participants nor the study's administrators would know who
had gotten the actual medication and who had gotten the placebo until all
participants had completed the study. Double-blind, placebo-controlled
studies are the gold standard for experimentation in the scientific community, as they are the best guarantee we have that neither the people taking
the pills nor those studying these people will be affected by their attitudes,
unconscious and otherwise, toward the substance being studied. So, as to
whether Lidia would get medication or placebo, she and I would both be
in the dark until the entire study was complete, which could take years.

When Lidia completed her term in the study, she said she wasn't feeling any worse but couldn't say that she felt much better, either. Inferring
that she had probably gotten the placebo, I offered her a prescription for
bupropion, which she agreed to try. Over the next month, she said she
thought she might be feeling a little better and that she wanted to continue taking the drug. But there had not been the kind of improvement I
would have expected had she been clinically depressed.

When a patient doesn't improve very much over the course of a study
and you figure it's because she was given the placebo, and then you give
her the drug and there's not that much difference, you go back, revisit the
case, and look for something else.

The end of Lidia's pregnancy had coincided with the abduction of her
aunt, and Lidia drew a connection between the disappearance of her aunt
and that of her sex drive. Her theory was plausible; her aunt's murder was
a calamity for the family, and a loss of sexual appetite is not unheard-of in
persons who suffer intense emotional distress. But Lidia's behaviors were
not consistent with those of a person suffering from clinical depression:
she was interacting amiably with her husband, managing the household, and taking care of her children, who, she told me on numerous

occasions, were a source of great joy to her. The fact that she could imagine the concept of joy, let alone experience it, told me that Lidia was not clinically depressed—grief-stricken and wounded, perhaps, but not depressed.

I ordered some tests, and when I looked at the results, I noticed something: it seemed to me that Lidia's testosterone level was probably a bit low for a woman of thirty-three. If I sound a bit cautious, it's because I am cautious when I put "woman" and "testosterone" together in a sentence, let alone in the flesh. The fact is, we don't have reliable data about testosterone levels in women. We have guidelines that indicate a range of normal for women in various stages of life, but we simply do not have rock-solid information as to how much testosterone a woman should have when she's eighteen compared to when she's twenty-five, forty, or sixty. That said, according to the guidelines we were using, Lidia's testosterone level was low for a woman still in the prime of her sexual life. I had a hunch that while Lidia's grief for her aunt was real, it was not emotional trauma but testosterone insufficiency that was causing her desire to ebb so low.

I told Lidia I wanted to put her on supplemental testosterone, but, since the FDA had not yet approved its use for women, we would have to do it on an experimental basis. She was all for it, and I chose a gel formula that she could use by applying it anywhere on the skin (except on the genitals). The biggest variable in the therapy was figuring out how much gel to use, because the concentration of hormone in the product was calibrated for men, and we would probably have to experiment a bit to find the right dosage. When treating women with testosterone, I prefer using gel to a pill or injection because it affords better control over the dosing. Once you get an injection, the substance is in your body, and there's nothing you can do except wait for it to work its way through your system. If the dosage is too low, you can always inject more, but if the dosage is too high, you're stuck with the outcome, so to speak, which may not be what you had in mind. As I mentioned in Chapter 7, a woman whose testosterone level is above the normal range (whatever that is) may develop hirsutism and sprout hair in places where men usually have it and women usually don't (face, back, buttocks) or find that the hair she already has starts growing in darker and denser. Also, her voice may deepen and her clitoris may enlarge (although there is still no evidence that she will develop an aversion to asking for directions). Though some of these symptoms will subside along with the body's testosterone level, others, such as excess hair, will do so only if you catch them early enough and adjust the dosage accordingly.

That's why I prefer to work with a gel: the patient can control how much she rubs into the skin and how frequently she applies it, and, by paying attention to her body's responses—and telling her doctor about them—a dosage that provides the desired results without unwanted side effects can be worked out. Although there is an element of uncertainty involved at the beginning of treatment, this is not a hit-or-miss proposition: physicians monitor cholesterol and testosterone levels in the patient's bloodstream as well as the patient's bodily reactions in order to determine a suitable dosage.

More and more women are agreeing to undergo experimental testosterone therapy and giving special permission to be treated with gels formulated for men. They know the treatment is not yet approved by the FDA, but they also know that approval is likely to be forthcoming and are willing to take a chance. Soon they may not have to: as I write this, a testosterone patch for women is in the testing phase; by the time you read this, they may be popping up in TV commercials and sticking in your memory (and perhaps to your biceps). Also, some women are using over-the-counter preparations of DHEA (dehydroepiandrosterone), a steroid hormone created by the adrenal glands from cholesterol, and which is the precursor of testosterone and estrogen. Some people claim that DHEA enhances sexual functioning, among other things; others say it does nothing of the kind. Though it is available at health food stores and requires no prescription, I do suggest you acquaint yourself with both sides of the DHEA debate before using it. We don't have enough information about it to ensure that it is safe to use, and, as with any steroid, there are risks involved.

Lidia responded very well to the therapy, reporting that her libido had increased enough for her to enjoy sex several times a week, which was a big improvement over the way she felt before. It is worth mentioning that her sex drive did not return to its explosive adolescent level, but that was not the objective; what Lidia hoped for was to be able to want sex again, to feel desire, and testosterone brought that ability back to her.

Lidia remained my patient for several months after the study so I could monitor her progress on the testosterone; when we were both satisfied that she was doing well, she left my care and returned to her primary care physician, who would continue to keep an eye on her. Her case was particularly satisfying because it was one in which I partnered with a patient to do good medicine: by using a study as a starting point rather than a finish line and administering a judiciously calibrated dose of hormone, Lidia and I were able to help her reclaim her sex life and liberate her from the belief that she had suffered grievous and irreversible psychological harm.

It's the dawning of self-awareness in a patient that makes me love my work. That look on her face when she realizes, No, it's not just in my head; it's in my body, my blood, my bones—*and I can make it better.* To be sure, not all patients have the moxie and the will to do it, as we saw with Toni. But most of the people I treat come away from our work with a sense of revelation about themselves, and it's because they've put their selves on the line, body and soul, to illuminate the darkness within that makes them, and all of us, human.

To a casual observer, Lidia had good reason to be depressed: a band of brutes had kidnapped a beloved relative and dispatched her with unspeakable barbarity, a calamity that coincided with the arrival of Lidia's third child. Now she was at home with three young children, with little to distract her from her anguish and loss. Depression was the logical culprit, so why look further?

Because it wasn't the real culprit. It was the most obvious choice, and also wrong. That is the point my teacher made so long ago: when you hear hooves, think horse; but if you see stripes, be open to zebra. Over and over again, we learn that there may be many elements to a problem, and the most logical conclusion may not be the right one. When a woman comes in distressed about her life in general and her sex life in particular, we need to stand back, look at the big picture, and then examine the details in the context of that woman's life to find a way to help *her:* this woman, with this partner and these children, this upbringing and this history and this spiritual belief, in this culture, at this moment. No book will give us all the answers; we must look to women themselves, and keep looking until we actually *see* them, each and every one. And we shouldn't tell them, "Well, there's nothing in the book that matches what you're describing, so you'll just have to suffer."

In my book, that's ridiculous. If we find something that can help women, we should offer it to them, and they can either take it or leave it. We're pretty clever that way; we can handle the choice.

SEXUAL INVENTORY

Could It Be Your Body After All?

Take a broad look at your sexuality, examining your overall health as well as your psychological well-being.

1. **Do you suffer from a medical condition (such as diabetes, epilepsy, or heart illness) that is or may be affecting your libido or sexual functioning?** Have you discussed this with your physician? If not, why not?

2. **Are you taking any medication(s) (such as an antidepressant, antihypertensive, or antianxiety drug) that might affect your libido or sexual functioning?** If so, have you discussed this with your physician? If not, why not?

3. **Are you trying to get healthy or stay healthy by eating right, exercising regularly, and limiting your intake of caffeine and alcohol?**

4. **Has anything happened to you that you believe may be affecting your sexual desire or functioning?** This could include medical illness, emotional distress, or excessive stress associated with family or work issues.

5. **Are you experiencing or have you ever experienced a sexual difficulty that seemed more rooted in the body than in the mind?**

Acknowledgments

First, I want to thank my patients, who opened their hearts and minds to me over the years. Specifically, thanks to those women who were willing to also share their stories with the world.

Thanks also to:

My colleagues at the University of Virginia, Elizabeth McGarvey and Adrienne Keller, who worked with me even when few thought this area was clinically important, and to my colleagues around the world who were brought together through the International Society for the Study of Women's Sexual Health, who discuss, debate, and challenge ideas, then do research to find the facts.

My administrative assistant, Teresa Woodson, who kept all the disparate areas of my work organized and on track, and did so with good humor.

My editor, Caroline Sutton, and her assistant, Christina Duffy, for their enthusiasm and encouragement. Thanks also to Beth Pearson, Lynn Anderson, and Robbin Schiff.

My literary agents, including Gail Ross and Howard Yoon, who first suggested I write a book, and Kara Baskin, who helped with the proposal.

Pamela P. Boggs of the North American Menopause Society, for patiently faxing copies of their instructive polls.

My sister-in-law, Barbara Clayton, whose early reading of the book proposal provided confidence that my views and voice would resonate with women.

My sister, Kathy Sarosdy, for her example of a strong and gentle woman.

My husband, Michael, for giving me room to write my opinions without embarrassment or reservation.

Robin Cantor-Cooke, whose tireless devotion to understanding my ideas, and to expressing them so others could understand, helped make this book such a great read.

And finally, my children and Robin's children, for putting up with the humiliation of having a mother writing a book about sex.

Notes

PREFACE: *Just a Few Words Before I Get Going*

1. A. H. Clayton, J. F. Pradko, H. A. Croft, C. B. Montano, R. A. Leadbetter, C. Bolden-Watson, K. I. Bass, R. Donahue, B. D. Jamerson, and A. Metz, "Prevalence of Sexual Dysfunction Among Newer Antidepressants," *The Journal of Clinical Psychiatry* 63 (2002): 357–66.

CHAPTER 1: *Am I Normal?*

1. As reported by E. O. Laumann, A. Paik, and R. C. Rosen in "Sexual Dysfunction in the United States: Prevalence and Predictors," *The Journal of the American Medical Association* 281, no. 6 (1999): 537–44. For a lively and readable account of the National Health and Social Life Survey and its findings, see Edward O. Laumann, Robert T. Michael, John H. Gagnon, and Gina Kolata, *Sex in America: A Definitive Study* (Boston: Little, Brown, 1995).

2. "This ABC News survey was conducted by telephone, by female interviewers only, August 2–9, 2004, among a random national sample of 1,501 adults"; see http://abcnews.go.com/Primetime/print?id=156921 (accessed June 20, 2006).

3. Published in the August 2004 issue of *Journal of Sex Research,* as reported at http://search.cnn.com/pages/search/advanced.jsp?Coll=cnn_xml&QuerySubmit=true&Page=1&QueryText=asexual&query=asexual (accessed October 15, 2004; now defunct).

4. Gardiner Harris, "Pfizer Gives Up Testing Viagra on Women," *The New York Times,* February 28, 2004.

5. With apologies to *The Velveteen Rabbit* by Margery Williams (Garden City, N.Y.:

Doubleday Books for Young Readers, 1958), available at http://digital.library
.upenn.edu/women/williams/rabbit/rabbit.html (accessed February 24, 2005).

6. For a spirited, in-depth tour, I recommend *Woman: An Intimate Geography*
(Boston: Houghton Mifflin, 1999), by Natalie Angier, who won the Pulitzer Prize
for science reporting.

7. Sound good? See www.epicurious.com/recipes/recipe_views/views/231869
(accessed June 8, 2006).

CHAPTER 3: *To Risk or Not to Risk: Our Uneasy Relationship with
the Truth*

1. Journal entry, October 14, 1922, in *The Journal of Katherine Mansfield*, as cited in
Robert Andrews, *The Columbia Dictionary of Quotations* (New York: Columbia
University Press, 1993).

2. S. MacNeil and E. S. Byers, "Dyadic Assessment of Sexual Self-Disclosure and
Sexual Satisfaction in Heterosexual Dating Couples," *Journal of Social and
Personal Relationships* 22, no. 2 (2005): 170–81.

3. As asserted by Alvy Singer in *Annie Hall*, written and directed by Woody Allen.

CHAPTER 4: *Unsexy Sex: The Egg and the I*

1. From "Motherhood: Who Needs It?," *Look*, May 16, 1971, as cited in Robert
Andrews, *The Columbia Dictionary of Quotations* (New York: Columbia
University Press, 1993).

2. H. Matsubayashki, K. Iwasaki, T. Hosaka, Y. Sugiyama, T. Suzuki, et al.,
"Spontaneous Conception in a 50-Year-Old Woman After Giving Up *In-vitro*
Fertilization (IVF) Treatments: Involvement of the Psychological Relief in
Successful Pregnancy," *Toaki Journal of Experimental & Clinical Medicine* 28,
no. 1 (April 2003): 9–15.

3. "DES Exposure," at Health A to Z, Your Family Health Site, www.healthatoz.com/
healthatoz/Atoz/ency/des_exposure.jsp (accessed June 20, 2006).

CHAPTER 5: *From Teddies to Teddy Bears: Sex During Pregnancy
and Beyond*

1. S. Gokyildiz and N. Beji, "The Effects of Pregnancy on Sexual Life," *Journal of
Sex & Marital Therapy* 31 (2005): 201–15.

2. Ibid.

3. Isabel Kallman, founder of Alpha Mom TV, as quoted in Randall Patterson, "Empire of the Alpha Mom," *New York,* June 20, 2005.

4. "FDA Official Quits over Plan B Pill Delay," as reported by the Associated Press in *The New York Times,* September 1, 2005.

5. Keith Ablow, M.D., "A Perilous Journey from Delivery Room to Bedroom," *The New York Times,* August 23, 2005.

6. J. E. Byrd, J. S. Hyde, J. D. DeLamater, and E. Ashby Plant, "Sexuality During Pregnancy and the Year Postpartum," *The Journal of Family Practice* 47, no. 4 (October 1998): 305–8.

CHAPTER 6: *After Puberty: Not with My Daughter!*

1. C. M. Grello, D. P. Welsch, M. S. Harper, and J. W. Dickson, "Dating and Sexual Relationship Trajectories and Adolescent Functioning," *Adolescent & Family Health* 3, no. 3 (2003): 103–12.

2. T. Van Elderen, S. Maes, and E. Dusseldorp, "Coping with Coronary Heart Disease: A Longitudinal Study," *Journal of Psychosomatic Research* 47, no. 2 (August 1999): 175–83.

3. "Sex Offenses Definitions from the National Incident-Based Reporting System," www.umaine.edu/security/sexoffenses.htm (accessed June 9, 2005). The legal age of consent varies from state to state.

CHAPTER 7: *What Lies, Roils, and Festers Beneath: Resentments, Fears, and Worries*

1. As reported by Melinda Page and Elizabeth Wells in "Healthy Habit: Why Arguing with Your Husband May Be Good for You," *Real Simple,* July 2005, p. 51.

2. "California, Vermont, Virginia, and Washington allow law readers to take bar examination after three or four years in apprenticeships registered with the state." As reported by the Associated Press in "Skipping Law School: Lincoln Did It; Why Not the Valoises?," *The New York Times,* September 21, 2005.

CHAPTER 9: *"I Want It to Be Like It Used to Be": The Menopausal Transition and Getting Your Groove Back*

1. Christiane Northrup, M.D., *The Wisdom of Menopause: Creating Physical and Emotional Health and Healing During the Change* (New York: Bantam Books, 2001).

2. W. H. Utian and P. P. Boggs, "The North American Menopause Society 1998 Menopause Survey, Part I: Postmenopausal Women's Perceptions About Menopause and Midlife," *Menopause: The Journal of the North American Menopause Society* 6 (1999): 122–28.

3. W. H. Utian and Isaac Schiff, "NAMS-Gallup Survey on Women's Knowledge, Information Sources, and Attitudes to Menopause and Hormone Replacement Therapy," *Menopause: The Journal of the North American Menopause Society* 1 (1994): 39–48.

4. Alex Berenson, "Sales of Impotence Drugs Fall, Defying Expectations," *The New York Times,* December 4, 2005.

5. Dr. Michael A. Perelman, sexual medicine specialist, as quoted in ibid.

CHAPTER 10: *When It Really Is Your Body*

1. A. H. Clayton, J. F. Pradko, H. A. Croft, C. B. Montano, R. A. Leadbetter, C. Bolden-Watson, K. I. Bass, R. Donahue, B. D. Jamerson, and A. Metz, "Prevalence of Sexual Dysfunction Among Newer Antidepressants," *The Journal of Clinical Psychiatry* 63 (2002): 357–66.

ABOUT THE AUTHORS

ANITA H. CLAYTON, M.D., is the David C. Wilson Professor of Psychiatry in the Department of Psychiatric Medicine at the University of Virginia and holds a secondary faculty appointment as professor of clinical obstetrics and gynecology. She has chaired or served on twenty-five academic committees. Dr. Clayton is also a consulting editor for the *Journal of Sex and Marital Therapy* and writes a bimonthly column for *Primary Psychiatry*. She has been featured in numerous publications, including *The New York Times, The Wall Street Journal, Psychiatric Times,* and *Ladies' Home Journal*. She is a wife and mother and lives just outside of Charlottesville, Virginia.

ROBIN CANTOR-COOKE is the co-author of *Thriving with Heart Disease* and has worked as a writer, editor, and producer on more than forty books and tape programs. She is an adjunct instructor at the College of William and Mary and lives with her husband and two sons in Williamsburg, Virginia.